Multicultural Resources
on the Internet

2

Multicultural Resources on the Internet

THE UNITED STATES AND CANADA

Vicki L. Gregory
Marilyn H. Karrenbrock Stauffer
Thomas W. Keene, Jr.

◆ 1999 ◆
Libraries Unlimited, Inc.
Englewood, Colorado

LIBRARIES UNLIMITED, INC.
P.O. Box 6633
Englewood, CO 80155–6633
1–800–237–6124
www.lu.com

Library of Congress Cataloging-in-Publication Data

Gregory, Vicki Lovelady.
   Multicultural resources on the Internet. The United States and
Canada / Vicki Lovelady Gregory, Marilyn H. Karrenbrock Stauffer,
Thomas W. Keene, Jr.
    ix, 366 p. 19x26 cm.
    Includes bibliographical references and index.
    ISBN 1-56308-676-X (softbound)
    1. Minorities--United States--Computer network resources--
Directories.   2. United States--Civilization--Computer network
resources--Directories.   3. Pluralism (Social sciences)--United
States--Computer network resources--Directories.   4. Minorities--
Canada--Computer network resources--Directories.   5. Canada--
Civilization--Computer network resources--Directories.   6. Pluralism (Social
sciences)--Canada--Computer network resources--Directories.
   I. Stauffer, Marilyn H. Karrenbrock, 1936-   .   II. Keene, Thomas W.,
Jr.   III. Title.
E184.A1G874   1998
973'.04'0285--dc21   98-38291
                                        CIP

Contents

1

Introduction

VICKI L. GREGORY

The Internet and the World Wide Web offer a seemingly illimitable array of new information sources, but finding the truly good sources containing the precise information sought is often difficult, especially for users who have a limited amount of time to spend surfing the Web. The organization of knowledge, which has always been central to the practice of traditional librarianship as well as the contemporary field of information science, is even more critical in the electronic environment than in the print sphere; the Web's "book cover" (i.e., a site's name or domain) can be even less helpful than its print counterpart. What you see is not always what you get. This is especially so in areas of interest that range over a wide span of disciplines and activities.

The first question one might logically ask is whether the Web, given its essentially ephemeral nature, is truly a proper subject for a compilation such as this work. After all is said and done, immutability is not what the Web is about (though the failure of some site sponsors to properly update time-sensitive information, such as dates of upcoming events, is a problem, and one doubtless best appreciated by persons responsible for the daily site maintenance that the usability of such information demands). But such is more or less as true about any source of knowledge and information—in the case of the Web, the pace is just faster. Like the characters in the *Star Wars* motion pictures of the late 1970s and early 1980s, we've all made the jump to light speed, and it's an exciting ride, but if the Web is an information environment in which nothing is constant but change, it necessarily cries out for organization and classification. To accomplish this in a manner usable by those looking for information who are not already versed in the organization of the particular subject area in which they are interested is a challenge that the electronic search engines remain unable to overcome, owing primarily to the electronic medium's point of interface with the user, i.e., the cathode ray tube or flat panel display. Anyone who has ever attempted to read an online novel, encyclopedia article, court case, newspaper item, index, or other material that exceeds but a few pages has acquired an intimate familiarity with this "structural" ergonomic problem that presently exists with electronic resources generally. Clearly, there remains an important place for compilations that users can "get their hands on."

The problem of out-of-date sources is as old as reference work publishing generally, and certainly, with the explosion of the Internet, the authors can make no claim to the long-term comprehensiveness of the material presented. But again, there is really no greater problem presented with Web sites and addresses than is typically the case with any other printed list of materials. To obviate these difficulties, we have attempted to adjudge sites as to quality with an eye toward their likely permanence, based usually upon the type of information contained in them and their authorship. Flashy graphics, dancing icons, sound file overlays, and the like were not viewed as conclusive evidence of permanence or value. Substantial consideration was given to the site sponsor or owner. Government sites tended to be favored, but we were also on the lookout for those sites sponsored by organizations that have been around for many years and that can be expected to continue to be active indefinitely into the future, such as religious organizations, museums, and so forth. We believe that the users of this work will benefit from this approach and that the usability of this work as a resource in its area of concentration will be thereby assured for a considerable period of time, even if that time may arguably be less than it might be in some other spheres of endeavor.

As its title is intended to imply, this book organizes and brings together Internet and Web sources dealing with multicultural issues that are likely to be of interest to an English-speaking audience in the United States and Canada. The cultures represented here are a selection and certainly do not cover all ethnic groups represented in the United States and Canada. In future editions of this work, additional cultures such as Korean, Vietnamese, and Cambodian will be included.

In locating sites and resources, several means of searching were used, including monitoring of electronic mailing groups used by the ethnic groups in question with an eye toward references to Internet sources discussed, as well as the use of World Wide Web search engines. Occasionally, URLs were located in periodicals or other compilations. Every entry has been examined in some depth by the author or authors of the chapter to determine its appropriateness for inclusion.

Many of the sites described here are multilingual, meaning that they are available online in more than one language (usually only two, but always including English), with some minor differences in coverage between the English-language and other-language pages; in all cases an English-language version is cited. In a few instances, a small number of sites existing only in the vernacular language of the ethnic group under consideration may be mentioned in the introductory material to a particular chapter, but otherwise all sites mentioned offer English versions (even if the name of the actual site is in a language other than English, an English translation of the title is provided). Some English-language versions of sites may not include everything that appears on the site in the primary language.

A few general points about locating information on the Internet are important to keep in mind. First, as indicated, the Internet from its inception and still today remains surprisingly time-sensitive. Although many of the locations and organizations described in this work have existed and will most likely continue to exist for some time (perhaps indefinitely), that does not necessarily mean that their Web sites will not change location or name or domain address or, perhaps more critically for the user in a hurry, that the server on which the site resides will be up and working or not overloaded at all times. Also, of course, new information is added to (and subtracted from) existing sites, and new sites are created on the Internet every day. All too often, such changes are less the result of "editorial" decisions made by those persons who maintain the sites than simply artifacts of the technological aspects of the Web, such as limitations on available bandwidth, temporary site shutdowns for maintenance, installation of new servers, etc. Therefore, the wise user will conduct periodic, regular, but somewhat free-ranging searches for the information sought; this is not only a good idea, but it can be fun! You never know what you'll come across (even if what you find isn't immediately useful or directly relevant to your search). Another helpful approach is simply to ask questions of people who surf the Web regularly. Most will be able to offer suggestions or referrals. Having a few good contacts who stay informed about the issues in which you are interested can save you time by allowing you to go directly to the items needed. Just remember that someday you may be someone else's resource!

Second, when sites either move or are simply no longer available, use one of the many search tools to locate the new address of the site or to find similar sites. There are now many searching tools available, especially on the World Wide Web, but unfortunately they each work a bit differently and you still have to evaluate (and explore) for yourself the different sites that these online searching tools root up for you. There have been various reviews published outlining how these search engines work and why it is very important to use and compare the results from more than one search engine. Two good Web sources for information and tutorials for various search engines are Search Engine Resources, which has both reviews and tutorials (**http://searchenginewatch.com/resources.htm**) and Understanding WWW Search Tools by Jian Liu (**http://www.indiana.edu/ ~librcsd/search**). The best approach is simply to try out several of them and then decide which ones you find best; you will quickly discover also that a search that is best for one type of inquiry will not necessarily be as good for another.

A third point to keep in mind is that many of the old Internet mainstay Gophers are in the process of being converted to World Wide Web sites. Where Gopher sites still exist, it is possible in many cases to access them using your browser by simply prefacing the address with "gopher://" rather than "http://."

As anyone who has ever attempted to navigate the Internet quickly discovers, site locations, discussion groups and documents have an unnerving tendency to play hide-and-seek with the increasingly frustrated user. Although the authors and editors of this work have repeatedly checked the sites listed throughout the period involved in the writing and publishing of this book, there is no way to guarantee that a search for any particular item mentioned will in fact be successful. Nevertheless, the sites and discussion lists we have listed here should serve the interested Web browser well as starting points for searches in the various subject areas involved, and, it is hoped, will provide (or quickly lead to) the exact information sought.

This book is divided into chapters according to the various ethnic groups considered, with chapter 2, by Sharon Peregrine Johnson, constituting a comprehensive collection of resources to provide coverage for those sites that provide information dealing with multiple ethnic groups and cultures. The chapters were written and compiled by faculty, students, and former students in the graduate Library and Information Science program at the University of South Florida in Tampa, Florida. While, due to inherent differences in the various groups and cultures considered, the chapters vary somewhat in type or concentration of content, each chapter deals with the following major topics, if quality sites were available in these areas: general information; business; culture and humanities generally; education; fine arts; government, law, and politics; history, language arts and literature; popular culture; religion; science and technology; women's issues; and "other" (which provides coverage of sites that do not fall easily into the general topics listed).

In chapter 3, Claudia Rebaza and Paula Geist detail Native American sources, setting forth many examples of the variety of headings covering this subject. Sites devoted to many of the various indigenous peoples of North America are described, and extensive lists of subject headings under which searches might be conducted are set forth. Of special interest are the electronic discussion groups devoted to language, education, and health matters.

Sharon Peregrine Johnson details the large and swiftly growing area of African American Internet resources in chapter 4. She deals with a myriad of sites covering the full gamut of the wide range of diversity and complexity of this largest American ethnic minority. One of the fastest growing areas on the Web, Sharon notes that over 400 new relevant sites of interest have appeared in a recent 12-month period. Of special interest is her section on educational institutions, which contains an extensive listing of sites for museums and libraries devoted to or containing extensive African American collections, as well as sites respecting more than 100 historically Black universities and colleges.

Hispanic American Internet resources are reviewed in chapter 5 by Angelo F. Liranzo with an eye not only to listing resources meaningful to or representative of Hispanic Americans but also to highlight sites useful to non-Hispanic Americans interested in exploring this important and growing segment of the American populace. Variety is the keynote of this chapter, and many interesting sites are described.

Chapter 6 covers Asian American cultures in general. Chapters 7 through 9 cover three specific Asian American cultures: Chinese American, Japanese American, and Asian Indian American. The authors of these chapters found information on their specific topics within numerous more general sites covering Asia and Southeast Asia. These more general sites are included in chapter 6.

Traditional Chinese medicine, including acupuncture, plus Chinese literature, music and art are featured in Chapter 7, by Suzanne M. Saunders.

Chapter 8, by D. Russell Bailey and Vicki L. Gregory, focuses on Japanese American resources and includes interesting sites on Japanese fine arts (ikibana, netsuke, kabuki and wood-block printing sites), martial arts, and traditional Japanese culture, including the Buddhist and Shinto religions, as well as sites relevant to the Japanese American experience of World War II from the point of view of persons on both sides of the Pacific.

Chapter 9, by Cynthia A. Nuhn, covers Asian Indian American Web resources and provides an excellent background discussion of Indian and South Asian culture generally. She places emphasis on sources of information for Asian Indians living in the United States who wish to keep abreast of current events in the land of their origin and provides an extensive listing of newsgroups and electronic mailing lists containing information about the magical and exotic land of India. Her subsection on Indian food and drink is especially enlightening.

Emily K. Dunskar details Jewish American resources in chapter 10. The sites listed include many sources on the Sephardic and Ashkenazic Jewish heritages. The chapter includes sections dealing with Jewish foods as well as a listing of Holocaust resources.

Sites of interest to and regarding Americans of Middle Eastern and North African descent are detailed in chapter 11, which was authored by Alicia Barraqué Ellison and Thomas Keene. The religious diversity of the area receives special treatment and emphasis. Because of the broad geographical coverage of this chapter, most topics cover general, regional sites first, then specific countries.

Vicki L. Gregory describes French Canadian resources in chapter 12. English-language resources were difficult to identify for purposes of this chapter, owing to the fact that it is the use of the French language that is itself such an important part of what defines a French Canadian. Many of the sites included are primarily French language, with an English translation, or in some cases an abbreviated English version; all Canadian government sites are, however, bilingual. Government and politics are covered extensively, with special emphasis on the Quebec Canadian separatist movement, which has gained significant strength in recent decades.

Cajun and Creole resources are covered in chapter 13, by Marilyn H. Karrenbrock Stauffer. A number of interesting personal Web pages are included in this chapter, providing information about Cajun cooking, humor, music, and folk tales. Sites concerned with genealogical matters that emphasize the French Acadian heritage of this unique American ethnic group are also included.

Hawaiian American sites are described in chapter 14, which was written and compiled by Ardis Hanson. This chapter focuses on the varied ethnology of the diverse population of America's Polynesian heritage state. Of special interest are the sites concerned with the Hawaiian language.

Although we realize that this work will not satisfy everyone's needs, we began it to fill a void that we discovered through our teaching in a graduate program of library and information science. Through this work we are attempting to make it easier for teachers at all levels, students (particularly at the secondary and college levels), and individual researchers to find multicultural resources. In future editions, we will strive to include more cultures, but we hope this beginning is useful to you.

2

Comprehensive Internet Sites

SHARON PEREGRINE JOHNSON AND VICKI L. GREGORY

INTRODUCTION

This chapter contains listings for Internet resources where information about more than one culture, usually many different cultures, is represented on the site. The intent is to provide a few good resources, often a link or links to certain types of sites, to help you get started. Areas of multiculturalism receiving special emphasis and coverage here that are not necessarily covered in the other chapters of this book are those relating to gender and to sexual preference and disabilities.

GENERAL INFORMATION

- **American Ethnic Studies**

   http://weber.u.washington.edu/~maurice/ethnic.html

   American Ethnic Studies Department at the University of Washington. In addition to departmental information, the site contains links to numerous sites dealing with African American, Asian American, Chicano, and Native American peoples and their cultures.

- **American Studies Links to the Web**

   http://www.keele.ac.uk/depts/as/links.html

   Information on and links to resources on American studies, history, film, music, art, and literature.

- **American Studies Web**

   http://www.georgetown.edu/crossroads/asw/

   Links are arranged by category and by subcategory. Categories of primary interest in the area of multiculturalism include Race and Ethnicity: General

Resources, African American Studies, Asian American Studies, Native American Studies, Latino and Chicano Studies; and Other Ethnicities: Gender and Sexuality, Women's Studies, and Gay, Lesbian, and Bisexual Resources.

◆ **Area Studies**

gopher://marvel.loc.gov:70/11/global/socsci/area

Links are provided to resources dealing with African, African American, Asian, Deaf, European, Eastern European, Jewish, Latin American, Middle Eastern, Native American, Pacific Islanders, former Soviet Union Studies, and gay, lesbian, and bisexual cultures.

◆ **Balch Institute for Ethnic Studies**

http://www.libertynet.org:80/~balch/index.html

The Balch Institute for Ethnic Studies proclaims itself to be the nation's only museum, library and archive dedicated to collecting and interpreting materials drawn from America's ethnic, racial, and immigrant experiences. With education as its focus, the mission of the Balch Institute is to promote greater intergroup understanding.

◆ **Culture–Community**

http://www.einet.net/galaxy/Community/Culture.html

Links to Internet resources on various world cultures, including African American, Asian, Celtic, French, Jewish, Latino, and Native American.

◆ **Cultures**

ftp://rtfm.mit.edu/pub/usenet/soc.answers/index

Listing of newsgroups and Web sites for information on world cultures and other topics.

◆ **Ethnic Studies at USC: Video Recordings about Minorities at USC**

http://www.usc.edu/Library/Ref/Ethnic/videos.html

The holdings of the video recording collection at the University of Southern California library dealing with various ethnic cultures in the United States.

◆ **Resources for Diversity**

http://www.nova.edu/Inter-Links/diversity.html

Links to diversity resources organized in several major categories with subcategories under each.

- General: Intercultural Classroom Connection, JustCause Diversity Activism, Migration and Ethnic Relations, Minority Studies Page, Multicultural Pavilion, UM Diversity Database

- Ethnicity & Culture: African Studies Web, Chicano-Latino Net, Latin World, Latin American Information Center, NativeNet, NativeWeb, Disability, American Sign Language, Cornucopia of Disability Information
- Gender: Feminism Resources, Women's Studies Database, Women's Studies on the Web, Sexuality, Gay/Lesbian Resources, Rainbow Room – Lesbigay Resources
- Religion: Facets of Religion, including sections on Hinduism, Judaism, Buddhism, Zorastrianism, Jainism, Christianity, Taoism, Islam, Sikhism, Baha'i Faith, Religious Texts
- Other: Minority Experts Database, MOLIS—Minority Online Service, Standards: A Multicultural E-zine

◆ **Subject Guides to the Butler Reference Collection and Selected Sources on the Internet**

http://www.cc.columbia.edu/cu/libraries/indiv/butlref/ guides.html

Subject guides on a variety of topics including: American and English literature, American history, African American studies, Latin American history, Spanish and Latin American literature, and British and U.S. government documents.

◆ **University of California-Santa Barbara: Voice of The Shuttle**

http://humanitas.ucsb.edu/shuttle/minority.html

The Voice of The Shuttle, an ethnic studies page on world cultures, including African American, Asian American, Chicano, Latino, Hispanic, Jewish, Native American, Pacific, and European minority cultures.

◆ **Yahoo (Society and Culture): Ethnic Groups**

http://www.yahoo.com/text/Society_and_Culture/ Minorities/

Yahoo's site on cultures and society of various ethnic groups (i.e., African American, Asian American, and Chicano/Latino American) with links to other sites and resources.

Current Events

◆ **DIVERS-L**

Subscription address: listserv@psuvm.psu.edu

DIVERS-L is an electronic mailing list that serves as an exchange for information on diversity concerns. "Persons of all backgrounds, including African American, Asian Pacific American, Hispanic/Latino American, Alaskan Native/ American Indian, Caucasian American, Foreign (non-immigrant), including genders are invited to participate. In terms of particular academic needs, discussion would like to have representative ethnic inputs into various academic programs.

Specific uses could be in terms of studio design problems, lecturers, exhibits, etc. They hope that discussion would enrich studies in this way rather than focusing on any particular group."

◆ **Telegraph Online**

**http://dspace.dial.pipex.com/town/square/de95/
newspaper.htm**

British online newspaper, which is self-proclaimed as Great Britain's oldest Internet newspaper, in operation online since 1987. It contains world news, including hourly and headline news, sports, science, book reviews, social issues, and more. *Telegraph Online* is associated with several print newspapers, including *The Disability Telegraph, The Asian Telegraph,* and *New World.* It offers a voice to London's ethnic minorities (33 percent of the city's population) and Britain's 6.2 million disabled people.

Newsgroups and Listservs

◆ **Newsgroup FAQs**

http://www.infinet.com/~sm/newsfaq.html

Site with FAQs (Frequently Asked Questions) and information on newsgroups, including those dealing with various world cultures.

◆ **soc.culture Newsgroups**

http://www.cl.cam.ac.uk/newslist/root.html

http://www.cl.cam.ac.uk/newslist/soc.culture.html

http://www.lib.ox.ac.uk/internet/news/soc.culture.html

These three sites contain listings of available newsgroups devoted to particular world cultures.

BUSINESS

◆ **The Economist**

http://www.economist.com/

This weekly journal deals with aspects of economics worldwide and in specific countries.

◆ **Yahoo: Business and Economy**

http://www.yahoo.com/Business/

Yahoo's links on world business, the economy, and international organizations.

CULTURE AND HUMANITIES, GENERAL

◆ **ABAA Booksellers' Specialties—Search Form**

http://www.clark.net/pub/rmharris/forms/searchca.html

**http://www.rmharris.com/pub/abaa-booknet/forms/
    searchca.html**

ABAA Booksellers' Specialties Subject Areas which include Africa, African Americana, American Historical Manuscripts, American Indians, American History, Arabia, Asia, and other topics.

◆ **The American Humanist Association**

http://www.infidels.org/org/aha/

Web site of the American Humanist Association with articles, essays, and other information about the organization, upcoming events, and humanist issues at this site.

◆ **ORTRAD-L**

Subscription address: listserv@mizzou1.missouri.edu

Send mail to: ortrad-l@mizzou1.missouri.edu

This electronic discussion group addresses issues related to oral traditions of many cultures. To join, send the message **sub ORTRAD-L your name** to the above address.

◆ **Yahoo: Arts: Humanities**

http://www.yahoo.com/Humanities/

Links to information on history, languages and linguistics, and more.

Anthropology

◆ **ANTHRO-L**

Subscription address: listserv@ubvm.cc.buffalo.edu

ANTHRO-L is an electronic mailing list, founded in 1988, that is generally about anthropology. It is "dedicated to providing information and an arena for discussion on any anthropoligical subject. It spans archaeology, social and cultural anthropology, linguistic anthropology, and physical anthropology. However, it is truly multidisciplinary in nature, and frequently drifts into related areas of other social and hard sciences." ANTHRO-L provides information about current anthropological events, employment opportunities, and research questions. The list has subscribers from a wide range of backgrounds and all are welcome.

◆ **ETHNOHIS**

http://listserv.surfnet.nl/archives/ethnohis.html

ETHNOHIS covers the intersection of two disciplines: ethnology and history. Interested researchers are encouraged to discuss relevant themes, such as the anthropology of museums, missionary photography, and methodological issues.

◆ **FOLKLORE**

Subscription address: listserv@tamvm1.tamu.edu

The FOLKLORE electronic mailing list is open to all topics within folklore and bibliographic information. Occasionally questions about Native Americans are asked.

◆ **ORTRAD-L**

Subscription address: listserv@mizzou1.missouri.edu

ORTRAD-L is an electronic mailing list that serves as an interdisciplinary forum for open discussion and exchange of resources in the general field of studies in oral traditions. "All those interested in the world's living oral tradition or in texts with roots in oral tradition (the Old and New Testaments, the *Mahabharata,* the *Iliad* and *Odyssey, Beowulf,* etc.) are invited to join the conversation. This e-conference should be useful for specialists in language and literature, folklore, anthropology, history, and other areas. Sponsored by the Center for Studies in Oral Tradition at the University of Missouri, Columbia, it is intended as an electronic companion to the journal *Oral Tradition* and seeks to address the same agenda: interdisciplinary communication across boundaries established by modern academic institutions, and specifically an exchange of views and information on the world's oral traditions and works with roots in oral tradition." Possible topics for discussion include: similarities and differences among oral traditions, fieldwork methods and results, strategies for editing, strategies for translation, texts and oral tradition, genre, performance in all its aspects, prosody, melody, musical accompaniment, oral-formulaic theory, the ethnography of speaking, ethnopoetics, computer applications, ongoing projects (work in progress), collections and archives, conferences, and publications (recent articles or books, also focused bibliography). "To facilitate further communication and encourage direct correspondence between members, a cumulative profile of all members is being compiled for this list. Each subscriber is asked to send a short message that indicates his or her background and interest in comparative oral tradition."

sci.anthropology

Usenet newsgroup discussion of all aspects of the study of humankind.

EDUCATION

- ◆ **Minority Institution List**

http://web.fie.com/web/mol/text/minlist.htm

List of US-accredited post-secondary minority institutions, with mailing addresses and telephone numbers.

- ◆ **Minority On-Line Information Service (MOLIS)**

http://web.fie.com/web/mol/sql/molis.htm

Information on minority educational institutions and their programs and staff. A search engine is provided to allow keyword searching on the site's database.

FINE ARTS

Dance

- ◆ **Dance Links**

http://www.dancer.com/dance-links/

Links are organized under the following categories: Ballet Companies; Modern/Contemporary Dance Companies; Other (Flamenco, Tap, Butoh, Multimedia, Jazz, World, etc.); Dance Presenters & Performance Listings; Newsgroups, Dance Publications, Dance FAQs, etc.; Dance Organizations, Coalitions, etc.; Funding Resources; Miscellaneous Dance Resources; University Dance; Dance Schools; Dancers; and Dance Web Indices.

- ◆ **Sapphire Swan Dance Directory**

http://www.SapphireSwan.com/dance/

Extensive links to a number of dance styles, including: Balkan, Ballet, Ballroom, Belly Dancing, Cajun Dancing, Chinese Dance, Clogging, Contra Dancing, Country Western, English Country, Flamenco, Folk Dancing, Greek Dance, Historical Dance, Hungarian, Indian Dance, Irish Dance, Jazz Dance, Latin Dance, Lindy Hop, Modern Dance, Morris Dancing, Salsa, Samba, Scandinavian, Scottish, Square Dancing, Swing Dancing, Tango, Tap Dance, Vintage Dance, and Zydeco.

Music

- ◆ **Allmusic**

Subscription address: listserv@vm1.nodak.edu

Electronic mailing list with discussions on all forms and aspects of music. To subscribe send a message, **subscribe allmusic your name** to the subscription address.

◆ **Gospel and Spiritual Music at the Southern Folklife Collection**

http://ils.unc.edu/liz/gospel.html

The Southern Folklife Collection at the University of North Carolina documents the history of gospel music with photographs, articles, playbills, and hundreds of sound recordings. The collection preserves the music of gospel quartets, soloists, jubilee singers, "sanctified" singers, and more.

◆ **International Music Council of UNESCO Conference**

http://inet.uni-c.dk/~janole45/imc/

This site contains a report on the 1998 International Music Council of UNESCO conference, Music Education in a Multicultural Society, which includes: lectures from Africa, America, Asia, and Europe; demonstrations of music lessons and concerts based on music from Africa, America, Asia, and Europe; and discussions with representatives and participants in the conference from all over the world. Also included on this site are materials from the council's first conference (in 1996), titled Rhythmic Music Education; which explored the subject of education in jazz, rock, and world music. Materials offered here include the conference program, proceedings, and papers.

◆ **Yahoo: Entertainment and Music**

http://www.yahoo.com/Entertainment/Music/Genres/

World music and artists, links to other sites containing information on new releases, tour dates, and interviews.

GOVERNMENT, LAW, AND POLITICS

◆ **Government Documents Homepage**

http://www.library.yale.edu/govdocs/gdchome.html

Document collections included are: U.S. Federal, United Nations, Canadian Federal, European Union, and more.

◆ **United Nations Scholars' Workstation Homepage**

http://www.library.yale.edu/un/unhome.htm

The United Nations Scholars' Workstation, developed by the Yale University Library and the Social Science Statistical Laboratory, is a collection of texts, finding aids, data sets, maps, and pointers to print and electronic information. Subject coverage includes disarmament, economic and social development, environment, human rights, international relations, international trade, peacekeeping, and population and demography.

◆ **Yahoo: Government: Politics**

http://www.yahoo.com/text/government/politics/

Yahoo's links to sites dealing with world politics and governments.

Human Rights

◆ **Amnesty International USA**

http://www.igc.apc.org/amnesty/

Information on human rights issues around the world. Amnesty International was founded in 1961 and is dedicated to human rights issues.

HISTORY

◆ **Art Glenn's Homepage: Famous Quotations**

http://www.chesco.com:80/~artman/index.html

Quotations of famous individuals and world leaders, including Maya Angelou, Muhammad Ali, James Baldwin, Winston Churchill, and more. A search engine is provided to allow you to search the database of quotations by keyword.

◆ **Internet Discussion Groups: H**

http://tile.net/listserv/h2.html

List of Internet discussion groups (i.e., H-AFRICA, H-NET, H-ALBION, H-NET, etc.) on world history. When you click on the name of a particular list, you get information as to how to subscribe, the e-mail address of the person responsible for the list, etc. This particular URL leads you to a list by title, but other links from this page allow you to search by name, subject, sponsoring organization and more.

◆ **National Archives and Records Administration: Still Pictures**

http://gopher.nara.gov:70/inform/dc/audvis/still

Information and photographs of African Americans and other ethnic groups during World War II; information and photographs of Native Americans and other groups throughout American history from the National Archives and Records Administration. Information concerning the purchase of copies of the photographs is available.

sci.archeology

Usenet newsgroup concerned with the study of antiquities.

◆ **Yahoo: Arts: Humanities: History**

http://www.yahoo.com/text/social_science/history/

Links to Yahoo's site on history, including specialties such as economic history, maritime history, oral history, history of science and technology, and more.

LANGUAGE ARTS AND LITERATURE

Language Arts

◆ ETHNOLOGUE DATABASE
http://www.sil.org/ethnologue/

Contains information about more than 6,500 languages spoken in the world, including alternate names, number of speakers, locations, dialects, linguistic affiliations, and other sociolinguistic and demographic data. Information may be accessed by country or territory, then by the following indexes: languages used within that country; language name; language family; languages of special interest; Gypsy languages; and language or dialect name.

POPULAR CULTURE

Food and Drink

◆ Diana's Links to International Recipes
http://www.citeweb.net/duvel/

From this page you will be able to go to alphabetical country lists (A–Z) and then to each country you are interested in. At the present there are about 3,300 links, and more countries and their recipes are continually being added. The alphabetical lists include states as well as countries, so under the letter *C* you will find California, Cambodia, Cameroon, Canada, Cape Verde, Caribbean (General), Cayman Islands, Chile, China, and many more.

Music

◆ Aardvark's Archive of Bands
For A–G: http://www.stl-music.com/bands1.html

Index to Internet sites for bands and musicians.

◆ Acid Jazz
http://www.cmd.uu.se/AcidJazz/
http://acidjazz.cmd.uu.se/

These sites enables you to search an interactive database of stores worldwide to get specialized music, including a lot of relevant information for acid jazz fans. Users can update the database by telling about specialty shops that the user knows of and writing comments about shops.

◆ **Rock and Roll Hall of Fame, Cleveland, Ohio**

http://www.rockhall.com/induct/index.html

Inductees Index page for the Rock and Roll Hall of Fame. Please note that the index to inductees provides information on musicians, singers, and their music (over 140). The index has an alphabetical listing and it is possible to download some audio sound tracks.

Sports

◆ **Australian Sports Commission Olympic Fact Sheets**

http://www.ausport.gov.au/factmenu.html

Contains historical information about the Olympics, nutrition for athletes, drug testing, political issues and the Olympics and much more.

◆ **ESPN.com**

http://ESPN.SportsZone.com/

Information about basketball, baseball, football, soccer, hockey, tennis, and much more.

◆ **International Association of Olympic Gold Medalists**

http://www.medalists.com/aboutgmi.htm

Information about Olympic gold medalists.

RELIGION

◆ **Facets of Religion**

http://www.christusrex.org/www1/religion/religion.html

This site contains information about Buddhism, Christianity, Hinduism, Islam, Judaism, Taoism and more. There is also a link to the Virtual Library of Religion.

SCIENCE AND TECHNOLOGY

◆ **Humbio-L**

Subscription address: mailserv@acc.fau.edu

Humbio-L is an unmoderated discussion group dealing with biological anthropology, adaptation, environmental stress, biological race, growth, genetics, paleoanthropology, skeletal biology, forensic anthropology, paleodemography, paleopathology, and primate biology and behavior. This discussion is open to all interested individuals or organizations. To join, send the message **sub Humbio-L your name** to the address above.

◆ **NSF: International**

http://www.nsf.gov/home/int/start.htm

Information about National Science Foundation grants, programs, awards, and news dealing with international efforts and collaboration with scientists from other countries. For example, there is a link to a program where U.S. and Japanese scientists are collaborating in regard to research in urban earthquake disaster mitigation.

Health

◆ **Family Health International**

http://www.fhi.org/

Information is provided about AIDS/HIV/STD, family planning, reproductive health and women's studies. Family Health International works to improve reproductive health around the world, with an emphasis on developing countries.

◆ **World Health Organization**

http://www.who.ch/

Links are provided to the reports of the World Health Organization since 1995 plus there are links to other resources on health topics, including Diseases: Communicable/Infectious; Diseases: Tropical Diseases; Diseases: Vaccine Preventable Diseases; Diseases: Non-Communicable; Environment and Lifestyle; Family and Reproductive Health; and Health Policies, Statistics, and Systems. Each of these major categories are further subdivided to provide information on specific diseases and conditions. Links are also provided to publications of the World Health Organization, its governing documents, policies, and press releases.

WOMEN'S ISSUES

◆ **Center of Concern**

http://www.igc.apc.org/womensnet/beijing/ngo/coc.html

The Center of Concern is a 25-year-old nonprofit education and resource center dedicated to global issues, including women's global justice initiatives.

◆ **DIOTIMA**

http://www.uky.edu/ArtsSciences/Classics/gender.html

This site is devoted to the study of women and gender in the ancient world. In addition to information and links to Internet resources, some course materials are provided, and there is a search engine provided to assist the user in locating information available from the Web site.

◆ **The Ethnic Woman International**

http://www.thefuturesite.com/ethnic/index.html

Information about women's issues around the world.

◆ **Feminist Majority Foundation Online**

http://www.feminist.org/home.html

Information and news reports on women's rights and feminist issues. Sections of the Web site include such topics as feminist news and events, feminist research center, breast cancer center, global feminism, and much more.

◆ **National Organization for Women**

http://www.now.org/

Information and links to key feminist issues such as: Abortion and Reproductive Rights, Affirmative Action, Economic Equity, Sexual Harassment, Electoral Politics, Promise Keepers Mobilization Project, Global Feminism, Legislation, Lesbian Rights, Racial and Ethnic Diversity, Violence Against Women, Women in the Military, Women-Friendly Workplace, and Young Feminism. In addition, there is, of course, information about the National Organization for Women and its activities.

◆ **Virtual Sisterhood**

http://www.igc.apc.org/vsister/vsister.html

Virtual Sisterhood, which describes itself as "a global women's electronic support network, is dedicated to strengthening and magnifying the impact of feminist organizing through promotion of electronic communications use within the global women's movement." In addition to English, the site is available in Chinese, French, German, Hebrew, Italian, Japanese, Russian, and Spanish.

◆ **Women and Minorities in Science and Engineering**

**http://www.ai.mit.edu/people/ellens/Gender/
    wom_and_min.html**

Extensive links to sites dealing with women, minorities, and science or engineering. Some sample links include: Women, Minorities, and Persons with Disabilities in Science and Engineering: 1996, from the NSF, The National Science Foundation's Partners in Science, Engineering, and Mathematics Education's brochure on Building a Diverse Community, Education Grants for Minorities and Women, The Mathematical Association of America's (MAA) information on women and minorities, including Strengthening Under-represented Minority Mathematics Achievement (SUMMA), The Association for Women in Mathematics (AWM), Women and Mathematics (WAM), DataLine (a newsletter on the glass ceiling faced by women and minority men), and The Library of Congress's bibliography on African-American women in the sciences.

- **women.com**

http://www.women.com

Women.com contains links to various items of interest to and about women, including *Women's Wire*, an online magazine for women.

- **Women in Politics**

http://www.glue.umd.edu/~cliswp/

Women involved in U.S. politics. Includes sections on the Women as Politicians, History, and Electing Women to Political Office.

- **Women's Studies (R)e-Sources on the Web**

http://scriptorium.lib.duke.edu/women/cyber.html

Very extensive listing of links to Web resources dealing with women's studies, women's organizations, and various feminist issues.

OTHER

Exhibits

- **Museums from Around the World**

http://www.internet.com.mx/bartes/MusLink.html

Links to the homepages of museums in the United States and around the world.

Travel and Tourism

- **CITY.NET**

http://www.city.net/

Searchable by countries or regions, this site combines the features of an atlas, a gazetteer, and an almanac, with those of local guidebooks and newspapers. It locates information on communities around the world, incorporating a wide variety of different sites for each locality, and a wide range of perspectives on each community. It includes Country Information from the latest CIA World Factbook, culture and languages, maps, and travel and tourism information from the U.S. Centers for Disease Control and the U.S. State Department.

- **Foreign Languages for Travelers**

http://www.travleng.com/languages/

This site is a nifty idea. It provides a basic-level online dictionary for translating words to and from English. It also provides sound files for some common foreign words. It includes about 45 foreign languages. As of this writing, the dictionary is directed at travelers and other beginners, but foreign language students will find the collection of languages impressive.

◆ **Great Outdoor Recreation Pages**

http://www.gorp.com/default.htm

These pages feature recreation possibilities worldwide. It is an attractive site, with lots of information, even if you don't intend to go to any of the locations.

◆ **Travel Warnings and Consular Information Sheets, U.S. Department of State**

http://www.travel.state.gov/travel_warnings.html

This site is searchable alphabetically by country name. Travel Warnings are issued when the State Department recommends that U.S. citizens avoid travel to a certain country. Consular Information Sheets on every country in the world include such information as the locations of the U.S. embassies or consulates, unusual immigration practices, health conditions, minor political disturbances, unusual currency and entry regulations, crime and security information, and penalties for violating drug laws.

◆ **U.S. Centers for Disease Control Home Travel Information Page**

http://www.cdc.gov/travel/travel.html

Contains reference material for international travel, from the Centers for Disease Control, including vaccination requirements and food and water pre-cautions. Search for destination-related information under Geographic Health Recommendations.

◆ **World Guide**

http://www.flynwa.com/wgspec/

This is a source of extensive travel information from Microsoft.

3

Native American Resources
CLAUDIA REBAZA AND PAULA GEIST

INTRODUCTION

The indigenous peoples of North America include Native Americans (or, conventionally, American Indians) plus a number of Arctic peoples, most of whom are variously known as Eskimos or Inuit but also including such other groups as Aleuts. Although all of these peoples had their origins in Asia and have generally retained some physical similarities with modern Asiatic peoples, they have been isolated long enough to evolve into a distinct group, generally called the American Indian geographic race. The differences between Asiatic and American have blurred somewhat in extreme northeastern Siberia and northwestern Alaska, where the indigenous peoples of that region have exhibited greater affinities with each other than with the other Native American races. This chapter focuses primarily upon Native Americans but some information is included concerning other indigenous peoples of North America.

At the time of initial European contact there were probably as many as 240 different tribes in North America. The indigenous peoples of this continent had developed very differently from those in Europe and Asia during their many thousands of years of isolation. Some European and Asian practices such as the use of the wheel, plow, and manufacture of iron implements did not emerge, and others such as pottery making, sculpture, basket-making and other art forms reached high levels of sophistication in the Americas. Many cultures depended on hunting and gathering, while others depended more upon an agricultural base.

In general, Native American tribes placed a premium on the visual world, as opposed to the people from Europe and Asia, who placed a high importance on textual materials as well as artistic achievement. The mission of the Native American artist is the same as that of an artist in any other culture, that is, to arouse an emotional response in his or her audience. In Native American cultures, the artist's ability to communicate successfully with his or her tribe is dependent largely upon the recognition of the force of tradition. Yet within this concern for tradition, a great deal of originality and freedom of expression is found. Many of the Native American Web sites demonstrate the power of the visual in the culture of the tribe.

Searching Strategies

This is a beginning, but by no means a comprehensive, bibliography of some sites and resources available online in the field of Native American studies and interests. Where possible, we have had organizations describe themselves and their missions in their own words.

When conducting searches on the Internet, be prepared to both sort through a lot of information and to find nothing. At the moment the Internet is like a giant bulletin board with notes pinned to it haphazardly. Because the most broadly used terms, Native Americans and American Indians can be linked to so many things, the net you throw out is as likely to be filled with junk as it is with fish. When dealing with the Internet, patience is not only a virtue but a necessity.

Books are still a prime source of information. When searching the Internet, check publishers' Web sites, bookstores, and online catalogs. Two sites that link to publishers' homepages and e-mail addresses are AcqWeb (**http://www.library.vanderbilt.edu/law/acqs/pubr.html**) and Publishers' Catalogues Homepage (**http://www.lights.com/publisher**).

Subject Heading Tips

One problem with searching for Native American material, whether online or not, is the various terms used for the cultures and subjects related to them. Jeanette M. Mueller-Alexander and Helen J. Seaton give examples of problems one can encounter in their article, "Researching Native Americans" (*DATABASE,* April 1994, pp. 45–56). The lack of standardization in terminology and the absence of indexing and cataloging in most online material is a question still unaddressed by the library and information science communities.

One area in which there is relative standardization is library catalogs. Most academic and large public libraries use Library of Congress (LC) classification, and most libraries in general will use *LC Subject Headings*. Unfortunately, these are only as good as the last update. Since 1991, LC subject headings have been changing in the area of aboriginal peoples. Online catalogs have made updating catalogs to reflect these changes much simpler than in the card catalog days, but the priority of this work varies from library to library.

Despite the growing wealth of materials available online, the value of information on paper is often higher. Many libraries now provide online access to their library catalogs, and these can be browsed for special collections on Native American culture or history, or individual works in certain areas. In general, Native American material can be found under the broad headings "Indians of North America," "Indian [subject]" (i.e., Indian craft), and "[Subject] [comma or two hyphens] Indian" (i.e., Athletes, Indian or Athletes--Indian). However, libraries with good collections on Native Americans may have vast amounts of material under these basic headings (especially the Library of Congress), so it pays to be as specific as possible.

It also pays to remember that these subject headings are not, in and of themselves, concepts that spring readily to mind (i.e., "Indians of North America as Seamen" or "Indian agents' wives"). What makes these subject headings particularly confusing is the seeming duplication of headings. For example, "Blacks--Relations with Indians" appears indistinguishable from "Afro-Americans--Relations with Indians." Or consider "Indian literature" and its broader heading "Literature--Indian authors." The first refers to the literature, the second to the ethnicity of the authors—which may have nothing to do with the content of their work. Following are some examples of the variety of headings in this area, along with some terms that do not fall under the three basic headings discussed above.

Headings: Indian [subject]

Indian agents
Indian craft (also try specific tribal works)
Indian drama
Indian literature—United States (also use [tribal name] literature)
Indian newspapers
Indian outlaws
Indian physicians
Indian poetry
Indian veterans

Indian warfare—North America (also try specific wars and battles)
Indians—Government relations
Indians in medicine
Indians in motion pictures
Indians in the motion picture industry
Indians—Languages
Indians—painting (use this for traditional art)
Indians, Treatment of—North America

Headings: [Subject] Indian

Alcatraz Island (Calif.)—History—Indian occupation, 1969–1971
American fiction—Indian authors
American poetry—Indian authors
Art, Indian (for Modern Indian art)
Arts, Modern—Indian influences
Athletes, Indian
Authors, Indian
Blacks—Relations with Indians or Afro-Americans—Relations with Indians
Canadian fiction—Indian authors
Canadian poetry—Indian authors
Children's poetry, Indian
Cookery, Indian
Folk songs, Indian

Libraries and Indians
Literature—Indian authors
Love poetry, Indian
Man, Prehistoric—America
Numeration, Indian
Painting, Indian
Paleo-Indians
Picture-writing, Indian
Prints, Indian
Religious poetry, Indian
Riddles, Indian
United States—Civilization—Indian influences
United States—([Navy], [Marines], etc.)—Indians

Other Terms

Eskimo craft	Kitchen—middens
Indigenous church administration	Kivas
Indigenous labor	Mound-builders
Kachinas	Wampum belts and Plumbate ware

Subdivisions Under "Indians of North America"

Subdivisions can be tried under specific tribal names and also under state subdivisions (i.e., "Indians of North America—Indiana—Antiquities"). You may wish to consult an LC subject heading book for specific terms you will use often.

GENERAL INFORMATION

◆ Aboriginal Studies

http://www.ciolek.com/WWWVL-Aboriginal.html

This is an academic, virtual library site with links to study centers, books, online databases, ftp archives, history documents, an aboriginal language library, government servers, and more.

◆ BJ's Native American Links

http://arginine.umdnj.edu/~swartz/nativam.html

Excellent directory listing nations and tribes, organizations, arts, biography, education, health, museum, legends and stories links, and even links to several search engines.

◆ Duster's Place

http://www.specent.com/~duster/volc2.html

This directory is distinguished by its inclusion of a brief write-up or glimpse into the offerings at the links listed. Features include: White Buffalo Calf; Native American Artists' Homepage; Native American Resources; Native American Home; Native American Art Styles: Pottery, Jewelry, and Religion; Native American Tribes; ENAN HotList; Native American Spirituality; Native American On-line Resources; SAIIC South and Meso-American Indian Rights Center!; *The First Perspective*, Canada's source for aboriginal news and events; Akwesasne Mohawk Information Service; The Sisseton Wahpeton Sioux Tribe; Cherokee Roots Search; and Information on Kahnawake and the Kanien'kehaka People.

◆ Index of Native American Resources on the Internet

http://hanksville.phast.umass.edu/misc/NAresources.html

Listing of sites grouped into cultural, historical, archaeological, educational, legal, musical, commercial, government, and artistic resources. Links also to individual homepages, bibliographies, announcements and job notices.

◆ **Links to Aboriginal Resources**

http://www.bloorstreet.com/300block/aborl.htm

Directory to U.S., Canadian, Latin American, New Zealand, and Australian links. Also lists human rights, cultural, and law links, aboriginal newsgroups. Lists court decisions, conferences and events. There are many good access points.

◆ **Native America**

http://www.mstm.okstate.edu/students/jjohnson2/ ok-native.htm

Features include The Five Civilized Nations, Calendar of Events, Education, Tribes and Nations, Collections, Art, Culture, Personal Homepages with a Native Focus, NativeTech (devoted to traditional technologies, arts, and crafts, with sources for supplies), The People's Homepage (on the Moccasin Telegraph Network), Repatriation and Reburial Issues, and Telecommunications Technology and Native Americans.

◆ **The Native American Page**

http://ns.gower.net/lee/nativeam.htm

Features include Newsletters from Chief Utsidihi Hicks of the Texas Cherokee, Tsalagiyi Nvdagi.; The Renewal of a Nation and a Tsalagi History; Information on Finding Your Native American Ancestors; Historic Dates Important to the Cherokee; TsaLaGi Dictionary (translates English words into Cherokee); The Messenger (history source); History of the Citizen Band Potawatomi Indian Tribe; Prairie Potowatomi; Wabimeguil Art Homepage; Environmental and Native links; Directory of Native American Sites; American Tribal Directory; Dineh Alliance Homepage; and *The Cherokee Advocate*, October 12, 1883.

◆ **Native American Resource Map**

http://echm10.tuwien.ac.at/inst/tk/tk.native.html

Listing of random sources, directories, history, medical, geographical, legal, ecological and cultural sites.

◆ **Native American Tribes: Information Virtually Everywhere**

http://www.afn.org/~native

Directory to organizations, electronic mailing lists, radio stations with Native American programming, a list of federally recognized tribes with links to their homepages, films and videos, Native American studies programs, and other directories.

◆ **NativeWeb**

http://www.nativeweb.org

Directory to gopher and ftp sites, bibliographies, organizations, literature, languages, education, geographic regions, nations/peoples, newsletters and journals, historical material, electronic mailing lists and newsgroups, an electronic store of Native-owned businesses, a calendar, and an electronic mailing list about the Web page itself.

- ◆ **Tribal Voice**

http://www.tribal.com/

Site attempts to present a united forum for Native American voices. Features include: The PowWow Page, PowWow White Pages, New Kids PowWow!

- ◆ **The Village of First Nations**

http://firstnations.com/

This site proclaims itself to be "a starting point for information on First Nations Peoples, native art, native life and culture." The site includes a Native Art Gallery, an On-line Political Forum, a Native Kids Education and Resource Centre, and Native Stories and Articles. Features include The Village Store (Exclusive Native-made Goods); Canadian Native Arts Gallery; Spiritual Places; First Nations News and Stories; First Nations Events, Shows, and Activities; and Search Links to: Other First Nations Resources.

- ◆ **Yahoo: Society and Culture: Native American**

http://www.yahoo.com/Society_and_Culture/Cultures/ Native_American

Directory to variety of sources such as specific tribes, issues, organizations, historical documents, other directories, the Native American Chat Channel, a page on the Pocahontas debate, a New England powwow schedule, etc.

Current Events

- ◆ **AMERICAN INDIAN-L**

Subscription address: listserv@cornell.edu

This is an electronic mailing list for Native Americans/American Indians only. It serves as the Native American Information Exchange. For assistance, contact the list owner at **idoy@crux1.cit.cornell.edu**.

- ◆ **Costanoan Indian Research Quarterly**

http://www.ucsc.edu:80/costano/nosonpage.html

Newsletter from the Mutsun Band of Costanoan People in San Benito County, California, which contains current general information for the living California Indian Community.

- ▼ **Native American News**

ftp://ftp.cit.cornell.edu/pub/special/NativeProfs/
    Choose newsletters.

Native American News is a current events newsletter distributed weekly. Part B is taken from the moderated lists nat-chat and native-l. Part A is composed of posts to alt.native, soc.culture.native, FidoNet, Indian Affairs and e-mail sent directly to the editor. To receive part A, part B or both, all a person has to do is submit a personal e-mail request from the account where he or she will receive the weekly mailings.

Newsgroups and Listservs

alt.culture.alaska

This Usenet newsgroup is concerned with Alaska studies.

alt.culture.hawaii

This Usenet newsgroup deals issues in the area of Hawaiian studies.

alt.native

This Usenet newsgroup contains messages concerning people indigenous to an area before modern colonization.

- ◆ **NAHUAT-L**

Subscription address: mailserv@acc.fau.edu

NAHUAT-L is an occasionally active electronic mailing list which deals with Nahuatl and Aztec studies in general. Most of the subscribers are professionals in the field, but it includes interested amateurs as well.

- ◆ **NativeNet**

http://niikaan.fdl.cc.mn.us/natnet

NativeNet is made up of a number of discussion groups and sources:

Native-l provides a general forum for exchanging information and perspectives on matters relating to the indigenous peoples of the world.

Natchat exists to provide a forum for general discussion.

Nat–1492, deals specifically with the 500-year anniversary of the voyage of exploration of Christopher Columbus to the "New World" and the havoc that ensued for the Native peoples of the Americas.

The nat-lang list is for exchanging information concerning the languages of indigenous peoples.

Nat-hlth list is for discussing health issues.

"A list called nat-edu, which deals with issues regarding the provision of culturally sensitive educational programs for Native people and better and more accurate educational materials concerning Native people for mainstream students has been established at Indiana University's INDYCMS site in Indianapolis.

All of these lists are self-administered, in the sense that subscribers can come and go at will by means of the commands provided by the LISTSERV software."

You can subscribe to any of the mailing lists below by sending a message to the indicated subscription address (the character at the end of the native-l list name is the letter *l*, and the last character of the host name tamvm1 is the numeral one).

List Name	Description	Subscription Address
native-l	General information exchange	**listserv@tamvm1.tamu.edu**
natchat	General discussion	**listserv@tamvm1.tamu.edu**
nat–1492	Columbus quincentenary	**listserv@tamvm1.tamu.edu**
nat-edu	Native education	**listserv@indycms.iupui.edu**
nat-hlth	Native health	**listserv@tamvm1.tamu.edu**
nat-lang	Native language	**listserv@tamvm1.tamu.edu**

◆ **Newsgroup Archives**

http://www.dejanews.com

This site allows you to search the archives of newsgroups.

soc.culture.native

This is a Usenet newsgroup for the discussion of issues relating to native populations throughout the world and is intended to provide an inclusive vehicle for exchange among native peoples and between native and non-native peoples. It provides not only a forum for the discussion of such issues as sovereignty, religion, education and philosophy, but also news stories and bulletins which pertain to current events relating to indigenous peoples, intended to alert readers to situations that require immediate responses, such as human rights cases and imminent encroachments upon native populations. This newsgroup is for native people in all parts of the world—North and South America, South Asia, etc. Weekly files of soc.culture.native posts and many other interesting and useful files (list of tribal addresses, court cases and more) are available by typing **ftp.cit.cornell.edu** at the login prompt, entering **FTP** at the password prompt, and entering your user ID (e.g., mlw@). The command to get to the correct directory is: **cd pub/special/NativeProfs/usenet**. Type **get filename** to obtain a copy of the file.

soc.culture.native.american

This Usenet newsgroup has discussion of Native American topics.

◆ **Updated Directories of Electronic Mailing Lists**

http://www.afn.org/~native/mlists.htm

http://www.nov.edu/Inter-Links/listserv.html

The first site listed provides an explanation of electronic mailing addresses and descriptions of mail lists. Includes lists not mentioned in this chapter. The second site offers a current directory of electronic mailing lists.

◆ **Updated Lists of Newsgroups**

http://www.liszt.com

Provides current directory of available newsgroups, searchable.

CULTURE AND HUMANITIES, GENERAL

◆ **Galaxy Native American Culture & Community**

http://galaxy.einet.net/galaxy/Community/Culture/Native-American.html

Directory listing articles, guides, art, periodicals, directories, and organizations.

◆ **Indian Pueblo Cultural Center**

http://hanksville.phast.umass.edu/defs/independent/PCC/PCC.html

Features include the following pueblos: The Acoma Pueblo, The Cochiti Pueblo, The Isleta Pueblo, The Jemez Pueblo, The Laguna Pueblo, The Nambe Pueblo, The Picuris Pueblo, The Pojoaque Pueblo, The Sandia Pueblo, The San Felipe Pueblo, The San Ildefonso Pueblo, The San Juan Pueblo, The Santa Ana Pueblo, The Santa Clara Pueblo, The Santo Domingo Pueblo, The Taos Pueblo, The Tesuque Pueblo, The Zia Pueblo, and The Zuni Pueblo.

Additional features of the site include: The Murals Project, Facilities offered by the Pueblo Cultural Center, Pueblo Etiquette and Rules, Directions to the Pueblos, 1996 Calendar of the Indian Pueblo Cultural Center, and 1996 Calendar of Dances and Events at the Pueblos.

EDUCATION

◆ **Community Learning Network's Aboriginal Education**

http://www.etc.bc.ca/coop2/aborg.html

Subsection of British Columbia's Learning Network pages. Features include Law and Legislation, Aboriginal Youth Network, Historical Images on File, Assembly of First Nations, British Columbia's Ministry of Aboriginal Affairs, Canadian Aboriginal Law, Canadian First Nations, Extension Indian Reservation Program, First Perspective, and Native Science Connection.

◆ **Educational Native American Network**

http://shaman.unm.edu/enan/texthome.htm

ENAN is a nationwide telecommunications network based at the University of New Mexico Center for Technology and Education, which is sponsored by the Bureau of Indian Affairs (BIA) and the Office of Indian Education Programs (OIEP). ENAN serves teachers, students and administrators in BIA and OIEP schools and certain professionals in the field of Native American Education. The ENAN system allows participants to send electronic mail, participate in online conferences, download data from ENAN libraries and engage in a variety of interactive educational activities. Features include:

- Access to information bulletin boards on important BIA/OIEP activities, state and regional education activities, and other professional data.

- Sharing of instructional ideas, lesson plans and other materials with teachers in other schools around the nation.

- Providing students opportunity to communicate with peers in other schools, participate in online interactive projects, and learn a variety of telecommunications skills.

- Downloading materials such as software reviews, articles for classroom use and a curriculum materials catalog.

- Finding online support and advice regarding administrative and other computer application questions.

A few ongoing projects include Sister School Project with New Zealand Schools; Online university course offerings; The Native American Public Broadcasting Materials Catalog; Administrative Training Sessions at the University of New Mexico; Online reviews of educational software; Macintosh user assistance; The National Laboratories Rural Assistance Program; "Only the Best," an online database guide to the highest-rated educational software and multimedia products; New Zealand Project, in which participants exchanged videotapes and used ENAN and the Internet to exchange mail and other information about their schools and communities; The *Native Monthly Reader,* containing news articles written for Indian students (available online and may be downloaded).

◆ **native.edu**

Usenet newsgroup concerning native education.

◆ **NATIVEPROFS-L**

Subscription address: contact the list manager at listmgr@cornell.edu

NATIVEPROFS-L is an electronic mailing list for and about the American Indian and Alaska Native Professorate. This discussion group was created in response to the need for continued communication among native professors expressed at the annual conference for the American Indian and Alaska Native Professorate in 1993, sponsored by Arizona State University. Persons using this electronic discussion group are members of this organization or those who will eventually become members of this organization. This discussion group is not intended for use by the general public.

Student Organizations

http://www.clas.ufl.edu/CLAS/american-universities.html
http://www.utexas.edu/world/univ

These two sites provide listings of university homepages. The homepages often provide links to, or lists of, student organizations. Native American student organizations may be cultural, political, social, or centered around minority issues.

FINE ARTS

Art

◆ **Apache Arts**
http://www.eskimo.com/~miller/apache

Apache Arts offers Native American artistic, educational and reference materials. Native American owned, started in 1993. Features include Directory of Native American Tribes of the United States; United States Wall Map of Native American Tribes; Wall Map of Native American Tribes in Washington State; Traditional Art; Native American Resources; and American Indian Internet Resources.

◆ **Native Fonts**
http://www.maxwell.syr.edu/nativeweb/language/
    fonts.html

A guide to commercially available fonts and Native fonts available on the Internet, including Native American fonts, Readme file to Cherokee fonts, Tsalagi font for Macintosh and Windows, Cree font, Inuit font, and font family made for Puget Salish.

GOVERNMENT, LAW, AND POLITICS

Government

◆ **Bureau of Indian Affairs**
http://www.doi.gov/bureau-indian-affairs.html

This is the official site of the Department of the Interior subdivision. Included are press releases, a biography of the assistant secretary, genealogical information, area offices, a newsletter, and a description of the bureau's mission.

◆ **The National Indian Policy Center**

http://gwis.circ.gwu.edu/~nipc/

The National Indian Policy Center Planning Office was established by congressional initiative and authorized by Public Law 101-301. The legislation, supported by a number of tribal leaders, provided for a policy center planning office to be located at the George Washington University in Washington, D.C. The policy center undertook a year-long consultation process with American Indian and Alaska Native governments and individuals to develop the purpose, structure and function of a research analysis institution for social, economic and legal policy development on Native issues. The ultimate goal of the consultation process was to develop a final report on the feasibility study that served as a framework for federal authorizing legislation in the 102nd Congress.

This site contains a Bureau of Indian Affairs (BIA) reservations map and links to other Web resources.

◆ **Nunavut Implementation Commission**

http://www.nunanet.com/~nic

This site is for the impending Nunavut Territory and Government (in northern Canada). It contains news releases, a FAQ, discussion papers, reports, and links.

Government Documents

◆ **Fourth World Documentation Project's Online Documents Archive**

http://www.halcyon.com/FWDP/

FTP: ftp.halcyon.com /pub/FWDP

The Fourth World Documentation Project, organized by the Center for World Indigenous Studies in 1992, has a mission to make the center's documents and resources available to tribal governments, researchers and organizations with an interest in the Fourth World. The FWDP collects documents from nations and organizations and converts them into electronic text for distribution on the Internet, Peace Net, and other computer networks. The FWDP also archives state governments' and international bodies' positions taken in regards to Fourth World nations and peoples, including over 300 documents on Fourth World nations in the Americas, Africa, Asia, Europe, Melanesia and the Pacific. The documents include essays, position papers, resolutions, organizational information, treaties, UN documents, speeches and declarations. The FWDP archives are an important resource for tribal officials, researchers, activists or anyone interested in the past and present struggles of Indigenous Peoples to regain their land and freedom.

Features include: Fourth World Documentation Project file directories and information; African Documents; North, Central and South American Documents; European and Asian Documents; Documents that discuss general Fourth

World issues or are global in scope; and Melanesian, Polynesian and Micronesian Documents. A sampling of American documents includes: Resolutions and Declarations; Affiliated Tribes of Northwest Indians Resolutions; Conference of Tribal Governments Resolutions; Navajo Nation's Navajo-Hopi Land Commission Papers; National Congress of American Indians Resolutions; Other Organization's Resolutions; and Tribal Government Resolutions.

◆ **U.S. Government Documents**

http://www.access.gpo.gov

http://www.fedworld.gov

Through these pages you can find the titles of publications or media items published by the U.S. government through the Government Printing Office (GPO). These items may be available at a government depository library near you. In certain databases you will be able to link to a list of libraries to find out which ones hold the item you want. Through these addresses you can find publications (and the libraries that house them), media, text of laws and regulations, etc. Try GILS, the Government Information Locator Service, or the Monthly Catalog online.

NOTE: When searching government documents, it is best to use the term "Indians of North America," because this is the heading still used by the Library of Congress.

Law

◆ **Alaska Natives and Native Americans—Justice and Law Links**

http://www.uaa.alaska.edu/just/links/natives.html

This site includes abstracts, government documents, articles, links to organizations and codes, dictionaries, and information on international, environmental, and religious freedom issues.

◆ **FindLaw**

http://www.findlaw.com/01topics/21indian/index.html

Handy legal reference listing laws, codes, regulations, cases, treaties, and constitutions. In addition, the site provides links to searching government resources using the Federal Web Locator and links to many Native American Web sites.

◆ **Library of Congress**

http://www.loc.gov/

The Library of Congress's homepage has links to a variety of sources, such as Thomas, which gives up-to-date information from the *Congressional Record*, what is happening on the House and Senate floors each week, the status of legislation, and so on. Also available are historical records online and materials being prepared for the digital archives; access to the Library of Congress catalog as well as other library catalogs; copyright and legal information; exhibitions, publications, and library services.

The Library of Congress Information System (LOCIS) contains several files which contain legislative information. These files are searched through the SCOR-PIO system, developed by the Library of Congress. Beginning with the 93rd Congress, a separate Bill Digest file exists in SCORPIO for each Congress. Each file provides information about the content and status of legislation introduced during that Congress. The LOCIS service provides summaries, abstracts, chronologies, and status information about legislation (bills and resolutions) introduced in the U.S. Senate and House of Representatives since 1973. In addition to digests of bills, the files identify sponsors, cosponsors, committees of referral, and detailed status (usually within 48 hours of the action). Since the 97th Congress, information about amendments, and the full text of most public laws, is also available.

- **THOMAS: U.S. Legislative Information from the Library of Congress**
http://lcweb.loc.gov

One cannot research information about Native Americans without bumping into a wide range of government documents and legislation. There are more than 4,000 pieces of legislation that concern Native Americans. This site provides full text of recent legislation. Updates are posted to follow any action taken until it is passed. The *U.S. Government Manual* and listings of committee members are also available.

This site provides access to U.S. Congress, Congressional Gophers, Congressional Directories, Federal Legislation, Guide to US Government Legislative Documents at LC, Online Legislative Databases at the Library of Congress, Other Legislative Support Agencies, and Government Information (Federal, State and Local Government Information).

The Legislative Resources area contains listings of major floor and committee actions taken in the House and Senate, as well as joint committees, for the last three legislative days. It is updated only when the House is in session, so does not include committee actions taken during recess. The Joint Committee Actions section includes information for the last three legislative days on which joint committees met and acted.

Menu selections are provided on this server for both senators and Senate committees, including a Full Listing of Files Available, Available Documents Distributed by Member, Available Documents Distributed by Committee, and Full Text Search on All Available Documents.

Organizations

- **American Indian Heritage Foundation**
http://www.indians.org

"The American Indian Heritage Foundation was founded in 1973 by Princess Pale Moon, a Cherokee/Ojibwa writer, activist, and concert/recording artist, to meet the physical and social needs of the American Indian tribes by providing emergency relief and educational opportunities and to foster economic development by providing forums on a national and international scale."

"The Foundation hosts many special programs, such as the monthly Washington Indian Leadership Forum on Capitol Hill, and it assisted in the passage of a Congressional bill designating November as National American Indian Heritage Month." The site utilizes advanced multimedia technologies available on the Net such as: live video, high-speed 3D virtual reality environments, "Internet radio," audio and keyboard chat, Netscape 2.0 and JAVA applications.

Features include: Foundation History and Highlights, Gifts-In-Kind Program, Past Projects, Human Development Awards & Grants, Cultural Preservation, Landmark Bill Signing, National American Indian Heritage Month, Operating and Program Expenses, and Interactive Charitable Contribution Form.

◆ **The INDIANnet Census Information and Computer Network Center**
http://indiannet.indian.com/

The INDIANnet Census Information and Computer Network Center was the first national computer network to provide civic information useful to American Indian and Alaskan Natives. The INDIANnet Census Information Center began as a joint project of California State University Monterey Bay, The United States Census Department, and Americans for Indian Opportunity. This project coordinates American Indian CIC centers in several locations nationwide. INDIANnet is a computer communication network similar to an Indian radio station, television station, or Indian newspaper. It is an Indian owned and operated nonprofit organization "dedicated to establishing and developing free, public access, computerized information and communication services for American Indians and Alaskan Natives." INDIANnet is multipurpose, acting as a clearinghouse for federal information and opportunities that pertain to Indians, as well as creating a setting for tribes to develop profiles on themselves. INDIANnet services include computer conferences and private electronic mail for Indian tribes, nonprofit organizations and individuals. Federal information such as the *Federal Register*, Employment Opportunities, Environmental Protection Agency data, US Census data and Geographic Information System (TIGER) files is available. There is also a specialized collection of American Indian and Alaskan Native research reports extracted from the Educational Research Information Clearinghouse (ERIC), and a number of public domain software programs that can be downloaded for free as well as a collection of authentic electronic Indian artwork and graphics.

INDIANnet supports an electronic mailing list. To subscribe send an e-mail message addressed to **LISTSERV@spruce.hsu.edu**. In the message area, type the command **sub INDIANnet-L your name**.

◆ **Native American Rights Fund**

http://www.narf.org

This site includes a mission statement (the organization provides legal representation to Native American tribes, villages, organizations and individuals), history, plans, press releases, a link to a Japanese site, reports, archives, and profiles of fund officers.

◆ **Planet Peace**

http://www.teleport.com/~amt/planetpeace/

Planet Peace is run by indigenous community organizers and activists dedicated to the worldwide distribution of information regarding indigenous and environmental grassroots initiatives. It's their mission to convey, inform, educate, and promote those principles which are dedicated to the protection and preservation of our cultures, traditional customs and ceremonies.

Features include Defense of Homelands, Sacred Site Protection, Cultural Preservation, Environmental Justice, AIDS Related Issues, Human Rights Situations, Treaty Obligations, Sovereignty Issues, Prison Issues, Permaculture, Ecological Restoration, Grassroots Activism, Action Alerts, Columns, and Artists.

HISTORY

◆ **AMWEST-H**

Subscription address: listserv@vm.usc.edu

AMWEST-H is an electronic mailing list dealing with American western history from the Lewis and Clark expedition to the battle of Wounded Knee and the treatise of Frederick Jackson Turner on the end of the frontier of 1893.

native.1492

This Usenet newsgroup contains discussion in reference to the observation of the quincentenary of the voyage of Columbus.

LANGUAGE ARTS AND LITERATURE

Language Arts

◆ **IROQUOIS**

Subscription address: listserv@utoronto.bitnet

IROQUOIS is an electronic mailing list dedicated to the discussion and dissemination of information concerning the Iroquoian languages, including Cayuga, Cherokee, Mohawk, Oneida, Onondaga, Seneca, and Tuscarora. Contributions and questions about any Iroquoian language or linguistic matter are welcome, as well as any matters pertaining to Iroquoian culture, music, etc.

native.lang

Usenet newsgroup with discussion of the traditional languages of aboriginal or indigenous peoples.

◆ **NEHINAWE Speak Cree**

http://arpp1.carleton.ca/cree/

Features include mailing list for Cree-related discussion; Technical requirements for using the special features of the site; Education Resources and Institutes; Cree Syllabics (alphabet/letters); Language Lessons; Stories and Poems; Readings and Resources; and Event Listings.

◆ **SSILA: The Society for the Study of the Indigenous Languages of the Americas**

http://trc2.ucdavis.edu/ssila/

The Society for the Study of the Indigenous Languages of the Americas (SSILA) was founded in December 1981 as the international scholarly organization representing American Indian linguistics. Membership in SSILA is open to all those who are interested in the scientific study of the languages of the native peoples of North, Central and South America. A quarterly *SSILA Newsletter,* contains news, announcements, notices of recent publications, current journal contents, and a listing of recent dissertations, and a "Computer Users' Corner." A monthly *SSILA Bulletin,* with late-breaking news and announcements, is sent to all SSILA members who are accessible on the Internet.

Literature

◆ **NATIVELIT-L**

Subscription Address: listserv@cornell.edu

NATIVELIT-L is an electronic mailing list for the discussion of Native American literature. For the purposes of this list, native refers to autochthonous peoples of the North Americas (the United States, Canada, and Mexico). This list is open to discussions about any aspect of native literature. The list welcomes book reviews, articles about poetry, fiction, and criticism; information about publications, talks and conferences; and general conversation about native literature.

RELIGION

soc.religion.shamanism

This Usenet newsgroup provides a forum for discussion and exchange of questions, ideas, views, and information about historic, traditional, tribal, and contemporary shamanic experience. There is no provision in the charter of soc.religion.shamanism for the general discussion of native religion.

SCIENCE AND TECHNOLOGY

♦ **AISES: American Indian Science and Engineering Society**
http://aises.uthscsa.edu/

American Indian Science and Engineering Society (AISES) provides educational opportunities for Native Americans and Alaska Natives in the areas of science, engineering, business, and other academic fields. This site is available in frames or no frames versions. There is information on the society and its educational programs as well as access to AISESnet, which is a moderated distribution list distributed by the University of Montana in Missoula. The purpose of the list is to provide communication and information for AISES chapters, students and faculty associated with AISES, and for members of industry and government. AISESnet discussions are open to all, including non-AISES members. Currently, the list is split into four groups:

- AISESnet General: This list's topics include AISES issues, position openings, scholarship announcements, AISES chapter communications, conference information, AISES events and announcements, Pow Wow info, topics of general interest to the entire subscription list, and chapter newsletters.

- AISESnet Discussions: This list is intended to discuss topics not suitable for the AISESnet General list. Examples are discussions of Native American issues, engineering and science issues, public opinion, creative writing, etc.

- AISESnet Drums: The AISESnet distribution list dedicated to drum groups addresses only issues concerning drum groups, pow-wow drum groups, drum building, pow-wow singers, etc.

- Alcohol & Drug: This list addresses only issues related to drugs and alcohol. It provides information as well as support. Participation is anonymous, and return address labels are not shown in the messages.

To subscribe, send your e-mail address to: **aisesnet@selway.umt.edu** with a request to be added to the distribution list. Your e-mail address will be added automatically to the AISESnet General and AISESnet Discussions lists. Please indicate if you would like to subscribe to the AISESnet Drums and/or the Alcohol & Drug list as well.

Health

♦ **Indian Health Service**
http://www.ihs.gov

Official page of an agency within the U.S. Department of Health and Human Services. Of particular interest are the various links under the Indian Country page (add **/1AmerInd/AI.html** to the address given above). Includes documents, books reviews, tribal pages, etc.

◆ **NAT-HLTH**

Subscription address: listserv@tamvm1.tamu.edu

Health issues of Native Peoples. To subscribe, send message **sub NAT-HLTH your name** to the above address.

native.health

Usenet newsgroup dealing with the health of indigenous peoples.

OTHER

Tribal Pages

◆ **Choctaw Nation Homepage (Unofficial)**

http://www.toners.com/choctaw

Listing of current tribal officers, books about the Choctaw Nation, genealogical information, information on the Choctaw language, etc.

◆ **Oneida Indian Nation**

http://one-web.org/oneida/

The Oneida Indian Nation, one of the original members of the Iroquois Confederacy, enjoys a unique role in America's history, having supported the colonies in the struggle for independence from England. The Nation exists as a sovereign political unit which predates the Constitution of the United States.

Features include News from the Oneida Indian Nation, Cultural and Historical Information, Oneida Indian Nation Police Homepage, Economic Enterprises, Destination Oneida Nation, and Information Links.

◆ **Seminole Tribe of Florida**

http://www.seminoletribe.com/

Features include Tribal Council, Tribal FAQs, Genealogy & Anthropology, Legends of the Seminole Tribe, AH-THA-THI-KI Museum, *Seminole Tribune*, and Seminole Tribe Education Department.

REFERENCES

Baldwin, George D. "Networking the Nations: The Emerging Indian Network Information Systems." *Journal of Navajo Education* (Winter 1992).

Carter, Kent. "Sources for Research on Tribal History in the National Archives Regional System." *American Indian Culture and Research Journal* 17 (Fall 1993): 107–11A.

Curtis, Jean M. "Symposium on the Summary Report of the White House Conference on Library and Information Services: Information 2000: Library and Information Services for the 21st Century." *Government Information Quarterly* 9 (1992): 323–63.

Mander, Jerry. *In the Absence of the Sacred: The Failure of Technology and the Survival of Indian Nations.* San Francisco, Sierra Club Books, 1991.

Mueller-Alexander, Jeanette M. and Helen J. Seaton. "Researching Native Americans: Tips on Vocabulary, Search Strategies and Internet Resources." *Database* 17 (April 1994): 45.

National Indian Policy Center. *Native Communications Survey.* George Washington University (Summer 1993).

Rayl, A. J. S. "New Technologies, Ancient Cultures." [use of computer and information technology by Native Americans] *Omni* 15 (August 1993): 46.

Rhind, David. "Why GIS." *ARC News* 11 (Summer 1989).

Sunderman, Tracy. "The Tribal Telecommunications Network: Economic Growth through Satellite Technology." *Winds of Change* 4 (Spring 1989): 45–46.

Taylor, Rhonda. "Profiles: Four Native American Libraries." *Wilson Library Bulletin* 67 (December 1992): 38–39.

United States. Senate. Select Committee on Indian Affairs. *Native American Libraries, Archives, and Information Services: Hearing, December 10, 1991.* 102nd Cong., 2nd Sess. 1991. S. hrg. 102–229.

Winchell, Richard. "Tribal Implementation of GIS: A Case Study of Planning Applications with The Colville Confederated Tribes." *American Indian Culture and Research Journal* 16 (Fall 1992): 175–84.

4

African American Resources
SHARON PEREGRINE JOHNSON

INTRODUCTION

The 1990 census indicated that 12.1 percent of the U.S. population (29,986,060 of 248,709,873) were African American, the largest racial group after white. According to recent estimates, the African American population continues to increase in number and cultural diversity, with a complexity that belies a single label.

This chapter provides a listing of significant Internet resources concerning the African American community. The main subject divisions are General Information; Business; Culture and Humanities, General; Education; Fine Arts; Government, Law, and Politics; History; Language Arts and Literature; Popular Culture; Religion; Science and Technology; and Women's Issues. Entries for directories and organizations are included at the end of the chapter. General Information covers World Wide Web sites for electronic journals and up-to-date reports. Fine arts include visual art, dance, and music. The section on music within the Fine Arts category concentrates on general music resources and classical music, blues, and jazz. The section on music under Popular Culture covers the significant contributions of African Americans in the popular music idiom. Of special interest is the Education section, which offers an extensive listing of museums, libraries, and more than 100 historically Black universities and colleges, and the Web sites under Government, Law, and Politics, which cover African American political interests, including such sites as NAACP, Nation of Islam, and National Rainbow Coalition, with special attention to civil rights. The listings are mainly World Wide Web sites, and unless otherwise stated, it is assumed the URL is a Web address.

The research for this chapter began in 1995 as a quest for African American Internet resources available on the World Wide Web and ended with a 110 page listing of sites. This research continued throughout 1996, when it became evident that an update was necessary.

There had been many changes since 1995: 50 percent of the 1995 sites were discontinued, the number of Web sites increased dramatically, and more sites have added sophisticated visual images. Meanwhile, gopher sites decreased significantly. Also since 1995, research on the Internet has become easier and more efficient due to a greater abundance of improved search engines with advanced Boolean logic for searching. Consequently, more than 400 new Internet sites for Black educational institutions, performers, musical groups, significant African Americans, organizations, and other topics were located in 1996. However, due to space limitations, the final version that follows contains listings selected on the basis of importance, quality, and educational significance from over 300 pages of current listings researched in 1996 and 1997.

The Web is constantly changing and supplies a near limitless array of information. Due to the evolving nature of the Web and the difficulty of providing a complete, up-to-date listing of Internet sites, this chapter is a mere snapshot of what is available on the Internet at a specific point in time. For further research, please use one or more of the following search engines.

Excite (**http://www.excite.com/**)

G.O.D. (**http://www.god.co.uk/**)

Infoseek (**http://www.infoseek.com/**)

Lycos (**http://www.lycos.com/**)

MetaCrawler (**http://www.metacrawler.com/**)

MetaSearch (**http://www.stpt.com/**)

Yahoo (**http://www.yahoo.com/**)

GENERAL INFORMATION

◆ **African American Directory**

http://www.igc.apc.org/africanam/africanam2.html

African American directory with a different theme every month (for example, the theme for October 1995 was the Million Man March, and the themes for November 1996 were Mumia and Black Church Fires).

◆ **African American Interest**

http://home.earthlink.net/~anthony/african.html

A listing of resources, such as the *African American Newspaper,* Universal Black Pages, African Artist, African American Homepage, African American Mosaic, Afrinet (The African & African-American Internet Community), *Lee Bailey's RadioScope* (The Entertainment Magazine of the Air), *Black Film & Video Guide,* and links to other African American Web sites.

◆ **African American Internet Resources**

**http://http2.sils.umich.edu/HCHS/Afroam/
Afroam_sources.html**

Links to archival, historical, and cultural resources dedicated to documenting African Americans and the African Diaspora, such as Universal Black Pages, African American Newspapers, African American News Service, the Onyx Page, Black/African Related Resources, the Drum, African American History, Black Information Network, newsgroups, and much more.

◆ **African American Population Census Data**

http://www.thuban.com/census/index.html

This site provides tables and graphs reflecting the latest information available from U.S. census data regarding the U.S. African American population. The categories of information provided include: General Population; Education; Marital, Family, and Household; Economics; Employment; and Poverty. The tables provided at this site are only legible with browsers that use HTML version 3.0 extensions. The material is compiled, prepared, and presented by Leonard Johnson, III, of Thuban Consulting, Inc., using only data obtained from the U.S. Census Bureau.

◆ **African American Resources**

http://www.igc.apc.org/africanam/resources/

Links, often with annotations, to Internet resources arranged in categories, which include business, education, entertainment, environmental, general, exhibits and gallery works, news and news services/papers and more.

◆ **African American Space**

**http://www.mbb.cs.colorado.edu/~mcbryan/bb/321/
summary.html**

Current listing of African American information resources, numerous links to related issues, and historically Black colleges and universities.

◆ **African Americana**

http://www.lib.lsu.edu/hum/african.html

Louisiana State University Webliography (guide to on-line resources). Extensive links to Web resources.

◆ **African World Community Network**

http://www.he.net/~awe/

African American culture site with links to resources such as Aframian Webnet, Virtually Afrocentric and other significant Internet sites.

◆ **Bibliography**

**http://www.sas.upenn.edu/African_Studies/Bibliography/
menu_Biblio.html**

The African Studies Bibliography has links to bibliographies on African American culture at the University of Pennsylvania, New York State Library, and other libraries and institutions in the United States and Canada. This is an excellent source of bibliographic information about African Studies.

◆ **Green Eggs Report**

http://www.ar.com/ger/soc.culture.african.american.html

The Web links on this list were found within the messages on the Usenet newsgroup soc.culture.african.american, a Usenet newsgroup featuring African American cultural perspectives and issues.

◆ **Links N' Such**

http://www.engr.wisc.edu/~hassrick/links.html

Links to numerous African American sites, including African American studies, Martin Luther King, Jr.'s "I Have a Dream" speech, Nelson Mandela's October 6, 1994, speech to Congress, the journal *Meanderings* (now called *Gravity)*, and more.

◆ **MelaLink**

http://www.melanet.com/melalink/

Source of Afrocentric Web sites and homepages, scholarship information, banking, demographics, organizations, and other topics.

◆ **Rest Stops on the Highway**

http://www.ai.mit.edu/~isbell/links.html

Links to other African American sites (The Skin I'm In, The Drum, The NAACP, The Universal Black Pages, The National Civil Rights Museum, The Library of Congress Resource Guide for Black History and Culture, African American Web Connection, Club Nubia, Brown Eyed Intelligence, Index to African American [by and for] Software Products, Black Planets, and more).

◆ **Selected Internet Resources**

http://www.lib.umich.edu/libhome/services/diversres.html

Selected Internet resources on diversity, multiculturalism, and African American issues such as Federal Information Exchange, Inc., MOLIS Homepage Resources, Tulane's Amistad Center, The Universal Black Pages, Isis, Drum Web Server Homepage, Black Information Network WWW, and others.

- ◆ **Universal Afrocentric Calendar**

http://www.melanet.com/afro_today.html

Important happenings in the African American world, on and off the Net, are found here. "Today in the Diaspora" lists events day by day. Readers can add events to the list from the site. A potentially useful site, but not many events are listed yet and some links do not work.

- ◆ **The Universal Black Pages**

http://www.gatech.edu/bgsa/blackpages.html

Internet resource for and about Black America. Categories of the information provided include: art, businesses, events, entertainment, history, music and many more.

- ◆ **Virtually Afrocentric**

http://www.tawcnet.com/~awe/va.htm

African American Internet resources divided by categories which include: art, music, business, news, communications, organizations, education, people, entertainment, places, information, politics, institutions, shopping, and sports.

- ◆ **W. E. B. Du Bois Institute**

http://web-dubois.fas.harvard.edu/

The W. E. B. Du Bois Institute for Afro-American Research at Harvard, founded in 1975, is the oldest such center for the study of African American history, culture and social institutions. This site features events, research projects, publications, and more.

- ◆ **Yahoo: Social Science: African American Studies**

http://www.yahoo.com/Social_Science/ African_American_Studies/

Yahoo's site for information on significant sociological issues, including African American studies, Black Cultural Studies Web sites, and more.

- ◆ **Yahoo: Society and Culture—African American**

http://www.yahoo.com/Society_and_Culture/Cultures/ African_American/

Yahoo's site on electronic sources about African American organizations, businesses, and culture. There are links to other Internet sites, such as AfriNET, Afro-American Newspapers, Black Experience, Black Information Network World Wide Web, Coalition of African American Organizations, and *Elam World Technology Review.*

Current Events

◆ **African American News Service**

gopher://gopher.igc.apc.org/11/race/aanews

African American News Service is an electronic news service presenting world news of importance to African Americans. It is provided by the African American Desk of the Institute for Global Communications and maintained by Debra Floyd and Art McGee. It contains historical material of interest to educators as well as current events.

◆ **AFRO-Americ@: The Afro-American Newspapers Homepage**

http://www.afroam.org

Afro-American Newspapers Homepage has listings of news stories on African Americans divided into categories and links to other sites dealing with African American issues.

◆ **Meanderings**

http://www.newsavanna.com/meanderings/

Meanderings is an African American journal of politics, arts, and culture. Back issues are available here. See also *Gravity.*

◆ **" 'Report the Crime—Not the Color,' Panelists Say"**

http://www.ccrc.wustl.edu/spj/newsletter/1095-color.html

The site is an article on the news media's reportage of crime, discrimination, and racial relations. It reports a program at a meeting of the St. Louis chapter of the Society of Professional Journalists.

Newsgroups and Listservs

◆ **ABSLST-L**

Subscription address: listserv@cmuvm.csv.cmich.edu

An electronic mailing list for members of the Association of Black Sociologists and other scholars. To subscribe send the message **subscribe ABSLST-L your name** to the subscription address.

◆ **AFAM-L**

Subscription address: listserv@mizzou1.missouri.edu

This electronic mailing list is devoted to discussions on African American research and contemporary issues of significance to African Americans. To subscribe, send the message **SUBSCRIBE AFAM-L your name** to the subscription address.

◆ **AFAS-L**

Subscription address: listserv@kentvm.kent.edu

AFAS-L is an African American Studies and Librarianship electronic mailing list. To join, send the message **subscribe AFAS-L your name** to the subscription address.

soc.culture.african.american

Usenet newsgroup on African American issues.

Newspapers, Magazines, and Newsletters

◆ **African American Newspapers**

http://199.186.169.35

A number of African American newspapers from around the country are represented, with features that are of interest to the African American community. This site includes a Kids Zone with myths and fables, as well as games, brainteasers, and other activities.

◆ **Afronet Times**

http://www.afronet.com/AFRONET-TIMES/frontpage.html

This online publication of *LA Watts Times* claims to be weekly. It does change occasionally, but is usually months out of date. The stories are interesting and may be useful, even though not current.

◆ **Atlanta Tribune Online**

http://www.atlantatribune.com/index.shtml

Online version of one of the leading minority newspapers in the Southeast. Coverage is available for features, columns, travel, business and more.

◆ **BOBC**

Subscription address: BOBCNEWS@aol.com

Black On Black Communications, BOBC, is an electronic newsletter that reports on the arts, business, medicine, law, technology and politics. To subscribe, type the word **subscribe** in the subject line of a message and send to the subscription address.

◆ **EUR**

Subscription address: EURmailroom@afrinet.net

An electronic newsletter, *EUR* offers urban infotainment. To subscribe, send the message **subscribe EUR** to the subscription address.

◆ **Gravity**

http://www.newsavanna.com/gravity/contents.shtml

An electronic journal dealing with issues of interest to or about African Americans.

◆ **Skanner On-line Newspaper**

http://www.theskanner.com

The Skanner Newspaper, established in October 1975, is published each Wednesday by IMM Publications, of Portland, Oregon, and Seattle, Washington. This site offers both editions of the paper, plus special editions and other information, such as a list of ethnic newpapers in the United States, arranged by state.

BUSINESS

◆ **African American Businesses in Indianapolis**

http://www.spcc.com/ihsw/aabus.htm

Based upon the resources of the Society and the Historic Landmarks Foundation of Indiana, this exhibit of African American Businesses presents the variety of African-American-owned businesses that blossomed in Indianapolis following the Civil War to 1970.

◆ **Bay Drum**

http://www.tomato.com/~baydrum/

Subscription: bay-drum-admin@love.corp.hp.com

Directory of African American businesses in the San Francisco Bay Community. A part of this site is a link to the African American E-mail Network which serves the San Francisco Bay Area.

◆ **Black Enterprise On-line Magazine**

http://www.blackenterprise.com/

Business news, strategies, information and resources for African American entrepreneurs, executives, managers, and professionals.

◆ **Local (Paperbound) Black Pages**

http://www.gatech.edu/bgsa/blackpages/paperblack.html

This sites provides the contact addresses of the "paperbound" Black Pages which are specific to a given area. These Black Pages are essentially like the phone company business directories, except they specifically target Black businesses and enterprises.

◆ **Melanet: The Uncut Black Experience**

http://www.melanet.com/

Links to African American businesses, an online marketplace, and much more.

◆ **Unite-Us: Black Business Database**

http://www.scbbs.com/~unite-us

Unite-Us, a listing of Black-owned businesses worldwide available via any resource on the Internet, with links to business sites.

CULTURE AND HUMANITIES, GENERAL

◆ **African American Resource Guide**

**http://www.usc.edu/Library/Ref/Ethnic/
    black_study_guide.html**

African American resource guides (dictionaries, encyclopedias, atlases, directories, indices, biographical works, bibliographies, literature, music, art, and more) for undergraduates interested in studying African Americans' influence on American life. From the libraries of the University of Southern California.

◆ **Afro American Culture–Community (from Galaxy: The
   Professional's Guide to a World of Information)**

**http://galaxy.tradewave.com/galaxy/Community/Culture/
    Afro-American.html**

The page consists solely of links to African American culture sites, arranged by topic.

◆ **Guide to the African American Heritage Preservation Foundation**

http://www.preservenet.cornell.edu/aahpf/homepage.htm

This site provides information concerning the goals and projects of the African American Heritage Preservation Foundation.

◆ **Kwanzaa Information Center**

http://www.melanet.com/kwanzaa

This site provides information about Kwanzaa, the African American spiritual holiday. It covers the Kwanzaa celebration, history, and other Internet sites, links, and resources.

◆ **On-Line African Wedding Guide**

http://www.melanet.com/wedding/

This site includes a great deal of information about weddings for African Americans, including a list of wedding consultants.

◆ **Schomburg Center**

http://www.nypl.org/research/sc/sc.html

http://gopher.nypl.org/research/sc/sc.html

New York Public Library's Schomburg Center for research in African American culture, its collections, programs, and resources.

EDUCATION

◆ **African Education Research Network (AERN)**

gopher://ra.cs.ohiou.edu/11/dept.servers/aern

This site provides information about AERN (purpose, news, newsletters, committees), information on other organizations, and African American Studies at U.S. and international universities.

◆ **Black Excel: The College Help Network**

http://cnct.com/home/ijblack/BlackExcel.shtml

Black Excel (founded in 1988 by Isaac J. Black) is a college admissions and scholarship service for African American students. Its Web site has numerous links to other related sites.

◆ **Black Student Organizations**

http://www.gatech.edu/bgsa/blackpages/schools.html

Links and listings to schools and student organizations for universities and high schools located in the United States, South Africa, and other countries.

◆ **Columbia University: Institute for Research in African-American Studies**

http://www.columbia.edu/cu/iraas/

The Institute for Research in African-American Studies at Columbia University, and African American history and studies.

◆ **IOTA PHI THETA**

http://www.siu.edu/departments/iotaphi/national/ overview.htm

Historical overview of Iota Phi Theta Fraternity, Inc. (an African American fraternity established in 1963).

◆ **National Alliance of Black School Educators**

http://www.nabse.org/

NABSE, its members, activities, and projects.

- ◆ **"Students Get Hard Sell on Education"**

gopher://gopher1.cit.cornell.edu:70/00/files/CH072894/ CH07289419

Darryl Geddes's article, published in the *Cornell Chronicle,* on the need to increase the numbers of African American and other minority teachers.

- ◆ **United Negro College Fund, Inc.**

http://www.uncf.org/

This organization's purpose is to raise funds and provide services to support its member colleges, a consortium of 41 private, historically black colleges and universities.

Historically Black Colleges and Universities

- ◆ **Alabama A & M University, Normal, AL**

http://www.aamu.edu/
http://web.fie.com/htbin/Molis/MolisSummary?FICE=001002

Alabama A & M University (founded in 1875), its faculty, and programs.

- ◆ **Alabama State University, Montgomery, AL**

http://www.alasu.edu/
http://web.fie.com/htbin/Molis/MolisSummary?FICE=001005

Alabama State University (founded in 1874), its programs, and faculty.

- ◆ **Albany State College, Albany, GA**

http://web.fie.com/htbin/Molis/MolisSummary?FICE=001544

Albany State College (established in 1903), its programs, and faculty.

- ◆ **Alcorn State University, Lorman, MS**

http://academic.alcorn.edu/
http://web.fie.com/htbin/Molis/MolisSummary?FICE=002396

Alcorn State University (founded in 1871), its programs, and other details.

- ◆ **Allen University, Columbia, SC**

http://www.icusc.org/allen/auhome.htm
http://web.fie.com/htbin/Molis/MolisSummary?FICE=003417

Allen University (founded in 1870 by the African Methodist Episcopal Church), its programs, faculty, and other information.

◆ **Arkansas Baptist College, Little Rock, AR**

http://web.fie.com/htbin/Molis/MolisSummary?FICE=001087

Arkansas Baptist College (founded in 1901), its programs, faculty, and related information.

◆ **Barber-Scotia College, Concord, NC**

http://web.fie.com/htbin/Molis/MolisSummary?FICE=002909

Barber-Scotia College (founded in 1867), its programs, and related information.

◆ **Benedict College, Columbia, SC**

http://www.icusc.org/benedict/bchome.htm

http://web.fie.com/htbin/Molis/MolisSummary?FICE=003420

Benedict College (founded in 1870 by the Baptist Church), its programs, faculty, and other information.

◆ **Bennett College, Greensboro, NC**

http://www.bennett.edu/

http://web.fie.com/htbin/Molis/MolisSummary?FICE=002911

Bennett College (established in 1873), its programs, and faculty.

◆ **Bethune-Cookman College, Daytona Beach, FL**

http://web.fie.com/htbin/Molis/MolisSummary?FICE=001467

Bethune-Cookman College (established in 1904), its programs, faculty, and other information.

◆ **Bishop State Community College: Mobile, AL**

Main campus: http://web.fie.com/htbin/Molis/ MolisSummary?FICE=001030

Carver campus: http://web.fie.com/htbin/Molis/ MolisSummary?FICE=005117

Bishop State Community College, its programs, faculty, and other information. The Main campus was established in 1927 and the Carver campus in 1962.

◆ **Bluefield State College, Bluefield, WV**

http://www.bluefield.wvnet.edu/

http://web.fie.com/htbin/Molis/MolisSummary?FICE=003809

Bluefield State College (established in 1895), its programs, and faculty. Sponsor/Contact: **webslinger@bscvx1.wvnet.edu.**

- ◆ **Bowie State University, Bowie, MD**
http://www.bowiestate.edu/
http://web.fie.com/htbin/Molis/MolisSummary?FICE=002062
http://www.bsu.umd.edu/
Bowie State University (founded in 1865), its degree programs, and African American Studies information.

- ◆ **Central State University, Wilberforce, OH**
http://web.fie.com/htbin/Molis/MolisSummary?FICE=003026
Central State University (founded in 1887), its programs, and faculty.

- ◆ **Cheyney University of Pennsylvania, Cheyney, PA**
http://www.cheyney.edu/www/history.html
http://web.fie.com/htbin/Molis/MolisSummary?FICE=003317
Cheyney University of Pennsylvania (founded in 1837), its programs, faculty, and other information.

- ◆ **Claflin College, Orangeburg, SC**
http://www.icusc.org/claflin/cchome.htm
http://web.fie.com/htbin/Molis/MolisSummary?FICE=003424
Claflin College (founded in 1869), its programs, faculty, and other details.

- ◆ **Clark Atlanta University, Atlanta, GA**
http://galaxy.cau.edu/cau/
http://galaxy.cau.edu/cau/ctsps.html
http://web.fie.com/htbin/Molis/MolisSummary?FICE=001559
Clark Atlanta University (founded in 1865), its programs, and faculty.

- ◆ **Coahoma Community College, Clarksdale, MS**
http://web.fie.com/htbin/Molis/MolisSummary?FICE=002401
Coahoma Community College (established in 1949), its programs, faculty, and related information.

- ◆ **Concordia College, Selma, AL**
http://web.fie.com/htbin/Molis/MolisSummary?FICE=010554
Concordia College (established in 1922), its faculty, and programs.

- ◆ **Coppin State College, Baltimore, MD**
http://web.fie.com/htbin/Molis/MolisSummary?FICE=002068
Coppin State College (established in 1900), its programs, and faculty.

◆ **Delaware State University, Dover, DE**

http://www.dsc.edu/index.html

http://web.fie.com/htbin/Molis/MolisSummary?FICE=001428

Delaware State University, its programs, faculty, and other information. It was established on May 15, 1891, by the Delaware General Assembly under the provisions of the Morrill Act of 1890 as a land grant college for African Amercians.

◆ **Denmark Technical College, Denmark, SC**

http://web.fie.com/htbin/Molis/MolisSummary?FICE=005363

Denmark Technical College (established in 1948), its programs, and more.

◆ **Dillard University, New Orleans, LA**

http://web.fie.com/htbin/Molis/MolisSummary?FICE=002004

Dillard University (founded in 1869), its programs, and related information.

◆ **Edward Waters College, Jacksonville, FL**

http://web.fie.com/htbin/Molis/MolisSummary?FICE=001478

Edward Waters College (established in 1866), its programs, and more.

◆ **Elizabeth City State University, Elizabeth City, NC**

http://www.ecsu.edu/

http://www.ecsu.edu/cs/cs.html

http://web.fie.com/htbin/Molis/MolisSummary?FICE=002926

Elizabeth City State University is a traditionally Black university founded in 1891.

◆ **Fayetteville State University, Fayetteville, NC**

http://www.uncfsu.edu/

http://web.fie.com/htbin/Molis/MolisSummary?FICE=002928

Fayetteville State University (founded in 1867), its curriculum, faculty, courses, and other information.

◆ **Fisk University, Memphis, TN**

http://www.fisk.edu/

http://web.fie.com/htbin/Molis/MolisSummary?FICE=003490

Fisk University, its programs, and faculty. The University started as Fisk School in 1866 when it opened its doors to former slaves, and is known for its strong liberal arts and science programs.

◆ **Florida Agricultural and Mechanical University, Tallahassee, FL**

http://www.famu.edu/

http://web.fie.com/htbin/Molis/MolisSummary?FICE=001480

http://www.cis.famu.edu/black.html

FAMU (founded in 1887 by Thomas DeSaille Tucker and Thomas Gibbs), admission policies, courses, programs, faculty, and other information.

◆ **Florida Memorial College, Miami, FL**

http://www.fmc.edu/

http://www.fmc.edu/history.html

http://web.fie.com/htbin/Molis/MolisSummary?FICE=001486

Florida Memorial College, its programs, faculty, and other information. FMC, one of the oldest academic institutions in Florida, was founded in 1879 and is known as the birthplace of the Negro National Anthem.

◆ **Fort Valley State University, Fort Valley, GA**

http://web.fie.com/htbin/Molis/MolisSummary?FICE=001566

Fort Valley State University (founded in 1895), its programs, and more.

◆ **Grambling State University, Grambling, LA**

http://web.fie.com/htbin/Molis/MolisSummary?FICE=002006

Grambling State University (founded in 1901), its programs, faculty, and other information.

◆ **Hampton University, Hampton, VA**

http://www.cs.hamptonu.edu/

http://www.cs.hamptonu.edu/Links.html

http://web.fie.com/htbin/Molis/MolisSummary?FICE=003714

Hampton University (founded in 1868), its curriculum, faculty, and courses.

◆ **Harris-Stowe State College, St. Louis, MO**

http://web.fie.com/htbin/Molis/MolisSummary?FICE=002466

Harris-Stowe State College (founded in 1857), and its programs.

◆ **HBCU (Historically Black Colleges & Universities) Homepage**

http://eric-web.tc.columbia.edu/hbcu/

Information on historically Black colleges and universities, African American history and culture, and other resources.

◆ **Hinds Community College, Utica, MS**
http://web.fie.com/htbin/Molis/MolisSummary?FICE=002407
Hinds Community College (founded in 1903), and its programs.

◆ **Howard University, Washington, DC**
http://www.howard.edu/
http://web.fie.com/htbin/Molis/MolisSummary?FICE=001448
Howard University (established in 1867), its programs, and faculty.

◆ **Huston-Tillotson College: Austin, TX**
http://web.fie.com/htbin/Molis/MolisSummary?FICE=003577
Huston-Tillotson College (founded in 1875), its programs, and faculty.

◆ **Interdenominational Theological Center, Atlanta, GA**
http://web.fie.com/htbin/Molis/MolisSummary?FICE=001568
The Center (established in 1958), its programs, and related information.

◆ **J. F. Drake State Technical College, Huntsville, Al**
http://web.fie.com/htbin/Molis/MolisSummary?FICE=005260
J. F. Drake State Technical College (founded in 1961), and its programs.

◆ **Jackson State University, Jackson, MS**
http://WWW.JSUMS.EDU/
http://web.fie.com/htbin/Molis/MolisSummary?FICE=002410
Jackson State University (established in 1877), its programs, and faculty.

◆ **Jarvis Christian College, Hawkins, TX**
http://web.fie.com/htbin/Molis/MolisSummary?FICE=003637
Jarvis Christian College (founded in 1912), its programs, and faculty.

◆ **Johnson C. Smith University, Charlotte, NC**
http://www.jcsu.edu/index.html
http://web.fie.com/htbin/Molis/MolisSummary?FICE=002936
Johnson C. Smith University (founded in 1867), African American Internet resources, and links to other significant African American sites.

◆ **Kentucky State University, Frankfort, KY**
http://www.state.ky.us/ksu/ksuhome.htm
http://web.fie.com/htbin/Molis/MolisSummary?FICE=001968
Kentucky State University (established in 1886), its programs, and faculty.

◆ **Knoxville College, Knoxville, TN**
http://web.fie.com/htbin/Molis/MolisSummary?FICE=003497
Knoxville College (founded in 1875), its programs, and other details.

◆ **Lane College, Jackson, TN**
http://web.fie.com/htbin/Molis/MolisSummary?FICE=003499
Lane College (founded in 1882), its programs, and faculty.

◆ **Langston University, Langston, OK**
http://www.lunet.edu/
http://web.fie.com/htbin/Molis/MolisSummary?FICE=003157
Langston University (founded in 1897), its faculty, curriculum, and courses.

◆ **Lawson State Community College, Birmingham, AL**
http://web.fie.com/htbin/Molis/MolisSummary?FICE=001059
Lawson State Community College (founded in 1965), its programs, and related information.

◆ **LeMoyne-Owen College, Memphis, TN**
http://web.fie.com/htbin/Molis/MolisSummary?FICE=003501
LeMoyne-Owen College (established in 1862), its programs, and faculty.

◆ **Lewis College of Business, Detroit, MI**
http://web.fie.com/htbin/Molis/MolisSummary?FICE=003968
Lewis College of Business (established in 1920), its programs, and courses.

◆ **Lincoln University of Missouri, Jefferson City, MO**
http://www.lincolnu.edu/
http://web.fie.com/htbin/Molis/MolisSummary?FICE=002479
Lincoln University of Missouri, its programs, faculty, and other information. It was founded in 1866 by the 62nd and 65th Colored Infantries.

◆ **Lincoln University of Pennsylvania, Chester County, PA**
http://www.lincoln.edu/
http://web.fie.com/htbin/Molis/MolisSummary?FICE=003290
Lincoln University of Pennsylvania, its programs, faculty, and other information. It is a historically Black university that was charted on April 29, 1854, and is noted as the first institution to provide a higher education in the arts and sciences for African American youths.

- **Livingston College, Salisbury, NC**
http://web.fie.com/htbin/Molis/MolisSummary?FICE=002942
Livingston College (founded in 1879), its programs, classes, and faculty.

- **Mary Holmes College, West Point, MS**
http://web.fie.com/htbin/Molis/MolisSummary?FICE=002412
Mary Holmes College (established in 1892), its programs, and faculty.

- **Meharry Medical College, Nashville, TN**
http://web.fie.com/htbin/Molis/MolisSummary?FICE=003506
Meharry Medical College (established in 1876), its courses, faculty, and related information.

- **Miles College, Birmingham, AL**
http://web.fie.com/htbin/Molis/MolisSummary?FICE=001028
Miles College (established in 1905), its programs, faculty, and classes.

- **Minority Institution Information**
http://web.fie.com/web/mol/molinfo.htm
Web site for historically Black colleges and universities. An opening map shows the distribution of these institutions throughout the United States.

- **Mississippi Valley State University, Itta Bena, MS**
http://fielding.mvsu.edu/
http://web.fie.com/htbin/Molis/MolisSummary?FICE=002424
Mississippi Valley State University (established in 1946), its programs, faculty, classes, and other information.

- **Morehouse School of Medicine, Atlanta, GA**
http://www.msm.edu/
http://web.fie.com/htbin/Molis/MolisSummary?FICE=000003
Morehouse School of Medicine (founded in 1973), its programs, faculty, and other information.

- **Morgan State University, Baltimore, MD**
http://www.morgan.edu/
http://web.fie.com/htbin/Molis/MolisSummary?FICE=002083
Morgan State University (founded in 1867), its programs, and faculty.

- **Morris Brown College, Atlanta, GA**
http://web.fie.com/htbin/Molis/MolisSummary?FICE=001583
Morris Brown College (established in 1881), its programs, and faculty.

◆ **Morris College, Sumter, SC**

http://web.fie.com/htbin/Molis/MolisSummary?FICE=003439

Morris College (established in 1908), its faculty, programs, and classes.

◆ **Norfolk State University, Norfolk, VA**

http://cyclops.nsu.edu/

http://web.fie.com/htbin/Molis/MolisSummary?FICE=003765

Norfolk State University (founded in 1935), its programs, and faculty.

◆ **North Carolina A & T State University, Greensboro, NC**

http://www.ncat.edu/

http://web.fie.com/htbin/Molis/MolisSummary?FICE=002905

North Carolina A & T State University (established in 1891), its programs, faculty, and courses.

◆ **North Carolina Central University, Durham, NC**

http://www.nccu.edu/

http://web.fie.com/htbin/Molis/MolisSummary?FICE=002950

North Carolina Central University (founded in 1910), its programs, faculty, and other information.

◆ **Oakwood College, Huntsville, AL**

http://www.oakwood.edu/

http://web.fie.com/htbin/Molis/MolisSummary?FICE=001033

Oakwood College (founded in 1896), its programs, faculty, and classes.

◆ **Paine College, Augusta, GA**

http://web.fie.com/htbin/Molis/MolisSummary?FICE=001587

Paine College (founded in 1882), its courses, faculty, and related information.

◆ **Philander Smith College, Little Rock, AR**

http://www.philander.edu/

http://web.fie.com/htbin/Molis/MolisSummary?FICE=001103

Philander Smith College (founded in 1877), its programs, faculty, and classes.

◆ **Prairie View A & M University, Prairie View, TX**

http://web.fie.com/htbin/Molis/MolisSummary?FICE=003630

Prairie View A & M University (established in 1876), its faculty, programs, and courses.

◆ **Rust College, Holly Springs, MS**
http://web.fie.com/htbin/Molis/MolisSummary?FICE=002433
Rust College (founded in 1866), its courses, faculty, and related information.

◆ **Saint Augustine's College, Raleigh, NC**
http://web.fie.com/htbin/Molis/MolisSummary?FICE=002968
Saint Augustine's College (founded in 1867), its programs, and faculty.

◆ **Saint Paul's College, Lawrenceville, VA**
http://web.fie.com/htbin/Molis/MolisSummary?FICE=003739
Saint Paul's College (established in 1888), its programs, faculty, and classes.

◆ **Savannah State University, Savannah, GA**
http://www.peachnet.edu/inst/savstate.html
http://web.fie.com/htbin/Molis/MolisSummary?FICE=001590
Savannah State University (originally chartered in 1890 by the State of Georgia), its programs, faculty, and other information.

◆ **Selma University, Selma, AL**
http://web.fie.com/htbin/Molis/MolisSummary?FICE=001037
Selma University (founded in 1878), its faculty, programs, and classes.

◆ **Shaw University, Raleigh, NC**
http://web.fie.com/htbin/Molis/MolisSummary?FICE=002962
Shaw University (founded in 1868), its courses, faculty, and programs.

◆ **Shelton State Community College-Fredd Campus, Tuscaloosa, AL**
http://web.fie.com/htbin/Molis/MolisSummary?FICE=000005
Shelton State Community College, Fredd Campus (established in 1965), its courses, faulty, and related information.

◆ **Shorter College, Little Rock, AR**
http://web.fie.com/htbin/Molis/MolisSummary?FICE=001105
Shorter College (established in 1873), its programs, faculty, and classes.

◆ **South Carolina State University, Orangeburg, SC**
http://192.231.63.160/scsu/state.htm
http://web.fie.com/htbin/Molis/MolisSummary?FICE=003446
South Carolina State Univserity, its programs, faculty, and other information. It is a Black land grant institution/university founded in 1896.

◆ **Southern University & A&M College, Baton Rouge, LA**
http://www.subr.edu/
http://web.fie.com/htbin/Molis/MolisSummary?FICE=009636
Southern University & A & M College (established in 1880), its programs, faculty, and other information.

◆ **Southern University, New Orleans, LA**
http://www.gnofn.org/~zaire/suno4.htm
http://web.fie.com/htbin/Molis/MolisSummary?FICE=002026
Southern University, New Orleans (founded in 1959), its programs, faculty, and other information.

◆ **Southern University, Shreveport, LA**
http://web.fie.com/htbin/Molis/MolisSummary?FICE=004622
Southern University (established in 1967), its programs, faculty, and classes.

◆ **Southwestern Christian College, Terrell, TX**
http://web.fie.com/htbin/Molis/MolisSummary?FICE=003618
Southwestern Christian College (founded in 1949), its faculty, courses, and other information.

◆ **Spelman College, Atlanta, GA**
http://web.fie.com/htbin/Molis/MolisSummary?FICE=001594
Spelman College (established in 1881), its programs, faculty, and classes.

◆ **Stillman College, Tuscaloosa, AL**
http://www.stillman.edu/
http://web.fie.com/htbin/Molis/MolisSummary?FICE=001044
Stillman College (one of the oldest historically Black colleges in America, founded in 1876), its programs, faculty, campus, and other information.

◆ **Talladega College, Talladega, AL**
http://web.fie.com/htbin/Molis/MolisSummary?FICE=001046
Talladega College (founded in 1867), its programs, faculty, and classes.

◆ **Tennessee State University, Nashville, TN**
http://www.tnstate.edu/
http://web.fie.com/htbin/Molis/MolisSummary?FICE=003522
Tennessee State University (Black grant university founded in 1912), its programs, faculty, and other information.

◆ **Texas College, Tyler, TX**
http://web.fie.com/htbin/Molis/MolisSummary?FICE=003638
Texas College (established in 1894), its faculty, programs, and classes.

◆ **Texas Southern University, Houston, TX**
http://www.tsu.edu/
http://www.tsu.edu/tsu.html
http://web.fie.com/htbin/Molis/MolisSummary?FICE=003642
Texas Southern University (established in 1894), its programs, and faculty.

◆ **Tougaloo College, Tougaloo, MS**
http://web.fie.com/htbin/Molis/MolisSummary?FICE=002439
Tougaloo College (founded in 1869), its programs, classes, and faculty.

◆ **Trenholm State Technical College, Montgomery, AL**
http://web.fie.com/htbin/Molis/MolisSummary?FICE=005734
Trenholm State Technical College (established in 1963), its faculty, courses, programs, and other information.

◆ **Tuskegee University, Tuskegee, AL**
http://www.tusk.edu/
http://web.fie.com/htbin/Molis/MolisSummary?FICE=001050
Tuskegee University (founded in 1881), its programs, faculty, and courses.

◆ **University of Arkansas, Pine Bluff, AR**
http://web.fie.com/htbin/Molis/MolisSummary?FICE=001086
University of Arkansas (established in 1873), its programs, and faculty.

◆ **University of Maryland at Eastern Shore, Princess Anne, MD**
http://www.umes.umd.edu/
http://web.fie.com/htbin/Molis/MolisSummary?FICE=002106
University of Maryland at Eastern Shore (founded in 1886), its programs, faculty, and other information.

◆ **University of the District of Columbia, Washington, DC**
http://www.udc.edu/
http://web.fie.com/htbin/Molis/MolisSummary?FICE=029100
The University of the District of Columbia (established in 1976), its programs, faculty, and other information.

◆ **University of Virgin Islands, St. Thomas, VI**
http://www.uvi.edu/
http://web.fie.com/htbin/Molis/MolisSummary?FICE=008841
University of Virgin Islands (established in 1962), its programs, and faculty.

◆ **Virginia State University, Petersburg, VA**
http://www.vsu.edu/
http://web.fie.com/htbin/Molis/MolisSummary?FICE=003764
Virginia State University (established in 1882), its programs, and faculty.

◆ **Virginia Union University, Richmond, VA**
http://web.fie.com/htbin/Molis/MolisSummary?FICE=003766
Virginia Union University (founded in 1865), its faculty and programs.

◆ **Voorhees College, Denmark, SC**
http://www.icusc.org/voorhees/vchome.htm
http://web.fie.com/htbin/Molis/MolisSummary?FICE=003455
Voorhees College (founded by Elizabeth Evelyn Wright in 1897), its programs, faculty, and other information.

◆ **W. E. B. Du Bois Institute**
http://web-dubois.fas.harvard.edu/
The W. E. B. Du Bois Institute for Afro-American Research and the study of African American history, culture and social institutions.

◆ **West Virginia State College, Institute, WV**
http://wvscen.wvsc.wvnet.edu/wvsc.html
http://web.fie.com/htbin/Molis/MolisSummary?FICE=003826
West Virginia State College (founded in 1891), its programs, and faculty.

◆ **Wilberforce University: Wilberforce, OH**
http://www.wilberforce.edu/
http://web.fie.com/htbin/Molis/MolisSummary?FICE=003141
Wilberforce University (founded in 1856), its programs, faculty, and classes.

◆ **Wiley College, Marshall, TX**
http://web.fie.com/htbin/Molis/MolisSummary?FICE=003669
Wiley College (established in 1873), its programs, courses, and faculty.

◆ **Winston-Salem State University, Winston-Salem, NC**

http://uncecs.edu/UNC_Schools/WSSU_Profile.html

http://web.fie.com/htbin/Molis/MolisSummary?FICE=002986

Winston-Salem State University (established in 1892), its programs, faculty, and other information.

◆ **Xavier University, New Orleans, LA**

http://www.xu.edu/

http://web.fie.com/htbin/Molis/MolisSummary?FICE=002032

Xavier University (established in 1915), its programs, faculty, and courses.

FINE ARTS

◆ **African-American Bibliography on the Arts**

http://www.sas.upenn.edu/African_Studies/Bibliography/ AFAM_Arts.html

This African American Bibliography on the Arts is based upon resources of the New York State Library.

◆ **Artists and Musicians of the Harlem Renaissance**

http://www.usc.edu/Library/Ref/Ethnic/ harlem_references.html

A bibliography of materials from the libraries at the University of Southern California. Has links to other sites and resources.

Art

◆ **The Montclair Art Museum**

http://www.interactive.net/~upper/mam-col.html

The Montclair Art Museum and its collections, with an emphasis on the eighteenth century to the present, the Hudson River School, nineteenth-century portraits, American Impressionism, the American Scene, Modernism, and twentienth-century works by African American artists.

◆ **National Museum of African Art**

http://www.si.edu/activity/events/evafart.htm

Activities, programs, and exhibits related to African art at the museum.

◆ **The Organization of Black Designers: Washington, D.C.**

http://www.core77.com/OBD/welcome.html

The Organization of Black Designers, its membership, the contributions of African Americans and other people of color to design.

Visual Art

◆ **African American Art**

http://www.lainet.com/~joejones/art.htm

Excellent collection of African American art on the Web. The art is arranged by galleries and each gallery can be entered from the Gallery Title Bar. A quick view of images contained in each gallery is provided below each gallery's title bar.

◆ **African Art: Aesthetics and Meaning**

http://www.lib.virginia.edu/dic/exhib/93.ray.aa/African.html

The items selected for this exhibit were chosen to exemplify African aesthetic and moral principles. Most of the objects exhibited come from West African societies and are in the Bayly Museum at the University of Virginia.

◆ **African Art Homepage**

http://jirah.com/

Photographs of gallery items plus a discussion forum.

Dance

◆ **African Dance in the Diaspora Bibliography**

http://www.sas.upenn.edu/African_Studies/Bibliography/ African_Dance_19560.html

A dance bibliography with annotations by Wendy E. Cochran, related to a special research project (apparently for an African studies course) in San Francisco. The interview notes on the project probably will not be of interest to most people, but the bibliography at the end is extensive. It includes books, music, newspapers and periodicals, and videos. The subjects covered include not only dance, but African history and culture in general, especially in the Americas.

Music

◆ **AACM: Association for the Advancement of Creative Musicians, Inc**.

http://csmaclab-www.cs.uchicago.edu/AACM/ AACM_HOME_PAGE.html

Information about the Association for the Advancement of Creative Musicians, Inc. (AACM), its members, history, and goals. The group is dedicated to encouraging serious, original music and places special emphasis on Black music in the United States and throughout the world.

◆ **African American Music**

http://www.unix-ag.uni-kl.de/~moritz/music.html

This site contains links to information on African American musicians and groups (over 100). Some of the sites are incomplete, however, with only a photograph of the performer or group.

◆ **African American Music Resources**

http://www.usc.edu/Library/Ref/Ethnic/
  black_amer_music_ref.html

Reference sources from the University of Southern California's Library on African American music, culture, musicians, history, and significant individuals.

◆ **Afro-Latin, African, and Latin Music**

rec.music.afro-latin

Usenet newsgroup on music with Afro-Latin, African, and Latin influences.

◆ **Blues Access Online**

http://www.bluesaccess.com/ba_home.html

Online magazine devoted to the blues.

◆ **BluesNet**

http://dragon.acadiau.ca/~rob/blues/blues.html

BluesNet is a WWW-based repository for information on blues performers. Each artist summary on this site was written by a volunteer who is a fan of the performer, and some of the information is heavily opinionated. The Mentors section has links to experts who are willing to answer questions dealing with blues performers.

◆ **Delta Snake Blues News**

http://www.island.net/~blues/snake.html

Online newsletter dealing with the blues. The current issue, plus archives dating back to January 1994, are available.

◆ **Great Day in Harlem**

http://www.beatthief.com/greatday.html

Information about jazz musicians from Harlem. Based on Jean Bach's 1994 film.

◆ **Indiana University: Classical Music in Black and White**

http://ezinfo.ucs.indiana.edu/~afamarch/home.html

Information about African American musicians and composers and their effect on American classical music.

◆ **Maxwell Street Blues Home Sweet Homepage**

http://www.openair.org/maxwell/maxblu.html

This site features famous blues performers of Chicago's Maxwell Street Market. There is a section with news plus some historical information about the blues.

Musical Instruments

◆ **Alternative or Fair Trade Merchandise**

http://www.polaris.net/~chp/cultures/cuf1.htm

African American musical instruments and other merchandise.

◆ **Fun Kazoo Facts**

http://www.kazoobie.com/kazoofax.htm

This site is devoted to the African American folk instrument, the kazoo (created in the 1840s by Alabama Vest and Thaddeus Von Clegg).

Musicians

◆ **Armstrong, Louis (1901–1971)**

http://www.rockhall.com/induct/armslou.html

Louis Armstrong and his music. A short audio file is available in several audio formats.

◆ **Baker, Josephine**

http://www.classicalmus.com/artists/baker.html

Biographical information and portrait of the vocalist Josephine Baker.

◆ **Fitzgerald, Ella**

http://www.unix-ag.uni-kl.de/%7Emoritz/artistdatabase/ a_g/fitzgeraldella.html

http://www.acns.nwu.edu/jazz/artists/fitzgerald.ella/

http://jazzcentralstation.com/jcs/station/musicexp/artists/ ella/misc/links.html

http://www.ubl.com/artists/001731.html

The Web addresses are to different sites with information about Ella Fitzgerald's life and works.

◆ **Holiday, Billie**

http://www.cmgww.com/music/holiday/holiday.html

Biographical information, career summary, and photographs of Billie Holiday.

- **Milestones: A Miles Davis WWW Site**

  http://miles.rtvf.nwu.edu/miles/milestones.html

  Information about Miles Davis and his music. Audio and video clips are also available.

- **Sounds of Blackness**

  http://www.unix-ag.uni-kl.de/%7Emoritz/daten/uwp/ soblackn.uwp

  The gospel music of the Sounds of Blackness.

- **Taylor, Koko**

  http://www.cclabs.missouri.edu/~maneater/120195/ 11story1.html

  Biographical information on blues singer Koko Taylor.

GOVERNMENT, LAW, AND POLITICS

- **African-American Journey: The First Years of Freedom**

  http://www.worldbook.com/features/blackhistory/ bh060.html

  This site (from *World Book*) provides a history of the National Association for the Advancement of Colored People (NAACP), its activities and purposes.

- **African Americans in Politics and Government**

  http://www.usc.edu/Library/Ref/Ethnic/black_politics.html

  Black politicians, biographical sources, and references.

- **Pan African Political and Organizational Information**

  http://www.panafrican.org/panafrican/

  This site provides information about the Pan African movement, plus links to papers and documents written by Black leaders such as Malcolm X, Martin Luther King, Jr., Nelson Mandela, and many others.

Civil Rights

- **Birmingham Civil Rights Institute: Birmingham, AL**

  http://www.the-matrix.com/bcri/bcri.html

  Covers the course of civil rights activities in Birmingham, AL.

◆ **Civil Rights**

http://www.fred.net/nhhs/

Discussion page maintained by North Hagerstown High School dealing with Martin Luther King, Jr.'s Dream 30 years later. General topics include current racial relations, discrimination, and African Americans in the United States.

◆ **The National Civil Rights Museum: Memphis, TN**

http://www.mecca.org/~crights/ncrm.html

Information on the museum (located in Memphis, Tennessee) and civil rights in the United States.

◆ **Taking the Train to Freedom**

http://www.nps.gov/undergroundrr/contents.htm

In 1990, Congress authorized the National Park Service to conduct a study of the Underground Railroad and its routes and operations, in order to preserve and interpret this aspect of U.S. history. This Web site contains information from this study, which includes a general overview of the Underground Railroad, with a brief discussion of slavery and abolitionism, escape routes used by slaves, and alternatives for commemoration and interpretation of the significance of the phenomenon.

◆ **Timeline of the American Civil Rights Movement**

http://www.wmich.edu/politics/mlk

This site, which is an ongoing project at the University of Western Michigan, contains brief comments with striking images highlighting events in the American Civil Rights movement.

◆ **The Tuskegee Airmen**

http://www.afroam.org/history/tusk/tuskmain.html

When the United States entered War World II, Black leaders and the African American press intensified their protest of the separate and significantly inferior access to training, facilities and participation that was available to African Americans. Faced with the realities of war, the U.S. government established the 66th Air Force Flying School at the Tuskegee Institute in Tuskegee, Alabama. The site chronicles these first African American fighter pilots and their contribution to the U.S. war effort.

◆ **United States Colored Troops (USCT)**

http://www.itd.nps.gov/cwss/usct.html

United States Colored Troops and their involvement with the Civil War. This site was developed by the National Park Service and its partners and is a part of the Civil War Soldiers and Sailors project.

- **X, MALCOLM**

http://www.unix-ag.uni-kl.de/~moritz/

Malcolm X, his life, and writings.

Organizations

- **NAACP Online**

http://www.naacp.org/

Homepage of the National Association for the Advancement of Colored People.

- **National Association for the Advancement of Colored People: Encarta Online**

http://encarta.msn.com/index/concise/0vol28/04d8a000.asp

This site provides information about the structure of the NAACP, its history and activities.

- **The National Coalition on Black Voter Participation, Inc.**

http://www.bigvote.org/

This site provides information on African American voter participation.

- **National Urban League, Inc.**

http://www.nul.org

The mission of the National Urban League is to assist African Americans in the achievement of social and economic equality. This site provides information about the organization, its mission and activities.

HISTORY

- **AAGENE-L**

Subscription address: AAGENE-L@UPEOPLE.COM

AAGENE-L is an electronic mailing list for African American genealogy researchers. It is also appropriate to discuss African American history on the list. To subscribe, send a blank message with the word **subscribe** in the subject line, to the subscription address.

- **An African American Bibliography on History**

**http://www.sas.upenn.edu/African_Studies/Bibliography/
AFAM_History.html**

The bibliography lists selected resources of the New York State Library that document and comment on the experience of African Americans in the history of the United States. In addition to primary sources and significant historical works, the bibliography contains references to bibliographies and research aids.

◆ **African American Bookstore**

http://www.thomson.com/gale/avs/bookstor.html

Historical books on African Americans, plus much more.

◆ **African American Historic Texts On-line**

http://curry.edschool.Virginia.EDU/go/multicultural/sites/ aframdocs.html

This site provides access to a number of historically significant texts by or about African Americans.

◆ **African American History**

http://www.msstate.edu/Archives/History/USA/ Afro-Amer/afro.html

Historical archives site with links to significant African American historical sites.

◆ **African American Images**

http://www.npac.syr.edu/projects/ltb/ AA_photos_index.html

This collection of African American images features several hundred photographs taken from the mid-1800s to the present time. This historical archive documents the African American community in Syracuse, New York, in portraits, at weddings, proms, graduations, sporting events, and in everyday activities.

◆ **African-American Mosaic: Authors and the Federal Writers' Project**

http://www.loc.gov/exhibits/african/authors.html

A Library of Congress Web site dealing with the exhibits and research from the Federal Writers' Projects (WPA), such as *Drums at Dusk* by Arna Bontemps, *Highlights of Harlem, The Negro in Virginia Documents Black Contributions, Gumbo Ya-Ya,* and much more.

◆ **African-American Mosaic: Cavalcade of the American Negro**

http://www.loc.gov/exhibits/african/cav.html

Library of Congress site dealing with the Chicago Exhibition of 1940 which celebrated the emancipation of the American Negro and African American achievements over the 75 years since the conclusion of the Civil War in 1865.

◆ **African-American Mosaic: Colonization**

http://www.loc.gov/exhibits/african/acsbegin.html

Library of Congress site that describes the roots of the controversial colonization movement, the origins of which date back to various plans first proposed in the eighteenth century. There is discussion of the American Colonization Society (ACS), which was formed in 1817 to send free African Americans to Africa as an alternative to emancipation in the United States.

◆ **African-American Mosaic: A Library of Congress Resource Guide for the Study of Black History and Culture**

http://www.loc.gov/exhibits/african/intro.html

This site contains numerous materials which are significant to the study of the African American experience. This site offers some introductory text describing the exhibit. The exhibit is arranged in the following categories (a couple of which have been described in other entries to provide a feel for the range of materials at this site):

> Colonization
>> Liberia
>> Personal Stories and ACS New Directions
>
> Abolition
>> Influence of Prominent Abolitionists
>> Conflict of Abolition and Slavery
>
> Migration
>> Western Migration and Homesteading
>> Nicodemus, Kansas
>> Chicago: Destination for the Great Migration
>
> WPA
>> Cavalcade of the American Negro
>> Authors and the Federal Writers' Project
>> Ex-slave Narratives

This is an excellent site that should be of particular benefit to educators and their students.

◆ **African-American Mosaic: Migrations**

http://www.loc.gov/exhibits/african/migr.html

A significant feature of African American history has been migration from the South. This site from the Library of Congress documents some of those migrations, including those between 1879 and 1881, when 60,000 African Americans moved into Kansas and others settled in the Oklahoma Indian Territories.

◆ **African-American Museum in Philadelphia**

http://www.libertynet.org/iha/_afro.html

This page is part of the Virtual Tour of Philadelphia. It describes and provides information about the Museum's offerings.

◆ **African American Perspectives: Pamphlets from the Daniel A. P. Murray Collection**

http://lcweb2.loc.gov/ammem/aap/aaphome.html

This collection from the Library of Congress American Memory Project contains important African American materials published between 1875 and 1900 by Frederick Douglass, Booker T. Washington, Emanuel Love, and others.

◆ **Amistad America, Inc.**

http://www.amistadamerica.org/welcome.html

Amistad America, Inc., is a not-for-profit educational foundation created by Mystic Seaport. Highlights of this site include Exploring Amistad, Race and the Boundaries of Freedom in Antebellum Maritime America, and Amistad Links, a comprehensive listing of links to pages about the Amistad and the Amistad incident.

◆ **Black History Database**

http://www.ai.mit.edu/~isbell/HFh/black/bhist.html

This site allows the user to look at some interesting facts about Black History for a particular week. The information is updated weekly, usually on Sunday or Monday. There is also an associated distribution list, described on the Web page. One can search the database for information and find pointers to other resources on the Web. The calendar of facts about a particular month can also be searched. Clicking on a blue dot will start a search on the topic(s) discussed by the fact next to it. One can also search the calendar for facts about a particular year. The user can also submit new facts, biographies, corrections, and links to additional resources.

◆ **Black History Hotlist**

http://www.kn.pacbell.com/wired/BHM/bh_hotlist.html

This site is an excellent starting point for a study of African American history. Sites are categorized under significant events and time periods of African American history, and there is a biographical section dealing with outstanding African American individuals, both historical and present day.

◆ **Black History Month Page**

http://www.bethel.hampton.k12.va.us/history.africa.html

A homepage for Bethel High School in Hampton, Virginia, containing information on African history, and links to related sites. The background makes the initial page hard to read, but there are worthwhile links to other resources on the Web.

◆ **The Black History Museum**

http://www.afroam.org/history/history.html

Information about particular African Americans and African American organizations and their impact on history. Information is provided about the Tuskegee Airmen, Jackie Robinson, the Million Man March and more.

◆ **Boynton's Calendar of African American History**

http://www.global-image.com/boynton/calendar/

African American history in chronological order.

◆ **Guide to Historic Virginia: African-American History Sites**

http://freenet.vcu.edu/tourism/histrich/african.html

Historical information on the African American culture in and near Richmond, Virginia.

◆ **Living Schoolbooks**

http://www.npac.syr.edu/users/gcf/livingtextbook/

Photographs and images of African Americans in the 1940s.

◆ **Mardi Gras Indians: Soul of New Orleans**

http://www.neworleansonline.com/sno18.htm

Textual information about the background and culture of the Mardi Gras Indians. Over the years, the music and musical style of the Mardi Gras Indians has become part and parcel of the African-American New Orleans experience.

◆ **Martin Luther King Jr.**

http://www.seattletimes.com/mlk/

This Internet site, maintained by the *Seattle Times,* is about Dr. Martin Luther King, Jr.'s life and the civil rights movement, with articles, sound clips, photos, and a discussion forum. It is primarily an electronic classroom site, great for educators.

◆ **Martin Luther King Jr. Papers Project at Stanford University**

http://www-leland.stanford.edu/group/King/

This site contains secondary documents written about Martin Luther King, Jr., as well as primary documents written during King's life.

◆ **Mary McLeod Bethune Council House National Historic Site**

http://www.nps.gov/mamc/index.htm

This National Park Service site chronicles the National Council of Negro Women, established by Mary McLeod Bethune in 1935; and the African American women's rights movement from 1943 to 1949.

◆ **Museum of African American History**

http://ipl.sils.umich.edu/exhibit/maah/

The Museum of African American History in Detroit, Michigan, is dedicated to the preservation and presentation of African and African American history and culture.

◆ **New Orleans Online Catalog—ABOUT—MardiGras Indians**

http://www.noline.com/prprofile.htm

Colorful pictures and posters (which can be purchased) of the Mardi Gras Indians, along with information about their costumes and public displays on Mardi Gras.

◆ **Persistence of the Spirit: African American Experience in Arkansas**

http://www.aristotle.net/persistence/

Permanent exhibit on the study of African American history, people, and important events in Arkansas; includes photographs and links to other similar resources on the Internet.

◆ **Role of African Americans in the American Revolution**

http://www.ilt.columbia.edu/k12/history/blacks/ blacks.html

The information on this site is categorized by Important Facts, and Food for Thought. Each category provides information and questions that will be of value to everyone, but would probably be especially appreciated by educators.

◆ **Social Science and Historical Resources**

http://www.lib.lsu.edu/lib/chem/display/aasocsci.html

A selected bibliography of social science and historical resources on African Americans. This is a bibliography of print resources, not links to resources available on the Web.

◆ **Some Important Nineteenth-Century African Americans**

http://www.brightmoments.com/blackhistory/index.html

This site has biographical essays as part of the Internet African American Challenge. A quiz is provided to help you sharpen your knowledge of African American history.

Genealogy

◆ **Afrigeneas**

http://www.msstate.edu/Archives/History/afrigen/

Afrigeneas is an electronic mailing list focused on genealogical research and resources in general and on African ancestry in particular. This Web site serves as a focal point for information about families of African ancestry and for pointers to genealogical sources worldwide. There are links to the Frequently Asked Questions (FAQ) of the mailing list, the newsletter, selected postings, and much more. An excellent site to get started in African American genealogical research.

LANGUAGE ARTS AND LITERATURE

Literature

- ◆ **African American Bookstore**

http://www.thomson.com/gale/avs/bookstor.html

Historical books on African Americans are featured; some excerpts are published here. There is a useful timeline of important dates in African American history, with links to excerpts.

- ◆ **African American Literature**

http://www.usc.edu/Library/Ref/Ethnic/
     black_lit_main.html

Bibliography of materials in the libraries of the University of Southern California about the development of African American literature, from 1853 to the present, as well as bibliographies of the works listed by genre.

- ◆ **Poets of the Harlem Renaissance and Later**

http://www.poets.org/lit/exh/EX006.htm

Brief biographical sketches of a number of African American poets are provided.

- ◆ **Virginia Hamilton**

http://www.virginiahamilton.com/index.html

Writings, life, and pictures of Virginia Hamilton, award-winning children's author.

- ◆ **Writing Black**

http://www.keele.ac.uk/depts/as/Literature/
     amlit.black.html

This site contains information about literature and history written by and about African Americans. It offers links to resources on a number of African American writers such as Maya Angelou, James Baldwin, Saul Bellow, Frederick Douglass, Rita Dove, Alex Haley, Zora Neale Hurston, Terri McMillan, and Toni Morrison.

- ◆ **Zulu Folk Love Tales**

http://www.thecanyon.com/gardners/stories.htm

The folktale "How Zebras Got Their Stripes."

POPULAR CULTURE

Music

◆ **EUR WEB: Electronic Urban Report**
http://www.eurweb.com/
The news and the sounds of R&B, hip-hop, reggae, jazz and gospel, and various forms of African American music.

◆ **The Internet Ghetto Blaster**
http://www.igb.com/
Radio, recording reviews, and evaluations of the work of new musicians.

◆ **Jack the Rapper's Mello Yello On-line**
http://www.mello-yello.com/
The online edition of America's oldest African American-owned trade publication targeted to African American radio and the professions related to African American music.

◆ **Jammin Reggae Archives**
http://v-music.com/niceup/index.html
Reggae information, FAQs, lyrics, article transcriptions, GIFs, audio, discographies, clubs, and more.

◆ **Radioscope**
http://eurweb.netgate.net/radio.html
African Americans in entertainment and music.

◆ **Reggae Newsgroup**
rec.music.reggae
Electronic discussion group on reggae and related music.

◆ **The Totally Unofficially Rap Dictionary**
http://www.sci.kun.nl/thalia/rapdict/
Rap Dictionary plus additional information about rap music and musicians.

Musicians

◆ **Baker, LaVern**
http://www.rockhall.com/induct/bakelave.html
LaVern Baker and her music. A short audio file is available in several audio formats.

◆ **Berry, Chuck**

http://www.rockhall.com/induct/berrchuc.html

Chuck Berry and his music. A short audio file is available in several audio formats.

◆ **Brown, James**

http://www.rockhall.com/induct/browjame.html

James Brown and his music. A short audio file is available in several audio formats.

◆ **Caribbean Connection**

http://www.dtek.chalmers.se/~d2domer/intresse.html

Reggae, the Caribbean Archives, and other related topics.

◆ **Charles, Ray**

http://www.rockhall.com/induct/charray.html

Ray Charles and his music. A short audio file is available in several audio formats.

◆ **The Coasters**

http://www.rockhall.com/induct/coasters.html

The music of The Coasters. A short audio file is available in several audio formats.

◆ **Cooke, Sam**

http://www.rockhall.com/induct/cooksam.html

Sam Cooke and his music. A short audio file is available in several audio formats.

◆ **Fats Domino**

http://www.rockhall.com/induct/domifats.html

Fats Domino and his music. A short audio file is available in several audio formats.

◆ **The Four Tops**

http://www.rockhall.com/induct/fourtops.html

The music of The Four Tops. A short audio file is available in several audio formats.

◆ **Franklin, Aretha**

http://www.rockhall.com/induct/franaret.html

Aretha Franklin and her music. A short audio file is available in several audio formats.

◆ **Gaye, Marvin**

http://www.rockhall.com/induct/gayemarv.html

**http://www.unix-ag.uni-kl.de/~moritz/artistdatabase/a_g/
gayemarvin.html**

**http://www.polydor-atlas.com/motown/artists/
Marvin_Gaye/Albums.html**

Marvin Gaye and his music. A short audio file is available in several audio formats at the Rock and Roll Hall of Fame site. The three URLs are to different Web sites dealing with Marvin Gaye.

◆ **Gladys Knight and the Pips**

http://www.rockhall.com/induct/knigglad.html

The music of Gladys Knight and the Pips. A short audio file is available in several audio formats.

◆ **Gordy Jr., Berry**

http://www.rockhall.com/induct/gordberr.html

Berry Gordy Jr. and his involvement with rock and roll and African American music.

◆ **Grandmaster Flash & the Furious Five**

**http://www.unix-ag.uni-kl.de/%7Emoritz/artistdatabase/
a_g/gfff.html**

The music of Grandmaster Flash & the Furious Five.

◆ **Hammer, M. C.**

**http://www.unix-ag.uni-kl.de/%7Emoritz/artistdatabase/
h_m/mchammer.html**

M. C. Hammer and his music.

◆ **Hendrix, Jimi**

http://www.rockhall.com/induct/hendjimm.html

Jimi Hendrix and his music. A short audio file is available in several audio formats.

◆ **Houston, Whitney**

http://www.spd.louisville.edu/~carudo01/wh/

http://www.aristarec.com/whitney/

Two Web sites with information about Whitney Houston, her music and movies, and links to related sites.

◆ **Ice Cube**

http://www.unix-ag.uni-kl.de/%7Emoritz/artistdatabase/ h_m/icecube.html

The music of Ice Cube.

◆ **The Ink Spots**

http://www.rockhall.com/induct/inkspots.html

The music of The Ink Spots. A short audio file is available in several audio formats.

◆ **King, B. B.**

http://www.rockhall.com/induct/kingbb.html

B. B. King and his music. A short audio file is available in several audio formats.

◆ **Kitt, Eartha**

http://www2.ucsc.edu/people/irena/eartha.html
http://www.chaoskitty.com/b_kitty/kitt.html

Biographical information and more on the singer Eartha Kitt.

◆ **Little Richard**

http://www.rockhall.com/induct/richlitt.html

Little Richard and his music. A short audio file is available in several audio formats.

◆ **Martha and the Vandellas**

http://www.rockhall.com/induct/vandella.html

The music of Martha and the Vandellas. A short audio file is available in several audio formats.

◆ **The Michael Jackson Music Database**

http://www.canoe.ca/JamMusicMichaelJackson/home.html

Michael Jackson, his music, and events reported in the news.

◆ **Pickett, Wilson**

http://www.rockhall.com/induct/pickwils.html

Wilson Pickett and his music. A short audio file is available in several audio formats.

◆ **Rainey, Ma**

http://www.rockhall.com/induct/rainma.html

Ma Rainey and her music. A short audio file is available in several audio formats.

◆ **Redding, Otis**

http://www.rockhall.com/induct/reddotis.html

Otis Redding and his music. A short audio file is available in several audio formats.

◆ **Reed, Jimmy**

http://www.rockhall.com/induct/reedjimm.html

Jimmy Reed and his music. A short audio file is available in several audio formats.

◆ **Robinson, Smokey**

http://www.rockhall.com/induct/robismok.html

Smokey Robinson and his music. A short audio file is available in several audio formats.

◆ **The Shirelles**

http://www.rockhall.com/induct/shirelle.html

http://www.unix-ag.uni-kl.de/%7Emoritz/artistdatabase/ n_s/shirelles.html

The music of The Shirelles. A short audio file is available in several audio formats on the Rock and Roll Hall of Fame site.

◆ **Sly and the Family Stone**

http://www.rockhall.com/induct/slyfam.html

The music of Sly and the Family Stone. A short audio file is available in several audio formats.

◆ **Smith, Bessie**

http://www.rockhall.com/induct/smitbess.html

http://www.unix-ag.uni-kl.de/%7Emoritz/artistdatabase/ n_s/smithbessie.html

Bessie Smith's music and recordings. A short audio file in several audio formats is available on the Rock and Roll Hall of Fame site.

◆ **The Soul Stirrers**

http://www.rockhall.com/induct/soulstir.html

The music of The Soul Stirrers. A short audio file is available in several audio formats.

◆ **The Supremes**

http://www.rockhall.com/induct/supreme.html

http://bspaa.com/Artist/supremes/supremesbio.html

The music of The Supremes. A short audio file is available in several audio formats on the Rock and Roll Hall of Fame site.

◆ **The Temptations**

http://www.rockhall.com/induct/temptati.html

The music of The Temptations. A short audio file is available in several audio formats.

◆ **Turner, Big Joe**

http://www.rockhall.com/induct/turnjoe.html

Big Joe Turner and his music. A short audio file is available in several audio formats.

◆ **Turner, Ike and Tina**

http://www.rockhall.com/induct/turnike.html

The music of Ike and Tina Turner. A short audio file is available in several audio formats.

◆ **Turner, Tina**

http://www.geocities.com/SiliconValley/8360/tina.html

http://www.dotmusic.co.uk/MWtalenttina2.html

Spanish: http://www.las.es/tina/

Three sites that provide information about Tina Turner and her music.

◆ **Walker, T-Bone**

http://www.rockhall.com/induct/walktbon.html

T-Bone Walker and his music. A short audio file is available in several audio formats.

◆ **Wilson, Jackie**

http://www.rockhall.com/induct/wilsjack.html

Jackie Wilson and his music. A short audio file is available in several audio formats.

◆ **Wonder, Stevie**

http://www.rockhall.com/induct/wondstev.html

Stevie Wonder and his music. A short audio file is available in several audio formats.

Sports

♦ **National Brotherhood of Skiers**

http://www.nbs.org

Organization that brings together African American ski clubs to ski and socialize. One of the original purposes of the NBS was to help get an African American skier into the Olympics.

Professional Sports

♦ **National Bowling Association**

http://www.inlink.com/~tnbainc/tnbamenu.html

The National Bowling Association promotes friendship, sportsmanship, and fellowship among its members. In addition, it serves as a recruiting agency and point of entry for African American bowlers into competitive bowling.

♦ **Negro Baseball League**

http://www.blackbaseball.com

Site dedicated to the Negro Baseball League; includes historical information about the players, teams, museums, and other interesting information.

♦ **The Negro Leagues Ring**

http://www.webcom.com/%7Eblessed/negro.html

Black baseball history in the U.S. with links to other Internet sites.

Television and Film

♦ **California Newsreel**

http://www.newsreel.org/

California Newsreel produces and distributes documentary films, primarily but not exclusively from an African American perspective. The titles include: *Goin' to Chicago, At the River I Stand, The Road to Brown, Miles of Smiles, Years of Struggle, Race Against Prime*, and more.

RELIGION

♦ **Historical Notes on the African Methodist Episcopal Church**

http://www.andersonchapel.org/history1.htm

This site provides historical information about the African Methodist Episcopal Church (AME), one of the largest Methodist denominations in the United States. The church was founded by a group of African American Methodists, led by Richard Allen, who withdrew from Philadelphia's St. George Methodist Episcopal Church in November 1787.

◆ **Morehouse School of Religion**

http://www.cyberspacembchurch.org/morehouse.htm

Information on the only accredited African American Baptist seminary in the world.

◆ **Nation of Islam**

http://www.noi.org/index.html

Links are provided to access historical information and press releases of the Nation of Islam, plus information about its programs and membership and many more related topics.

SCIENCE AND TECHNOLOGY

◆ **African-American Bibliography on Science, Medicine, and Allied Fields**

http://www.sas.upenn.edu/African_Studies/Bibliography/ AFAM_Science.html

An African American bibliography on science resources of the New York State Library.

◆ **African-Americans in Science**

http://www.luc.edu/libraries/science/diversity/aasci.html

African Americans in science, women and minorities in science and engineering, plus links to other related sites and sources.

◆ **African Americans in the Sciences**

http://www.lib.lsu.edu/lib/chem/display/faces.html

African Americans and their contributions to science, past, present, and future. There is an alphabetical index of profiles provided if you are looking for a sketch of a particular African American scientist.

Health

◆ **The Balm in Gilead, Inc.**

ftp://hwbbs.gbgm-umc.org/library/african/balmgil.txt

The Balm in Gilead, Inc. has information on AIDS and its effect on the African American populace (especially male).

◆ **Documenting the African American Health Care Experience in Michigan**

http://http2.sils.umich.edu/HCHS/Afroam/Afroam.html

This site provides a guide to resources dealing with African American health care, with links and references to other Internet resources.

◆ **JNCI**

http://wwwicic.nci.nih.gov/jnci/issue11/87–793.html

Article on cancer research and the effect of cancer on African Americans from *JNCI* (vol. 87 [1995], issue 11).

◆ **National Black Deaf Advocates (NBDA)**

gopher://people.human.com/00/inc/alpha/nbda

The Mission of the National Black Deaf Advocates (NBDA) is to promote the well-being, culture, and empowerment of African American persons who are deaf or hard of hearing. This site provides information about NBDA programs and services, such as its forums and workshops, conventions, and much more.

Information Technology and Telecommunications

◆ **Black Data Processing Associates [BDPA]: Silicon Valley Chapter**

http://www-leland.stanford.edu/group/bgsa/bdpa/bdpa.html

BDPA is a network of information technology professionals who share information, provide education, and perform community service. This site provides information about this and other chapters of the association. Links are provided to newsletters, career leads and other topics.

WOMEN'S ISSUES

◆ **African-American Women: On-Line Archival Collections**

http://scriptorium.lib.duke.edu/collections/african-american-women.html

Materials from the Special Collections Library at Duke University and links to related Internet resources.

◆ **Essence Online**

http://www.essence.com/

Online version of *Essence,* a general magazine for African American women.

◆ **Global Women of African Heritage (GWAH)**

http://www.thefuturesite.com/ethnic/gwah.html

The stated purpose of the organization is to "further the development in social and economic involvement both nationally and internationally. In order to enable women of African Heritage around the world to join hands in developing a cohesive organization that will lend strength in advancing and preserving womanhood in the world of technology and energy of the coming century."

◆ **Isis Plus**

http://www.netdiva.com/isisplus.html

The art and culture of women of the African Diaspora.

◆ **National Council of Negro Women**

http://www.erols.com/trirose/ncnw.htm

Founded in 1935 by noted educator and human rights activist Mary McLeod Bethune, the National Council of Negro Women is the nation's broadest based organization of African American women. This site provides information about this nonprofit voluntary service organization, which has 34 national affiliated constituency-based organizations and 250 community-based sections. The stated mission of the National Council of Negro Women is to "advance opportunities and the quality of life for African American women, their families and communities."

◆ **Online Resources for African American Women and Womanist Studies**

http://www.uic.edu/~vjpitch/

This site provides hotlinks to Internet resources by and for all women, but specifically African American women.

◆ **A Woman's NIA on the Net**

http://robynma.simplenet.com/nianet/

This is a powerful and comprehensive cultural, computing and Christian resource guide for African American women.

Biography

◆ **Bethune, Mary McLeod (1875–1955)**

http://www.fas.harvard.edu/~felder/bethune.html
http://www.moore.net/~hrmoore/mcleod.htm
http://catalog.upapubs.com:70/1/newtitle/001a/
http://web.cr.nps.gov/nr/31.htm

The URLs above are to different sites that deal with various aspects of Mrs. Mary McLeod Bethune's life, writings, and achievements.

◆ **Browne, Marjorie Lee (1914–1979)**

http://www.scottlan.edu/lriddle/women/brown.htm

Brief biographical sketch on her life and accomplishments. She was one of the first African American women to earn a Ph.D. in mathematics.

◆ **Hale, Clara "Mother"**

http://www.wic.org/bio/chale.htm

Information about "Mother" Hale and her unselfish devotion to children.

◆ **Jackson, Shirley Ann**

http://www.lib.lsu.edu/lib/chem/display/jackson.html

Biographical sketch of Shirley Ann Jackson and her work in physics.

◆ **Jordan, Barbara**

http://www.utexas.edu/lbj/faculty/Jordan.html

This site provides information about the life and political career of Barbara Jordan.

◆ **Murray, Pauli (1910–1985)**

http://web.fie.com/~tonya/murray.htm

Brief biographical sketch of Pauli Murray and her involvement with law and sexism. She also became the first African American woman to be ordained an Episcopal priest.

◆ **Sudarkasa, Dr. Niara**

http://www.aed.org/more/sudarkasa.html
http://www.mala.bc.ca/~mcneil/sudarkas.htm

The two Web addresses are to different sites about Niara Sudarkasa, a renowned anthropoligist, and her accomplishments.

- Terrell, Mary Church (1863–1954)

http://www.webcom.com/~bright/source/mct.html
http://rs6.loc.gov/ammem/aap/terrell.html

These two sites provide information about Mary Church Terrell, her life and involvement with education and integration.

- Walker, Madame C. J. (Sarah Breedlove McWilliams Walker)

http://www.lib.lsu.edu/lib/chem/display/walker.html

Madame C. J. Walker (1867–1919) became one of the first American female millionaires through her own invention and business sense. This site documents her life and success.

- Wells-Barnett, Ida Bell (1862–1931)

http://info.umd.edu/Pictures/WomensStudies/
PictureGallery/wells.html

Ida Bell Wells-Barnett and her struggle to fight discrimination against African Americans.

OTHER

- Stamp on Black History

http://tqd.advanced.org/2667/Stamps.htm

Stamps commemorating African American men and women. Be sure to scroll down the page as there are numerous links to resources below the opening graphic.

Directories

- African Americans (from A San Francisco Bay Area Progressive Directory)

http://www.emf.net/~cheetham/kafans-1.html

The Progressive Directory (**http://www.emf.net/~cheetham/dir.html**) is a list of organizations of interest to progressive activists. This page lists many African American organizations. While specific to one urban area, many of the organizations listed will be of interest to people from other areas. Unfortunately, there is no indication of how current the site is, and there are no links to available Web pages for the organizations, although some such sites exist.

Organizations

◆ **Americans for African Adoptions, Inc.**
http://www.cyberspacepr.com/outreach2.html

Sponsoring an Angel, a program promoting African adoptions by Americans. This site provides information about the organization and its program and activities.

5

Hispanic American Resources

ANGELO F. LIRANZO

INTRODUCTION

This chapter is intended to serve as a brief guide for locating a variety of Hispanic American Internet resources quickly and easily. It has been compiled using a variety of search tools. Even so, it is not comprehensive. No Internet guide in print could possibly be comprehensive for long. The Internet is so dynamic that there is something new on it all the time, and so this guide should be seen as just a starting point. You will quickly notice that one Internet resource often links you to a number of related resources.

The idea for this chapter had its beginnings in a student project several years ago, and when work began to update it, it was amazing how many new things had appeared. The search methods employed for locating the resources in this guide include using commerical World Wide Web search engines such as Yahoo and Altavista; searching The Liszt and Deja News for newsgroups and electronic mailing lists; using a variety of keywords to find newsgroups and individual Web pages; and finally, analyzing some of the major gateways to Hispanic American/Latino/Chicano resources, some of which have improved greatly since the initial compilation of this information.

The keywords used included variations of Hispanic, Hispano, Latino, and Chicano. The author's training in Spanish language, literature, and culture allowed use of other Spanish-language terms, but for reasons of practicality, provision of a sample only of all that is available was the goal. While every attempt has been made to ensure that all the resources here were still current as of the date of submission of the manuscript by the editors, personal experience with each and every electronic mailing list and Usenet newsgroup would doubtless reveal both special gems and some peculiarities. Without going into detail about the particulars of electronic mailing lists, please bear in mind that some are private. They may be intended just for a particular class of students or just for the members of a particular association, etc. Find out from the group before you begin taking part in the discussions.

As for the method of selecting sites for inclusion in this guide, no attempt to limit the sites based on any vague notions as to which sites might prove most enduring has been made, nor have arbitrary notions of what is valuable or worthwhile been relied upon. Rather, the aim has been simply to provide a sample of the great variety of sites already available on the Internet with a focus on Hispanic Americans, with the hope that the sites would reflect the rich variety of experience that Hispanic Americans have enjoyed in the United States.

Perhaps this guide will result in two things. One good outcome would be to encourage its readers to investigate in greater detail the fields in which Hispanic Americans are already represented on the Internet. The other good result would be to encourage its readers to create Web sites and other Internet resources that both examine and celebrate the achievements for which Hispanic Americans are not yet well-represented on the Internet. Included here are sites that were either entirely in English or bilingual English/Spanish so that they would be useful to all Americans, including those Hispanic Americans who themselves have little knowledge of the Spanish language.

The main focus is Hispanic Americans themselves. While you may find some sites in this chapter that provide information on Latin American countries and cultures, a guide to resources about Spain, Latin America, and the rest of the Spanish-speaking world would constitute a different topic for a different guide. The intention here is to include a sample of resources that are meaningful to or representative of Americans of Hispanic heritage in the United States, as well as resources that will be useful to non-Hispanic Americans who are interested in the Hispanic American community. Many informational sites have had to be eliminated because they were written solely in Spanish.

For those readers who read Spanish, Ciber-Centro (**http://www.cibercentro.com**) is a large general site, Global Net Directory (**http://www.globalnt.com/**) is a Spanish-language Web subject catalog somewhat similar to Yahoo, and Mundo Latino: Buscadores e Índices (**http://www.mundolatino.org/internet/buscador.htm**) is an impressive listing of numerous Spanish-language Internet search engines. Israel en Español (**http://www.ilespnl.com/index.htm**) is a site for Spanish-speaking Jews from all over the world.

There were several excellent sites for art and museums which can be enjoyed visually even if the text cannot be read: Museos de Sevilla (**http://www.fie.us.es/Sevilla/museos.html**), Museum of Fine Arts (Museo Nacional de Bellas Artes), Santiago de Chile, at **http://www.puc.cl/faba/ARTE/ArteMuseo.html**; Pintores Mexicanos (Mexican Painters) at **http://mexico.udg.mx/Arte/Pintura/pintores.html**; and Web Museum of Latin America which connects to many museums (**http://museos.web.com.mx/awll.html**). There are numerous Usenet newsgroups listed under soc.culture (i.e., **soc.culture.argentina**, **soc.culture.caribbean**, **soc.culture.brazil**, **soc.culture.latin-america**, etc.), but these have not been listed since they are almost entirely in the native language of the country, i.e., Spanish, French, or Portuguese.

The author would like to thank several people for their suggestions, advice, and instruction. Dr. Kathleen de la Peña McCook, Dr. Vicki L.Gregory and Dr. Marilyn Stauffer were most helpful both in instructing me in the use of the Internet and in encouraging the compilation of this reference guide. Alicia Ellison and Paula Geist assisted through passing along any news they heard relating to Hispanic American Internet resources. Gina Persichini and Drew Smith were also very helpful, in the early days, in making me feel comfortable with navigating the Internet. and lastly, a special thanks to Goran Mimica, my co-author of the initial class project that has led to this guide. I am grateful to everyone for their suggestions and contributions, though I am solely responsible for any shortcomings in the finished product.

GENERAL INFORMATION

◆ andanzas al Web Latino

http://lib.nmsu.edu/subject/bord/latino.html

This directory, compiled by leading authority Molly Molloy, provides brief annotations to a variety of sites listed by type of Internet resource (WWW, Listservs, Newsgroups, etc.) and then by general topic, such as Major Latino Gateways; News; Music, Art, Theatre, & Travel; and Trade, Commerce, and Development.

◆ Aztlan

http://www.sscnet.ucla.edu/esp/csrc/index.html

Aztlan, published by the Chicano/a Studies Research Center at UCLA, is the foremost journal of Chicano studies. This site includes indexes to articles in current and previous issues.

◆ BiblioNoticias Series

http://www.lib.utexas.edu/Libs/Benson/bibnot/ bib_noticias_www.html

The BiblioNoticias series, from the Benson Latin American Collection at the University of Texas Libraries, is an annotated bibliography of materials on subjects concerning Latin America. Several new issues are added each year. This is a useful resource for researchers and scholars.

◆ Caribbean Supersite

http://caribbeansupersite.com/

This site contains information about all the islands of the Caribbean. It includes maps, news and weather reports, and links to other sites.

◆ **Chicana Studies Web Page**

http://clnet.ucr.edu/women/womenHP.html

Part of Chicano/Latino Electronic Network (CLEN), this page includes profiles, resources and topics, organizations and networks, and more.

◆ **Chicano/LatinoNet**

http://clnet.ucr.edu

This site is a virtual community of Hispanic/Latino/Chicano Internet resources. It provides information on job opportunities, research, the popular Bronze Pages, and much more! CLNet is a part of the Chicano/Latino Electronic Network (CLEN). Excellent!

◆ **Chicano Library Resource Center**

http://www.library.sjsu.edu/dept/chicano/chicano.htm

The Chicano Library Resource Center is located at San Jose University in California. This attractive Web site lists an impressive number of materials of all types. The information provided will suggest many materials to look for in other libraries.

◆ **EgoWeb: Felipe's Things Latino Page-Connecting to CyberRaza**

http://edb518ea.edb.utexas.edu/html/latinos.html

The eclectic look and feel of this site give it a nuance of mere playfulness. But not so! In fact, this is one of the largest and best developed Hispanic information gateways for accessing everything from serious cultural information to popular magazines and various people's idea of humor. Felipe's personality shines through! Highly recommended. Bilingual. Searchable.

◆ **EgoWeb: Latino Related Electronic Mail Discussion Groups/ Listservs**

http://edb518ea.edb.utexas.edu/html/latinlist.html

This Web page provides a convenient way to locate electronic mailing lists that focus on Hispanic-related topics. When you want to communicate on the Internet, not just browse, this is one of the best places to find the list you want!

◆ **Electric Mercado**

http://www.mercado.com

Electric Mercado is a Web design, commerce, hosting and translation company that provides a variety of links on its Web site, including links to shopping, literature, food, music, and youth.

- ◆ **Guide to Sources in the University of Illinois Library for Study and Research on Hispanic Americans**

http://www.staff.uiuc.edu/~ngonzale/hisbib.html

This site at the University of Illinois Library, included here because it is a handy listing organized by topics, is one example of the lists of available resources that can be found on Web sites of many university and other libraries. Topics in this list include Bibliography, Culture, Elderly, Health, History, Juvenile Books, Library Services, Periodicals, Statistics, Theater, and many more.

- ◆ **Hispanic.com**

http://www.hispanic.com

This site provides links to sites such as National Latino Peace Officers Association, Telemundo Television Network, *Hispanic Magazine,* Hispanic Association on Corporate Responsibility, LatinWorld, and more. It presents information on products and services relevant to Hispanic businesses, organizations, and associations.

- ◆ **Hispanic/Latino Telaraña**

http://www.latela.com/

A virtual cornucopia of Latino pages ranging from sports to electronic journals, employment, music, art, organizations, and much more. One of the largest gateways to Hispanic resources on the Internet. Bilingual homepage.

- ◆ **Hispanic Pages in the USA**

http://coloquio.com/index.html

Provides links to information on Famous Hispanics in the World and History, Los Países, Connections to all Hispanic Countries, A Defense of the Spanish Language in the U.S. Resources, the Bernardo de Gálvez Homepage and more.

- ◆ **Hispanic Research Center**

http://www.asu.edu/clas/hrc/index.html

Although under construction at the time of this writing, it is already obvious that this site may become one of the major gateways to Latino/Hispanic American Internet resources. Includes the HRC Art Gallery and *Hispanic Outreach Magazine.*

- ◆ **Hispanic Research Center Projects Homepage**

http://mati.eas.asu.edu:8421/mati/

Among other things, this site contains a great set of links to A World of Links to Minority Opportunities at **http://mati.eas.asu.edu:8421/mati/links.html**. This site is part of the Minority Advanced Technology Initiative at Arizona State University. (At this writing, this site seemed to be under construction. Even so, it is already useful.)

◆ **HLAS Online: Handbook of Latin American Studies**

http://lcweb2.loc.gov/hlas/hlashome.html

HLAS is an essential guide to resources on Latin America consisting of works selected and annotated by scholars around the world. HLAS is edited by the Hispanic Division of the Library of Congress and alternates annually between the social sciences and the humanities. HLAS is helpful for understanding the background of Hispanic American immigrants. The online version is updated monthly, and includes items to be included in future volumes, as well as those in current and retrospective ones.

◆ **InfoLatino**

http://infolatino.com/

This is a bilingual information source for Latino concerns. Unfortunately it has not been kept up to date, but it does list organizations and museums that may be of interest.

◆ **Internet Resources for Latin America**

http://lib.nmsu.edu/subject/bord/laguia

Possibly the definitive guide to Latin American Internet resources. A "must see" for serious researchers. Contains an excellent list of electronic mailing lists. Annotated. Complemented by Ms. Molloy's andanzas al Web Latino.

◆ **LANIC—Latin American Network Information Center,**
   Univ. of Texas

http://www.lanic.utexas.edu

gopher://lanic.utexas.edu/

Arguably the best gateway to information about Hispanic countries and cultures. Provides Hispanic-related information organized by countries and by subjects. Note: the main focus is Hispanic (Latin American) countries, not Hispanic Americans. Even so, this site is definitely worth a visit for all interested in Hispanic culture. Searchable.

◆ **LANIC Latino Links**

http://www.lanic.utexas.edu/la/region/hispanic/

Part of LANIC (above). Links on this page focus on Latino/Hispanic sites.

◆ **LaRed Latina of the Intermountain Southwest**

http://www.inconnect.com/~rvazquez/sowest.html

LaRed Latina (Latin Network) disseminates socio-political, cultural, educational, and economic information about Latinos in the Intermountain Region (New Mexico, Utah, Colorado, Arizona, Idaho, etc. Affiliated with it are the electronic mailing list LaRed-L and the online magazine *La Sierra Nevada News,* both accessed from this page. Other features include Did You Know? (Hispanic/Latino history) and Hispanic Holidays.

◆ **Latin American Perspectives**

http://wizard.ucr.edu/lap/lap.html

This is a scholarly and theoretical multidisciplinary journal that covers economics, political science, international relations, sociology, history, and philosophy in relation to Latin America. Each issue focuses on a single topic or country. Introductions or lists of articles are provided for recent issues.

◆ **Latino Connection**

**http://www.ascinsa.com/LATINOCONNECTION/
index95.html**

Primarily a country directory to Latin America, but this site also has an impressive collection of Latino Links. Contains individual country pages with links to country information, government, history and culture, economy and business, travel and tourism, arts and entertainment, cuisine, higher education, Internet, and other related Web pages.

◆ **Latino Resources at the Smithsonian**

http://www.si.edu/resource/tours/latino/start.htm

This useful page describes Latino resources and initiatives at the many museums and offices of the Smithsonian. Rather than sending the searcher to the homepages of each museum, this page sends one to information about offerings specific to the Latino community.

◆ **LatinoWeb**

http://www.latinoweb.com

This virtual reference guide for Hispanic American/Latino Internet resources provides information in the categories of Art & Music, Business, Government Agencies, Latino Books, Non-Profit Organizations, Radio Latino, and much, much more. Searchable.

◆ **LatinWorld**

http://www.latinworld.com

LatinWorld is a directory of Internet resources on Latin America and the Caribbean. Though not about Hispanic Americans specifically, it is surely targeted at them and at all Americans and speakers of English.

◆ **Library of Congress Hispanic Reading Room**

http://lcweb.loc.gov/rr/hispanic/

The Hispanic Reading Room is an access point for research in topics related to the Caribbean, Latin America, Iberia, and to people all over the world who are influenced by those areas.

◆ **Puerto Rico**

http://www-lib.usc.edu/~calimuno/puerto_rico.html

Surely this site contains everything you want to know about La Isla del Encanto! Has numerous links to a wide variety of information, including academic institutions, other Puerto Rican pages, and less-expected topics such as Gay Puerto Rico. Well-developed. A valuable resource for all students and enthusiasts of Puerto Rico.

◆ **Puerto Rico: Isla del Encanto**

http://www.princeton.edu/~accion/puerto.html

Another great site about La Isla del Encanto. Provides links to Puerto Rican resources, history, politics, and more. Look for the Puerto Rican Rum page and El Barrio, a gateway to Puerto Rican students and groups at Princeton, Penn, MIT, etc.

◆ **Queens Public Library Hispanic Experience Internet Resources (Queens, NY)**

http://mickey.queens.lib.ny.us/cdd/hispapub.htm

A brief set of links to other Internet resources, convenient because they are annotated. Pages in Spanish at this library can be helpful for mainstreaming recent immigrants.

◆ **U. of Florida Center for Latin American Studies List of Listservs**

http://www.latam.ufl.edu/listservers/lists.htm

Along with the EgoWeb list of electronic mailing lists, this is the best place to go for a convenient list of discussion groups on a variety of Hispanic-related topics.

◆ **U.S. Department of State Background Notes: Latin America and the Caribbean**

http://www.state.gov/www/background_notes/arabgnhp.html

State Department information for each of the countries in Latin America and the Caribbean. Topics include geography, people, government and politics, ecomony, history, foreign relations, relations with the United States, travel and business, and more.

◆ **Zona Latina**

http://www.zonalatina.com/

A site that covers the world of Latin American media, broadcast/cable/satellite television, magazines, newspapers, radio and advertising in Latin America. The site contains research data, photographs, schedules, discussions, book reviews, and many links to Latin American media resources. Provides copious links to current information about Latin America. Directed at speakers of English.

Current Events

◆ **CENTAM-L: Central America Discussion Group**

Subscription address: listserv@ubvm.cc.buffalo.edu

Just one example of an electronic discussion group, if you prefer to discuss current events and not just read about them. This is an active group for people from Central America and others interested in the region. To join, send the message **sub CENTAM-L your name** to the above address.

◆ **Conexión Latina**

http://www.conexionlatina.com/

This is a service for the worldwide Hispanic community from MCI. Topics include Sports and Entertainment, Travel, Latin Kitchen, Immigration, Community, Business Place, Kid's World, and Meeting Place.

◆ **IPRNet: The Information Service on Puerto Rican Issues**

http://www.iprnet.org/IPR/

This site is published by the Institute for Puerto Rican Policy. The information is primarily political and socio-cultural, but there are many other kinds of materials. Includes data on Puerto Ricans in the continental U.S.

◆ **LatinoLink News**

http://www.latinolink.com

This Web site provides a Latino focus on news, entertainment, books, jobs, chat, conferencing, and more. A great source for the Latino perspective on everyday news. Extensive coverage, valuable resource. Searchable. A less attractive text-only version is found at **http://headlines.yahoo.com/latinolink**.

◆ **Mexico Online**

http://www.mexicool.com/

An English-language directory to this great U.S. neighbor. Includes information on news, politics, business, travel, and more. The links to Mexican online newspapers and magazines indicate Spanish or English. Also provides links to worldwide online publications.

◆ **Spain Online—Daily News**

http://www.spainonline.com/menu.html

A curious mix of Spanish and English; click on the English word below a menu button to get the English version. Chock full of information and links. Interesting for Spanish enthusiasts and business travelers to Spain. It is worthwhile to get familiar with this site, which even has links to Web sites of major Spanish newspapers and the stock markets in Madrid and Barcelona. Also contains links to banks and businesses in Spain. Useful!

Newsgroups and Listservs

◆ **Linguistic Minority Research Institute Listservs**

http://lmrinet.gse.ucsb.edu:70/11/LMRI/lists

gopher://lmrinet.gse.ucsb.edu:70/11/LMRI/lists

This site provides a handy list of some 15 Linguistic Minority Research Institute electronic mailing lists that focus on Hispanic-related issues, including Reformanet, Mujer-L, LangPol, and TESOL

◆ **MUJER-L**

Subscription address: listproc@lmrinet.gse.ucsb.edu

Send mail to: mujer-l@lmrinet.gse.ucsb.edu

This electronic mailing list is a discussion group for Chicana/Latina-related issues. To join, send the message **sub MUJER-L your name** to the above address.

soc.culture.Mexican

This Usenet newsgroup discusses many aspects of Mexican life. Messages may be in either Spanish or English. Frequently Asked Questions for the newsgroup can be found at **http://www.public.iastate.edu/~rjsalvad/scmfaq/faqindex.html**.

soc.culture.us.southwest

This Usenet newsgroup is devoted to topics about the region.

Newspapers, Magazines, and Newsletters

◆ **La Estrella**

http://www.startext.net/today/news/estrella/index.htm2

This is the Web site of the bilingual online newspaper from the Fort Worth Star-Telegram. Well-developed site with a variety of news and other features. Extensive coverage, valuable resource.

◆ **Hispanic Online**

http://www.hisp.com/

Online version of the popular *Hispanic Magazine* with national circulation of 250,000. News, events, and issues of interest to the Latino community. Well developed, attractive. A great magazine and a great Web site! Look for the link to Tesoros: Top Latino Websites for monthly reviews of Web sites by the staff at *Hispanic Magazine*. This is a "must see" for all Hispanics and those interested in the Hispanic American community.

◆ **Latino Outreach**

http://www.asu.edu/clas/hrc/latino/

This electronic magazine provides information about Hispanic life in the United States. At the time it was examined, there were two articles available: one on Cesar Chavez and one on Home Altars.

◆ **La Prensa on the Web**

http://www.hispanic.com/LaPrensa/LaPrensa.html

This is a bilingual online newspaper from San Antonio, Texas, providing local, national, and international news. The site also contains material relevant to business, commentary, entertainment, sports, and much more. Articles are in English or Spanish, but usually not in both languages.

◆ **La Raza**

http://www.laraza.com

Spanish-language weekly with some features in English. Attractive layout.

◆ **Vista**

http://www.vistamagazine.com/whtvist.htm

Vista is a magazine for all Hispanics, with the largest circulation of all Latino magazines. It is distributed primarily as a newspaper insert in areas with large Hispanic populations, although some copies are mailed directly to homes. The Web site articles are either in English or Spanish (but not in both). This is a sister publication to *Hispanic Magazine*.

BUSINESS

◆ **CLNet Employment Center**

http://latino.sscnet.ucla.edu/employment.html

Part of the great Chicano/LatinoNet. Links to Hispanic Experts Database, U.S. JobNet, Online Career Center, Career Mosaic Center, Saludos Web, and more.

◆ **Hispanic Association on Corporate Responsibility (HACR)**

http://www.hacr.org/

HACR is a coalition of 11 of America's largest national Hispanic organizations. Its purpose is to promote the inclusion of Hispanics in corporate America. It seeks market reciprocity, the inclusion of Hispanics in corporate America at a level comparable to their purchasing power.

◆ **Hispanic Business Magazine**

http://www.hispanstar.com/

This magazine is overflowing with useful information for business executives of Hispanic American heritage. Sophisticated research and statistics gathering.

◆ **HispanicBiz**

http://www.hispanicbiz.com

One-stop information service for Hispanic/Latino small businesses and professionals and students. Has links to Web resources on Marketing, Business, Technology, and Community.

◆ **MexPlaza; The First Virtual Shopping Center in Latin America**

http://mexplaza.com.mx/imagen-ingles/

For those who wish to shop Mexico from the comfort of their own home. Award-winning site offering a myriad of products and services. Impressive.

◆ **National Association of Hispanic Investment Bankers & Advisors (NAHIBA)**

http://www.neta.com/~1stbooks/nahiba.htm

This brief site expresses its message clearly and provides all the needed contact information for this organization. Of interest to Hispanic Americans in investment and banking.

◆ **National Hispanic Business Association (NHBA)**

http://piglet.cc.utexas.edu/~nhba/index.html

NHBA is a national network of Hispanic business students and alumni whose mission is to address educational and business issues and concerns related to Hispanics.

◆ **National Internet Community of Hispanic Entrepreneurs Network (NICHE-Net)**

http://www.matrixes.com/niche/nichenet.htm

This organization promotes awareness of and access to the Internet for Hispanic Internet businesses and communities.

◆ **Plaza Coquí, the Electronic Commerce Center of Puerto Rico**

http://www.plazacoqui.com/

This site hosts the Web sites of businesses in Puerto Rico, including education, computing, and telecommunications companies.

◆ **Saludos Web**

http://www.saludos.com/

This Web site, sponsored by *Saludos Hispanos* magazine, promotes Hispanic careers and education. Articles from the magazine, extensive job listings, career and educational information and more.

◆ **U.S. Hispanic Chamber of Commerce**

http://www.ushcc.com/

Provides information on the Hispanic market, governmental affairs, business opportunities, and more. A valuable resource.

CULTURE AND HUMANITIES, GENERAL

◆ **Are Chicanos the Same as Mexicans?**

http://www/azteca.net/aztec/chicano.html

This page discusses the question in the title, but also defines many terms such as Hispanic, Latino, Mexicans, Mexican American, and others. This is part of the Azteca Web Page (see next entry).

◆ **Azteca Web Page**

http://www.azteca.net/aztec/

Azteca provides much information and many links of interest to the Chicano/ Latino/Mexican-American Community. Information is related to Mexico and Chicano culture. Indigenous Mexican Images (**http://www.azteca.net/aztec/ prehisp/index.shtml**) has pictures of Native American people and historical places.

◆ **Blue Pearl Latin Links**

http://www.bluepearl.com/latinlnks/index.html

An attractive page consisting entirely of links to art, countries and traditions, dance, music, periodicals and webzines, literature, science and government, institutions, directories, universities, news, newsgroups, and other information.

◆ **Chupacabras Homepage**

http://www.princeton.edu/~accion/chupa.html

Is it a myth? A legend? Find out more about Puerto Rico's version of the Yeti, the Chupacabra. There are links to other Puerto Rico-related phenomena, including El Yunque, Puerto Rico Tunnel, and other Chupacabra sites. Relax and have fun at this well-developed site!

◆ **Culture and Society of Mexico**

http://www.public.iastate.edu/~rjsalvad/scmfaq/

This site includes Frequently Asked Questions for the Usenet group **soc.culture.Mexican** and a very attractive Mexican Heritage Almanac. Most of the other links on this page are either in Spanish or not particularly useful.

◆ **La Herencia Del Norte**

http://www.herencia.com/

La Herencia Del Norte, The Heritage of the North, is a quarterly magazine that highlights New Mexico's Hispanic culture, past and present, and discusses trends and issues affecting Hispanic citizens of the state. The Web site provides sample articles for those interested in New Mexico's Hispanic culture.

◆ **Hispanics Don't Exist**

http://www.usnews.com/usnews/issue/980511/11hisp.htm

This report, from *U.S. News* Online, makes the point that there is no single Hispanic culture. In fact, it discusses 17 different Hispanic cultural groups in the United States today.

◆ **Latino Culture—US**

http://latinoculture.miningco.com/

All kinds of information about Latino culture can be found in the Mining Company pages. A search engine is provided to help the user locate information available from this site.

◆ **Summary Results from the Latino Ethnic Attitude Survey**

http://www.azteca.net/aztec/survey/index.html

This survey, conducted by Daniel L. Roy of the Department of Geography at the University of Kansas, was concerned with middle class Latinos in the United States. The summary looks at Latino self-identity, how identity or ethnicity was an issue in the workplace or community, language preferences, and generational differences. It includes geodemographical information relating to gender, education, income levels, and zip codes. Tables, charts, and maps make this survey easy to use. This is part of the Azteca Web Page.

◆ **TAINO-L**

Subscription address: majordomo@corso.ccsu.ctstateu.edu

An electronic mailing list that is a forum for discussion of Taino and other Arawak-speaking peoples of the Caribbean, U.S. and South America. Promotes awareness of Taino people and culture. To join, send the message **sub TAINO-L your name** to the above address.

◆ **What Is a Hispanic? Legal Definition vs. Racist Definition**

http://www.worldculture.com/expert.htm#hispanic

A long, repetitive argument emphasizing the fact that the term Hispanic refers to a person whose culture has developed from that of Spain, rather than being based on geographical or ethnic grounds.

EDUCATION

◆ **Acción Puertorriqueña y Amigos: The Puerto Rican Students Organization at Princeton University**

http://www.princeton.edu/~accion/

Provides information about this campus group, as well as about Puerto Rico and its culture. Even has a collection of links for resources to the Latin world.

◆ **AmeriSpan**

http://www.amerispan.com/

AmeriSpan is a company that melds education and travel, specializing in Spanish immersion programs from many different schools. It also has a volunteer/intern program and educational tours and studies.

◆ **Baden-Powell Institute**

http://www.giga.com/~baden/

Web site of a Spanish language learning institute in Morelia, Mexico. Additional schools/institutes are easy to find using Yahoo or other Internet search engines.

◆ **Bilingual Education & Teaching English as a Second Language**

http://www.coe.tamu.edu/dept/edci/BilingPage/ BilingESL.html

Web site of the Bilingual/ESL Programs in the Curriculum and Instruction (EDCI) Department at Texas A&M University. The bottom of the page contains a useful, brief list of links to other resources.

◆ **Bilingual/Latino Links for Kids**

http://volvo.gslis.utexas.edu/~kidnet/biling.html

Links to many resources for students. Songs, people, recipes, folktales, stories are all found here. A valuable site for its intended audience!

- **Chicana and Chicano Space: A Thematic, Inquiry-Based Art Education Resource**

http://mati.eas.edu:8421/ChicanArte/html_pages/ Protest-home.html

This site is a resource for teachers, students, and others interested in Chicana/o art and culture. It includes artworks, information, and lesson ideas. This is a valuable resource for art educators.

- **Hispanic Scholarship Guide**

http://www.HispanicScholarships.com/

This attractive and valuable site is sponsored by Chrysler Corporation and *Vista* magazine. Most of the information is found under Resources. Not only does the site provide help finding scholarship money, but it also gives hints on what to do to qualify for aid and even gives a sample letter for requesting information from colleges. The links page provides additional sites at which college-bound students can find needed information.

- **Increasing Hispanic Participation in Higher Education: A Desirable Public Investment**

http://www.rand.org/publications/IP/IP152/

This 1995 Rand publication discusses the problem of a growing Hispanic population with low educational attainment.

- **IUP Online: Inter University Program for Latino Research**

http://latino.sscnet.ucla.edu/iup.html

Provides links to 11 Latino Studies programs at U.S. universities, including the Center for Chicano Research, Stanford University; Center for Mexican American Studies, University of Texas Austin; Centro de Estudios Puertorriqueños, Hunter College, CUNY; Chicano Studies Program, University of Texas, El Paso; Chicano Studies Research Center, UCLA; Cuban Research Institute, Florida International University; Hispanic Research Center, Arizona State University; Julian Samora Research Institute, Michigan State University; Mauricio Gastón Institute, University of Massachusetts; Mexican American Studies and Research Center, University of Arizona; and Southwest Hispanic Research Institute, University of New Mexico. Programs and positions of the group are included.

- **IUPLA: Inter-University Program for Latino Research**

http://iuplr.utexas.edu/

This site has more information than the IUP Web site at UCLA (see above). Thirteen universities are listed here, and there is extensive information about the IUPLA network, projects, resources, and other topics.

◆ **Latina/o Leadership Opportunity Program**

http://www.sscnet.ucla.edu/csrc/llop.htm

This program, sponsored by the Chicano/a Studies Research Center at UCLA and the Inter-University Program for Latino Research, is funded by the Ford Foundation. Its purpose is to prepare future policy advocates and leaders at local and national levels to serve the Latino community.

◆ **Latino-L**

Subscription address: latino-l-request@amherst.edu

The purpose of this electronic mailing list is to foster communication among Latino students. To join, send the message **sub Latino-L your name** to the address above.

◆ **Latino Resources on the Internet**

http://www.maxwell.syr.edu/geo/latino/lat.htm

No-nonsense Web page providing links to 19 Latino/Hispanic Centers at U.S. universities, plus Puerto Rican universities, and miscellaneous Latino sites. No link provided to Syracuse's program, but you know by the URL that that is where you are.

◆ **MCLR: Midwest Consortium for Latino Research**

http://38.15.30.162/glenwelk/mclr/

MCLR's mission is to provide leadership for the advancement of Latino scholars and to encourage and support research about Latinos in Midwestern institutions. The frames version of the page is at **http://www.indians.org/welker/framemcr.htm**.

◆ **MCLR-L: Midwest Consortium for Latino Research**

Subscription address: listserv@msu.edu

This electronic discussion group is for Latino scholars and others interested in Latino research in the United States. Announcements of Latino-related grants, academic jobs and more. To join, send the message **sub MCLR-L your name** to the address above.

◆ **Minorities and Women: Financial Aid and Scholarships**

http://financialaid.miningco.com/msub3.htm

Links to the Hispanic College Fund and the Hispanic Educational Foundation.

◆ **RETAnet, Resources for Teaching About the Americas**

http://ladb.unm.edu/www/retanet

RETAnet provides resources and curriculum materials for secondary educators, educational specialists, and scholars to use in teaching and studying about Latin America, the Spanish Caribbean, and the U.S. Southwest. It is produced by the Latin America Data Base, part of the Latin American Institute at the University of New Mexico. Funded by U.S. Department of Education. Good Internet links. Lesson plans and more!

FINE ARTS

◆ **Arts & History: Virtual Forum of Mexican Culture**
http://www.arts-history.mx/direc2.html

This site covers art, museums, theater, dance, and many other forms of fine arts. There is an English version of the homepage and some of the other pages, but many are only in Spanish. There are good representations of artworks.

◆ **Electric Mercado: Arts Groups**
http://www.mercado.com/grupos/

Electric Mercado is a Web design, commerce, hosting and translation company that provides a variety of links on its Web site, including links to several performing arts groups, such as Teatro Familia Aztlán, Alma, and Esperanza del Valle. Other links include shopping, literature, food, music, and youth.

Art

◆ **Christus Rex**
http://www.christusrex.org/www1/news/noticias.html

Christus Rex is a private, nonprofit organization whose Web page disseminates information on works of art preserved in churches, cathedrals and monasteries all over the world. This mostly English-language site provides religious (Catholic) news in Spanish and other languages.

◆ **Curare—Contemporary Mexican Art**
http://www.laneta.apc.org/curare/index.html

Good site for discussing art, instead of browsing for images. Web site of Curare, a nonprofit association in Mexico City for art and cultural criticism, historical research and new perspectives on Mexican contemporary art.

◆ **Recursos de Arte por País: Latin American Art Resources**
http://www.netlink.co.uk/users/amigos/level3/gallery/artepais.html

This site contains links to Latin American artists, galleries, and museums on the Web, arranged by country. Links may be in either English or Spanish.

Visual Art

◆ **Art from the Heart of Aztlan**

http://www.chicanoartist.com/

New Mexico artist Edward Gonzales is well known for his pictures of Chicano life. This Web site offers bilingual posters for home, classroom, and work, as well as books written and illustrated by Gonzales.

◆ **Chicano Murals in Tucson**

http://latino.sscnet.ucla.edu/murals/Sparc/muralhis.html

This page describes the mural scene in Tucson, Arizona. There are no pictures of the murals on the main page, but these can be found on the linked pages for each artist.

◆ **Chicano/LatinoNet's Virtual Museum**

http://clnet.ucr.edu/MUSEUM.HTML

This part of Chicano/LatinoNet is one of the major gateways to links for all major Latino cultural resources on the Internet, including Art, Music, Dance, Theater, and Film.

◆ **Contemporary Art from Cuba: Irony and Survival on the Utopian Island**

http://asuam.fa.asu.edu/cuba/main.htm

This exhibit, held at Arizona State University Art Museum in Fall 1998, was the first major exhibition of contemporary Cuban art in a U.S. museum. Nineteen artists, many of them Afro-Cuban working in Cuba today were featured. Examples of their work are shown on the site.

◆ **Cyberaza**

http://www.contrib.andrew.cmu.edu/usr/turcios/cyberaza.html

Cyberaza is a nonprofit organization that promotes Latino culture on the Internet. It provides free Web space for Latino/a artists to display their works.

◆ **Diego Rivera Virtual Museum**

http://www.diegorivera.com/diego_home_eng.html

Rivera's life and work are chronicled in a most attractive site, presented in both Spanish and English.

◆ **Frida Kahlo**

http://www.cascade.net/kahlo.html

Kahlo was a Mexican artist and wife of muralist Diego Rivera. This site includes biographical information and images of many of her paintings.

◆ **Hispanic Research Center Art Gallery**

http://www.asu.edu/clas/hrc/art/

The Hispanic Research Center Art Gallery provides a pictorial perspective of Hispanic art. Styles include campesina, folkloric, traditional, contemporary Chicano/Latino, and Magic Realism.

◆ **Legacy/Legado**

**http://www.nytimes.com/library/books/
    072098best-novels-list.html**

This page is an exhibition of Latino art that celebrated the bicentennial and restoration of the Old State House in Hartford, Connecticut. The exhibition explored the contemporary relevance of the State House, which is a National Historic Landmark. The themes of the exhibition were History, Culture, Family, and Childhood. Pictures of the artwork and information about the artists are available at this site.

◆ **Los Angeles Murals Homepage**

http://latino.sscnet.ucla.edu/murals/index1.html

Information about and photographs of murals in Los Angeles, many of which are of Chicano origin. The Social and Public Art Resource Center (SPARC) presents SPARC'S Tour of Chicano Murals in L.A. (**http://latino.sscnet.ucla.edu/murals/Sparc/sparctour.html**) and there is a Brief History of Chicano Murals (**http://latino.sscnet.ucla.edu/murals/Sparc/muralhis.html**).

◆ **Mayan Photo Adventures**

http://www.concentric.net/~yohon/english.html

This site contains interesting information and excellent photographs of Mayan monuments. Some of the pages include a table with links to other photo archives of the page's owner, John C. Mureiko.

◆ **MuralArt.com**

http://www.muralart.com/

This site includes sections on California murals and Los Angeles murals that include Chicano efforts. The Mural of the Month page has depicted several Chicano murals.

◆ **Pintores de Tigua: Indigenous Artists of Ecuador**

http://www.mip.berkeley.edu/tigua/

A notice announcing an exhibition of the work of indigenous artists of Ecuador. This Web page includes examples and descriptive information about the artists.

Dance

◆ **Flamenco Homepage**

http://solea.quim.ucm.es/flamenco.html

This site provides information about flamenco performances in Madrid and about flamenco resources on the Internet. Unfortunately, the material is not always up-to-date.

◆ **West Coast Flamenco**

http://www.flamenco.org/

This site is a well-developed resource for worldwide information about Flamenco.

Drama

◆ **COMEDIA**

Subscription address: listserv@arizvm1.ccit.arizona.edu

This electronic mailing list is a discussion group about Hispanic classic theater. To join, send the following message, **sub COMEDIA your name**, to the above address.

◆ **El Teatro Campesino**

http://www.mercado.com/grupos/campesin/index.html

Formed in 1965 by Luis Valdez, who joined César Chávez in organizing farmworkers. He organized El Teatro Campesino (The Farmworkers Theater) to popularize and raise funds for the grape boycott and farmworker strike. In 1968, El Teatro Campesino left the fields to create a theater that reflected the full Chicano experience. Site includes Film and Video Center and more. Note: clicking on the pictures or the captions under them takes you to the Electric Mercado homepage (**http://www.mercado.com/**). You must click on the links in the line just above the word ¡BIENVENIDOS! or on the links below it to get to the information about El Teatro Campesino.

Music

alt.music.afro-latin

This Usenet newsgroup discusses music with Afro-Latin, African, and Latin influences.

◆ **Caribbean Music and Dance Programs**

http://www.caribmusic.com/

This colorful site is that of a company that organizes cultural travel programs to the Caribbean and Brazil. There is a wide variety of programs in the categories of Workshops in Music & Dance, Music Seminars, Festivals & Events, and more!

◆ **Discóbolo**

http://204.183.116.8/discobolo/

This music store specializes in Hispanic music from all over the Spanish-speaking world.

◆ **Latin Music Online**

http://www.lamusica.com/

This is perhaps the best developed site on a great variety of Latin music resources. Includes music news, reviews, magazines, radio shows, TV shows, concerts, record stores, dance lessons, and more. An award winner!

GOVERNMENT, LAW, AND POLITICS

◆ **Affirmative Action: Where Do Latinos Fit In?**

http://latino.sscnet.ucla.edu/research/iup/aa.html

This paper by Frank Bonzilla is dated October 1995. It discusses affirmative action in general and as specifically related to Hispanic concerns.

◆ **AmericasNet**

http://summit.fiu.edu/americas/americas-frames-noblue.html

This site is maintained by the Summit of the Americas Center (SOAC) at Florida International University. SOAC was established to monitor, analyze, and disseminate information about the process of Western Hemisphere integration. Information about the Santiago Summit of the Americas (April 1998) and the Free Trade Area of the Americas can be found here.

◆ **Chicana Feminist Homepage / "Making Face, Making Soul..."**

http://www-leland.stanford.edu/%7Eslg/

While the main topic of this Web site is political in nature, the site itself is informational. Although aimed primarily at Chicana women, it welcomes anyone who wishes to examine the social and political inequalities of race, class, gender, and sexuality in U.S. society.

◆ **Hearing on Language Rights: Statement by Prof. Frank Bonzilla**

http://latino.sscnet.ucla.edu/research/iup/language.html

This statement describes the policy formulated in 1977 by the National Puerto Rican Task Force on Educational Policy, "Toward a Language Policy for Puerto Ricans in the U.S." The goal of this policy was educational bilinguality, with command of both English and Spanish. This is a very different goal than that formulated today by the critics of bilingual education, who seek to eliminate such programs.

◆ **IPRNET: The Information Service on Puerto Rican Issues**

http://www.iprnet.org/IPR/index.html

The Institute for Puerto Rican Policy (IPR) provides this award-winning site to present valuable information on a variety of issues of concern to Puerto Ricans and Latinos. The IPR-FORUM, available through this site, is an electronic mailing list on which interested persons can discuss policy.

◆ **North American Congress on Latin America (NACLA)**

http://www.serve.com/nacla/

NACLA is an independent, nonprofit organization that provides information on major trends in Latin America and its relations with the United States. It publishes a bimonthly magazine, *NACLA Report on the Americas,* the most widely read English-language publication on Latin America; its tables of contents for recent issues are given at the site.

◆ **The Official Summit of the Americas Implementation Page**

http://americas.fiu.edu/state/

The Summit of the Americas was held in Miami, Florida in December 1994. Thirty-four democracies in the Western Hemisphere were represented. This page, maintained by the U.S. Department of State, includes official documents, press releases, and other information from that summit, as well as information about subsequent actions taken by Summit members to further the initiatives developed at the Summit. A link to information about the April 1998 Summit in Santiago, Chile, was not working at the time this was written. Information about the 1998 Summit can be found at AmericasNet (see previous page).

◆ **Tomás Rivera Policy Institute**

http://www.cgs.edu/inst/trc.html

This organization conducts timely and objective policy-relevant research on issues of concern Latino communities in the U.S. Up to date!

◆ **Treaty of Guadalupe Hidalgo**

**http://www.asu.edu/clas/hrc/1848and1898at1998/
   treaty.html**

This site contains the text of the 1848 treaty, which ended the war between the United States and Mexico. As a result of the treaty, much of what is now the U.S. Southwest was acquired.

Organizations

◆ **Brown Berets National Organization**

http://www.brownberets.org

The primary goal of the Brown Beret Movement is to educate the general public and the Chicano community to participate in community action and awareness in order to improve the living conditions for La Raza in the United States. Currently, the organization is attempting to reduce barrio violence and to create a long lasting community organization.

Note: at the time this chapter was written, the above URL was not available, but History of the Brown Berets was available at **http://www.brownberets.org/history.html**, and other Brown Beret links were available at the bottom of that page.

◆ **Congressional Hispanic Caucus Institute, Inc. (CHCI)**

http://www.chci.org/home.html

CHCI is a nonprofit, nonpartisan, educational organization whose mission is to promote and encourage the next generation of Latino leadership through education and information. The site provides information about Hispanic members of the U.S. Congress, Hispanic leaders, educational programs, and current legislation.

◆ **Cuban American National Foundation**

http://www.canfnet.org/

This Cuban-American organization, based in Miami, is a nonprofit organization dedicated to re-establishing freedom and democracy in Cuba.

◆ **Hispanic Leadership Institute**

http://www.primenet.com/~valle/hliinfo.htm

The Hispanic Leadership Institute promotes the participation of Hispanics in leadership roles, increasing Hispanic participation in the development of public policy and creating leadership capacity in serving the Hispanic community. The Institute is a 14-week program held at Arizona State University.

◆ **League of United Latin American Citizens (LULAC)**

http://www.lulac.org

Founded in 1929, LULAC is one of the oldest Latino organizations in the U.S. This site provides information about LULAC's stands on political matters, education, language, jobs, and other topics. The LULAC National Convention, which draws over 6,000 people each year including top leaders from government, business, and the Hispanic community, is announced.

◆ **National Council of La Raza**

http://www.nclr.org/

The National Council of La Raza (NCLR) is a nonprofit, nonpartisan organization established to improve life opportunities for Hispanic Americans. It provides aid primarily through assistance to Hispanic community-based organizations and through research, policy analysis, and advocacy.

◆ **NHMC: National Hispanic Media Coalition**

http://www.latinoweb.com/nhmc/

This is the Web site of a coalition of Hispanic American organizations that addresses a variety of media related issues that affect the Hispanic American community, such as lack of coverage of Hispanic issues, lack of equal employment, stereotypes in programming, etc.

◆ **United Farm Workers**

http://www.ufw.org/

Press releases, history, regional offices, current actions and other information about this important labor organization.

HISTORY

◆ **Chicano!**

http://www.pbs.org/chicano/

Chicano! was a PBS series about the history of Mexican Americans, especially the period 1965–1975. The site features historical information, biographies of people profiled in the series, teaching/learning resources, and resources for use with the series.

◆ **Chicano/LatinoNet Folklore/Customs/Traditions**

http://clnet.ucr.edu/research/folklore.html

Provides numerous links to information on art, festivals, food, folklore, narratives, and more. This site is a part of the Chicano/LatinoNet.

◆ **Civilizations in America**

http://www.wsu.edu/~dee/CIVAMRCA/CIV.HTM

Mesoamerican (Aztec, Maya, Olmec, etc.) and Andean (Inca) civilizations are described and there are excellent photographs of ancient structures.

◆ **Hero Street**

http://www.neta.com/~1stbooks/hero.htm

A simple, elegant cyber-monument to Hispanics in America's defense: men who gave their lives for their country: Joe Gomez, Peter Masias, Johnny Muros,

Tony Pompa, Frank Sandoval, Joseph Sandoval, William Sandoval, and Claro Soliz. Links to Hispanic America USA.

◆ **Hispanic America USA**

http://www.neta.com/~1stbooks/

This site provides an overview of the role of Hispanic Americans in the history of the United States. Topics include Military, Hispanics in Politics, Historical Timelines, Hispanic Exploration of Canada, History of American Pioneers, Hispanic Living History, Hispanics in Space. Primarily in English, with some Spanish.

◆ **Hispanic America USA: Hispano History Links**

http://www.neta.com/~1stbooks/link0.htm

Provides state by state links to Hispanic history resources on the Internet.

◆ **Hispanics in America's Defense**

http://www.neta.com/~1stbooks/defense.htm

Click on Introduction to reach an index that lists Medal of Honor winners, Hero Street (see previous page), and Hispanics who fought in U.S. wars from the Revolutionary War onward. Some sites are still under construction. Some pages may be difficult to read.

◆ **Maya World**

http://www.stevensonpress.com/mwindex.html

Maya World is an electronic magazine produced by the Mesoamerica Foundation. It discusses the archaeology, history, culture, and societies of the Mayan peoples. The articles are varied, covering such topics as the Maya monkey, the city of Calakmul, the origins of Mesoamerican culture, Gonzalo Guerrero, the Olmecs, and different meanings of the word "macho."

◆ **Precolumbian Culture**

**http://udgftp.cencar.udg.mx/ingles/Precolombina/
    precointro.html**

This site contains material about the Mayans, Aztecs, and Olmecs, including legends, from the University of Guadalajara. It includes a map and illustrations.

◆ **SPAN 3323 Hispanic Area Studies**

http://saul.snu.edu/syllabi/language/span3323/

This site is a course, conducted in English, that traces Spain's influence on the Americas, especially on the United States. Although offered by the Spainish Department at Southern Nazarene University, it is basically a history course. It is listed here because the Schedule of Daily Activities has many links to information and pictures relating to Hispanics and their history.

◆ **SPANBORD: History and Archaeology of the Spanish Borderlands**
Subscription address: listserv@asuvm.inre.asu.edu

The focus of this electronic mailing list is on topics related to the history and contemporary culture of northern Mexico and areas of the United States that were once part of the Spanish Empire. To join, send the message **sub SPAN-BORD your name** to the above address.

◆ **Transhistoric Thresholds Conference**
**http://www.asu.edu/clas/hrc/1848and1898at1998/
    index.html**

This Web site contains information about the conference at Arizona State University in December 1998, as well as all other worldwide events relevant to the Treaty of Guadalupe Hidalgo (1848), the Spanish-American War (1898), and the U.S. annexation of Hawaii (1898).

◆ **World History Archive: History of the Americas as a Whole**
http://www.hartford-hwp.com/archives/40/index.html

This site includes a wealth of historical documents and other materials. This page links to pages for various regions of the Americas, which in turn link to pages for individual countries. Links are annotated, and full documents are provided.

◆ **The World of Mayan Culture**
http://www.sureste.com/mayas/mapaengl.htm

This site includes information about the ancient, colonial, and modern Mayan world. There is an excellent map. Also available in Spanish.

Genealogy

◆ **soc.genealogy.hispanic**
This Usenet newsgroup is devoted to genealogy of Hispanics.

LANGUAGE ARTS AND LITERATURE

Language Arts

◆ **Bilingual Books for Kids**
http://www.bilingualbooks.com

This site offers books written with Spanish and English appearing side-by-side, in order to increase bilingual skills, language and learning abilities and positive awareness of various cultures. Besides books, the site offers musical and language-learning tapes and games chosen for their educational value, quality of text and illustrations, and for depicting cultures affirmatively. There is also a category for adult books. This site is a place to order these useful bilingual materials. Neatly organized by categories. Attractive book covers are shown as well as a short synopsis of the contents.

◆ **Center for the Study of Books in Spanish for Children and Young Adults**
http://www.csusm.edu/public_html/yin/intro_eng.html

This Web site is maintained by Dr. Isabel Schon at California State University, San Marcos. Books can be searched in many ways, and in addition to full bibliographic information, the data includes subjects, a short annotation, and references to reviews.

◆ **Computer Spanglish**
http://www.actlab.utexas.edu/~seagull/spanglish.html

A high level of sophistication makes this a valuable resource. It is an online dictionary of Internet and computer terms that have been adapted into Spanish from the original English. Yolanda Rivas, the author, indicates that the site may not be comprehensive, though it sure looks like it might be! Useful explanations included. Interesting.

◆ **Ethnologue: Languages of the World—The Americas**
http://www.sil.org/ethnologue/countries/Americas.html

This site provides information on all languages spoken in each country, including number of speakers, language family, and areas where spoken. The information is much the same as that provided in Living Languages of the Americas (see below), but it is arranged in paragraphs, rather than in charts.

◆ **The Internet TESL Journal**
http://www.aitech.ac.jp/~iteslj/

This e-zine is for teachers of English as a second language. It features articles, projects, and teaching techniques.

◆ **Living Languages of the Americas**
http://www.sil.org/lla/

This site provides information on languages spoken in North, Central, and South America and the Caribbean, arranged by country. The language name, language family, number of speakers, and areas where spoken are given in chart form. Studies of the various languages are listed in a bibliography.

◆ **Webspañol: Spanish Language Resources On-Line**
http://www.cyberramp.net/~mdbutler/

Webspañol promotes the study and appreciation of the Spanish language by utilizing Internet resources. There are links to various language learning aids, including free language learning software, online sound files that help with basic pronunciation, on-line Spanish lessons, and even a link to "e-mail amigos," pen-pals via e-mail. This is a truly useful resource!

Literature

- ◆ **Annotated Bibliography of Children's Literature Focusing on Latino People, History, and Culture**

http://clnet.ucr.edu/Latino_Bibliography.html

This annotated bibliography, developed in Spring 1995, includes fiction, nonfiction, poetry, picture books, and resources for teachers and parents.

- ◆ **Bilingual Review/Press**

http://mati.eas.asu.edu:8421/bilingual/HTML/index.html

Bilingual Review/Press publishes significant works by Hispanic writers. Most are in English, although some bilingual and Spanish-only titles are published.

- ◆ **BookLink**

http://www.intac.com/~booklink/

BookLink is a book distributor in ESL (English as a Second Language) and multicultural materials. It also claims to provide any British book in print. Unfortunately, only two topics, ESL Books and Multicultural Books, list available materials.

- ◆ **Books con Salsa, etc.**

http://www.brainiac.com/gordon/

This company offers antiquarian, out-of-print, and scarce books and ephemera from Latin America and the Caribbean.

- ◆ **CHICLE: Chicano Literature Discussion Group**

Subscription address: chicle-request@unmvma.unm.edu

CHICLE is an electronic discussion group covering issues related to Chicano literature and heritage. To join, send the message **sub CHICLE your name** to the above address.

- ◆ **Howard Karno Books**

http://www.karnobooks.com/

Howard Karno is a bookseller dealing with new, rare, and out-of-print books about Latin America. Unfortunately, the page does not appear to have been updated since October 1997.

- ◆ **Latino Literature Pages**

http://www.ollusa.edu/alumni/alumni/latino/latinoh1.htm

The concept of this Web site is wonderful! As of this writing, however, much of it is still under construction. The aim is to create a Web site where Latino/Latina literature is discussed, reviewed, and analyzed. Currently, the list includes famous Latin American authors, but very minimal information about Latinos/Chicanos/ Hispanic Americans in the U.S., which is the stated aim. With continued development, this concept may become a valuable reality. Worth checking for updates.

◆ **Libros Latinos**

http://www.concentric.net/~libros/

Libros Latinos is the leading vendor of new and out-of-print scholarly material from Latin America. Catalogs and booklists can be ordered from this site.

◆ **Literature/Literatura**

http://www.mercado.com/literatura/

Poems and stories by Latino/a writers. Most are in Spanish, but some are in English.

POPULAR CULTURE

◆ **Frontera Magazine**

http://www.fronteramag.com/

Frontera is an irreverent, witty blend of Latino music, arts, culture and politics for those on the cutting-edge. Of interest to twentysomething Latinos and others. It includes audio files and an archive of past programs.

◆ **Moderna Online—the Latina Magazine**

http://www.hisp.com/moderna/

This Web site provides information of special interest to Hispanic-American women. *Moderna* is from the publishers of the popular *Hispanic Magazine*.

◆ **Ritmo-Y-Mas: Latino Music and Books**

http://www.ondanet.com:1995/tejano/tejads/ritmo/ ritmo.html

This site states that it specializes in Tejano music and Latino literature. It also sells T-shirts and sundries, which includes such items as comic books, videos, and calendars. Workers of America merchandise is also sold.

Food and Drink

◆ **Ajili-Mojili Restaurant**

http://www.icepr.com/ajili-mojili/ajili-mojili.html

A Puerto Rican restaurant which offers gourmet Puerto Rican cuisine.

Music

alt.music.reggae

This Usenet newsgroup discusses roots, rockers, and dancehall reggae.

◆ **Border Cultures: Conjunto Music**

**http://www.lib.utexas.edu/Libs/Benson/border/
    ConjuntoIndex.html**

This page celebrates the music of the Mexican/U.S. border. The links give access to sites on its history, cultural significance and artistry.

◆ **Mariachi Web in Cyberspace**

http://www.qvo.com/MariachiWeb.html

Your one-stop-shop for information on mariachi music in the U.S., Mexico, and the cyber-world! Colorful, with many links.

◆ **Rumba y Bembé**

http://www.princeton.edu/~accion/index3.html

A one-stop-shop for links to information about Puerto Rican/Latino music and dance, including Merengue, Salsa, Rock, and individual artists such as Ruben Blades, Juan Luis Guerra, Luis Miguel, and José Feliciano.

◆ **Tejano Music Awards**

http://www.sanow.com/ttma/

Texas Talent Musicians Association page featuring information on the best of Tejano music. Includes Tejano music news, merchandise catalog, pictures of Tejano music stars, and more.

◆ **Tejano Music Homepage**

http://www.ondanet.com:1995/tejano/tejano.html

Another fantastic collection of information and links for Tejano music resources. Includes news, reviews, photos, history, record labels, and more. A special tribute to beloved artist Selena. Updated regularly.

◆ **The Unofficial Selena's Web Site**

http://www.ondanet.com:1995/tejano/selena.html

This site is a tribute to the popular singer who was killed in 1995.

Radio

◆ **Latino USA: Radio Journal of News & Culture**

http://www.utexas.edu/coc/kut/latinousa/

This is a weekly news program from National Public Radio and the University of Texas, at Austin.

Sports

- **National Association of Latinos in Amateur Sports (NALAS)**

http://hrcweb.utsa.edu/html/nalas.htm

The National Association of Latinos in Amateur Sports was formed in 1996 to improve the quality of life of all Latino amateur athletes in the United States. Goals target all levels, from young people in disadvantaged neighborhoods to Olympic athletes.

Bullfighting

alt.culture.bullfight

This Usenet newsgroup is for anyone who wishes to discuss the art and sport of bullfighting.

- **Bullfighting**

**http://www.personal.isat.com/bullfights/Web97/
    index97.htm**

Explanation of bullfighting, photos, schedules and standings (Mexico only), even a discussion group about this sport/art. Interesting!

- **Bullfighting: Toros en Holanda!**

http://huizen.dds.nl/~legemaat/toros2/toros.html

This is a Dutch page on the art of bullfighting, which is partly in English and has some text. Also good pictures.

- **La Tauromaquia: The Art of Bullfighting**

http://coloquio.com/toros/bullhist.html

History, terminology, and culture of bullfighting. The site is in English, but some links are in Spanish.

Television and Film

- **Blue Pearl**

http://www.bluepearl.com/

Blue Pearl Entertainment is an innovative company which manages talent and creates television and film programming with a Latin slant. From the homepage, click on About Blue Pearl for more information and a link to the performers ("talent") managed by the company.

- **Coyote Pass Productions**

http://home.earthlink.net/~coyotep/

Coyote Pass Productions creates quality entertainment (documentaries, films, series, commercials) for theater and television. The productions feature Latino characters in stories appealing to both mainstream and Hispanic audiences.

◆ **KINT TV – Channel 26**

http://www.kint.com

Web page of the Univision affiliate in El Paso, Texas. Includes information about the station's programming, news, and weather.

◆ **The Movies, Race, and Ethnicity: Latinos**

http://www.lib.berkeley.edu/MRC/imageslatinos.html

From the Media Resources Center, Moffitt Library, UC Berkeley, this list of films about Latinos includes descriptions of the content and references to reviews; links to full-text online reviews are given when available. Very useful for educators.

RELIGION

◆ **The Aztecs: A Tradition of Religious Human Sacrifice**

http://www2.hmc.edu/~sbooth/aztecpaper.htmlx

Despite the sensational title, this is a fascinating, documented discussion of Aztec religion, wherein the victims were believed to be incarnations of gods and their bodies were eaten in a ritual communion.

◆ **Interlupe: A Message from Heaven**

http://spin.com.mx/~msalazar

This site, from Centro de Estudios Guadalupanos, provides information in Spanish and English on the theology, legend and art of the Virgin of Guadalupe, Patroness of the Americas.

SCIENCE AND TECHNOLOGY

◆ **SHPEASU**

Subscribe to: listserv@asuacad.bitnet

Send mail to: shpeasu@asuacad.bitnet

Listserv for the Society of Hispanic Professional Engineers. To join, send the message **sub SHPEASU your name** to the address above.

◆ **Society for the Advancement of Chicanos and Native Americans in Science (SACNAS)**

http://www.qvo.com/azteca.html

SACNAS is a society of science professors, industry scientists, K–12 teachers, and students. It promotes graduate science education for Chicano/Latino and Native American students. Teacher workshops and national conferences are featured. The Biography Project is a resource for educators who wish to teach students about the accomplishments of Chicano/Latino and Native American scientists. The *SACNAS Quarterly Journal* is included online.

◆ **Society of Hispanic Professional Engineers (SHPE)**
http://www.shpe.org/

SHPE promotes the development of Hispanics in engineering, science, and technical fields, focusing on education, professional development, community outreach, and development of the organization.

◆ **The Society of Mexican American Engineers and Scientists (MAES)**
http://tam2000.tamu.edu/~maes

A nonprofit, tax-exempt organization founded in 1974, MAES works to increase opportunities and recognition for Mexican Americans in engineering, computer technology, and science. Provides information about student chapters, *MAES National Magazine,* and more.

◆ **Volcano World—Mexico**
http://volcano.und.nodak.edu/vwdocs/volc_tour/mex.html

This is a tour of Mexican volcanoes, with extensive information and excellent photographs. At Volcano World (**http://volcano.und.nodak.edu/vw.html**), information on volcanoes in other countries, including many in Latin America, can be found.

Health

◆ **National Coalition of Hispanic Health and Human Services Organizations (COSSMHO)**
http://latino.sscnet.ucla.edu/community/cossmho.html

Web site of a nonprofit organization dedicated to improving the health and psycho-social well-being of the nation's Hispanic population. Its projects include demonstration programs, research, policy analysis, information provision, and technical assistance.

Information Technology and Telecommunications

◆ **Frontera/Borderlands Communications Seminar**
http://www.utep.edu/comm3459/fall97/

Technology-based communication videoconference seminar course at the University of Texas at El Paso taught simultaneously with UT-Austin that explores the U.S./Mexico Frontera (border) and new telecommunications media's effects in the area. Links to a variety of telecommunications resources.

- ◆ **Tomás Rivera Policy Institute: Latinos and the Information Superhighway**

http://www.cgs.edu/inst/trc_super1.html

A detailed report providing an analysis of the relationship between Latinos and the Internet/Computers.

- ◆ **Trans-Border Information Technology Collaborative**

http://www.utep.edu/~tbitc/

This is a report of a grant project funded by the Telecommunications and Information Infrastructure Assistance Program (TIIAP) of the National Telecommunications and Information Administration (NTIA) of the United States Department of Commerce. The purpose of the project was to plan the future of the information and telecommunications highway for West Texas, Southern New Mexico and Northern Chihuahua. This report can serve as a model for many types of projects.

OTHER

Organizations

- ◆ **Reforma, the National Association to Promote Library Services to the Spanish-Speaking**

http://clnet.ucr.edu/library/reforma/index.htm

Provides information about the organization and its listserv, Reformanet.

- ◆ **Reformanet**

Subscription address: listproc@lmrinet.gse.ucsb.edu

This is the electonic mailing list for Reforma, the National Association to Promote Library Services to the Spanish-Speaking. This is a great resource for librarians. To join, send the message **sub REFORMANET your name** to the address above.

- ◆ **Taino Inter-Tribal Council**

http://www.hartford-hwp.com/taino

The Taino Inter-Tribal Council is an organization of Taino and other Arawak-speaking people from the Caribbean islands who live in the U.S. This Web site is a central information source for members of the Council and for others interested in Taino-related issues. There are links to Taino community events, various tribal homepages, Taino culture, and Taino relationships with the world outside the Unites States.

Travel and Tourism

- ### The Civilized Explorer Travel Information Page: Caribbean
http://www.cieux.com/trinfo3.html#cu

This page contains links to resources for travelers to the Caribbean islands. It consists of a limited number of links for each island. Each link is well annotated.

- ### Eco Travels in Latin America
http://www.planeta.com/

Eco Travels provides information on environmental and eco-tourism issues. Contains travel tips, a directory of Spanish-language schools, and archives of the quarterly newsletter *El Planeta Platica (The Earth Speaks)*.

- ### Escape to Puerto Rico
http://escape/topuertorico.com/

This is the Internet's most comprehensive guide to Puerto Rico. It is updated daily with information for travelers, businesses, and anyone interested in almost any topic related to the island.

- ### Harry S. Pariser's Travel Guides
http://www.catch22.com/~vudu/bookd.html

The author of these pages has written guides to several countries in the Caribbean and Central America. Although the site is basically an advertisement for these books, some information about the countries is given. Not all the links work, but some, such as the one for Puerto Rico, are worth checking out.

- ### Mexico: An Endless Journey
http://mexico-travel.com/mex_eng.html

Virtually anything you might want to know about travel in Mexico is found here. The backgrounds may make the site hard to read, but there is a wealth of information.

rec.travel.caribbean

This Usenet newsgroup discusses travel to the islands of the Caribbean.

rec.travel.latin-america

This Usenet newsgroup discusses travel to the Caribbean and Central and South America.

6

Asian American Resources, General

D. RUSSELL BAILEY, VICKI L. GREGORY,
CYNTHIA A. NUHN, AND SUZANNE M. SAUNDERS

These sites cover Asian American cultures in general. For specific cultures, see chapters 7–9.

BUSINESS

- **Asia Central**

http://www.asiacentral.com/

Asia Central describes itself as the Internet outpost of Info Pacific, which offers sales and marketing assistance to companies wanting to sell to Asians living outside their ancestral country. The site focuses on China, Japan, Korea, Vietnam, and India. In the China section, there are detailed lists of contact addresses for Chinese American magazines, newspapers, radio stations and television stations, as well as some articles including demographics on Chinese Americans (and the other cultures mentioned above).

- **Asian Buying Consortium**

http://www.abcflash.com/

This group intends to be the largest buying group in North America that focuses on Asians, and it offers discounts to members, both organizations and individuals. To entice people to the Web site, a page of general Asian American-interest links is maintained and is very popular.

GOVERNMENT, LAW, AND POLITICS

◆ **The Sunday Group**

http://pantheon.yale.edu/~caase/sunday.html

The Sunday Group is the Internet equivalent of the weekend political TV talk shows, intended to "demonstrate the relevance of diverse Asian American perspectives to American current affairs" and make up for the lack of Asian Americans on the political TV talk shows. The group meets weekly and chats by telnetting to a particular server and entering a particular chat forum; the mechanics of so doing are explained clearly on the site. The Web site includes transcripts of previous chats, along with related articles for the subject of each chat, and information to prepare participants on the subject of the next chat. To participate, one does have to arrange in advance with the project's maintainer, but there is an e-mail link to do so on the site. Note: the site has not been updated since February 1997.

HISTORY

◆ **Angel Island: A Journey Remembered**

http://207.171.220.89/angelisland/index.html

This site includes both texts and pictures about Angel Island and the treatment of Asian immigrants. There is also a list of resources. Excellent site.

◆ **Angel Island: Ellis Island of the West**

http://www.kqed.org/fromKQED/Cell/Calhist/angel.html

This site is a lesson plan for teaching about Angel Island. Background information, activities, and resources are given. The plan is part of a series of history lessons developed by the San Francisco Unified School District. Age level was not given, but it seems to be upper elementary.

◆ **Asian American Center at Queens College, New York City**

http://www.qc.edu/Asian_American_Center/index.html

This address includes a bibliography on the history of print publications of the Center, an annotated list of films and videos, online articles on the history of various nationality groups in New York City, current and back issues of the *A/AC Newsletter,* and a description of the Translation Program, which translates materials from organizations in Queens into various Asian languages.

◆ **Different Voices, Different Choices**

http://naio.kcc.hawaii.edu/bosp/voices/index.html

This outgrowth of a journalism class at the University of Hawaii became a magazine about the voices of the many cultures which come together in Hawaii.

At least three of the essays listed are accounts of Chinese American experiences, and several others are about race conflicts in Hawaii.

POPULAR CULTURE

- ◆ **Dead Fish Online Magazine**
http://www.deadfish.com/

Dead Fish Online, "the place where your brains get stir-fried," is another Asian American-themed pop-culture online magazine aimed at college-age people, but this one is much more offbeat in tone—sections called Garbage Can and Atomic Rice prove that. It can't be viewed without a frame-capable Web browser, and some of the graphics which serve as links do not clearly indicate what they link to. But the content is amusing, and readers who like it can sign up to receive an e-mail notification when each new issue comes out, approximately each month.

- ◆ **RealizAsian Magazine**
http://www.nyu.edu/pages/pubs/realizasian/

This magazine from a club at New York University focuses on all sorts of issues of interest to college-age Asian Americans. The site is nearly unusable in a non-graphic Web browser, but with the proper software one can reach some very interesting articles. The editor notes that the supposedly monthly magazine may have to cut back on the frequency of its issues because the students who run it don't have time to produce issues, or money available for the print copies they distribute at their university. (The articles currently online are good insights into the lives and interests of its authors.)

- ◆ **TMIWEB**
http://www.tmiweb.com/

TMIWEB is the Web site for publishers of print magazines for Asian Americans. The web site includes selected articles from various magazines on Asian Americans' success and influence, style and fashion, makeup and cosmetics, entertainment and lifestyles, and men's interests, as well as an Asian-themed bookmart and an area to post free classified ads. Subscribers to some of the magazines can access extra parts closed to non-subscribers. But even non-subscribers can use the topical index to the articles available on the site, or revisit the What's New periodically to get an update on new features.

- ◆ **YOLK.com**
http://www.yolk.com

YOLK is another magazine for Asian Americans, for the "Generasian Next." The full magazine is available in print format, and selections from various back issues are online. Also available are talk forums about things that have appeared in the print magazine, on the Web site, or just concerning Asian Americans in general, and an online merchandise catalog.

Sports

◆ **The Martial Arts as I've Learned Them**

http://redtape.uchicago.edu/users/fun5/martial.html

The page deals mostly with the styles of martial arts and related practices that the maintainer (Kent, no last name given) has personal experience with: Tang Soo Do, Aikido, Qigong, Jeet Kune Do, and Chung Moo Doo. In addition to Kent's comments on each style, there are links to other resources on each subject (for example, philosophical works, magazine articles and the controversies they caused, and martial arts suppliers). Kent tries to be fair when dealing with controversy even when firmly biased.

◆ **The Martial Arts Network Online**

http://www.martial-arts-network.com/

An electronic forum dedicated to promoting martial arts of all styles, this site has discussion forums, lists of resources by country of origin, and other useful information for the practitioner of martial arts.

◆ **Sports in Asia**

http://home.ust.hk/~ke_kck/sport/asia.html

This is one of the few working general Asian sports pages in English that was found. For China and related countries, it lists pages for soccer, swimming, horse racing, and other sports.

◆ **Taijiquan (Tai Chi Chuan)**

http://www.neijia.org/taijiquan.html

A very easy-to-read basic outline of the history, basic philosophy and various styles of this martial/health art.

Television and Film

◆ **Asian Americans in TV and Movies—The Media Portrayal Project**

http://pantheon.yale.edu/~caase/menu.html

This site, though it is labeled "under construction," already has several thought-provoking essays on the portrayal of Asian Americans (and Asians) in U.S. television and movies. The author covers the portrayals of Asian Americans as foreigners to the U.S., and at other times, as the model minority, as well as Caucasian appropriation of Asian martial arts, of the one-sidedness of the interracial relationships involving Asian Americans shown in these media, the historical inaccuracy of portrayals of Asian history, and a list of positive portrayals of Asian Americans in TV and movies.

◆ Sawnet: South Asian Women's Cinema

**http://www.umiacs.umd.edu/users/sawweb/sawnet/
cinema.html**

This site is sponsored by the South Asian Women's Network and films are reviewed by Sawnet members. The site welcomes submissions, and non-Sawnet member reviews are included at the discretion of those who maintain the page. The movies reviewed are Asian, American, and from other countries as well. It was interesting to read reviews from people who were not professional movie reviewers. The movie titles are hypertext and the user clicks on the title of the desired film review. There are links to films and filmmakers, articles about South Asian cinema, and other related links.

RELIGION

Buddhism

◆ **Buddhist Studies WWW VL**

http://www.ciolek.com/WWWVL-Buddhism.html

This site is part of the WWW Virtual Library. It offers extensive information about Buddhism. The site is updated almost daily. Links include Buddhist Texts Input/Translation Projects; Buddhism Gopher; FTP; mailing lists and chat room resources; and Buddhism/Buddhist electronic newsletters and journals, which include catalogs, academic serials, and other serials. There are also links to Buddhist art and Buddhist WWW sites.

SCIENCE AND TECHNOLOGY

Health

◆ **Asian and Pacific Islander American Health Forum**

http://www.apiahf.org/apiahf/

This organization, which exists to promote improvement in the health status of all Asian and Pacific Islanders in the United States has a very informative site. In addition to health information, there is some demographic information on the appropriate ethnic groups, and immigration and welfare explanations (also available in several languages besides English).

Information Technology and Telecommunications

◆ **Newsbytes Pacifica Homepage**

http://www.nb-pacifica.com/

NB Pacifica provides high-tech news coverage of the entire Asia-Pacific region. This is a pioneering electronic publication offering both text and images. It has provided daily coverage of the dynamic and complex computer and telecommunications industries since 1983. The wire service reports, on average, 30 stories each day, filed by 19 correspondents worldwide.

WOMEN'S ISSUES

◆ **Journal of South Asian Women Studies**

http://www1.shore.net/~india/jsaws/index.htm

This online journal is directed to scholars of South Asian women's studies and women in and from South Asia. Topics covered are diverse and include civil rights, feminism and ecofeminism, gender issues, law, history, dance, music, drama, poetry, language, folklore, customs, and modern and classical literature. Users can perform a search of the World Wide Web using this site's search engine. Current and back issues are available for exploring. Many related links are offered from this site.

◆ **Sawnet: Books by and about South Asian Women**

http://www.umiacs.umd.edu/users/sawweb/sawnet/
   SAW.books.html

This site is part of Sawnet, but it is too wonderful not to have a description of its own. This site features writings by South Asian women. Hypertext links include Fiction and Poetry, Nonfiction, Magazines, Collections and Anthologies, and Articles. Reviews of books with photographs of the authors are included. Clicking on Write! offers helpful information on writing opportunities for aspiring authors. There is also a link to bookstores/publishers.

◆ **Sawnet: South Asian Women's Network**

http://www.umiacs.umd.edu:80/users/sawweb/sawnet/
   index.html

Sawnet is the South Asian Women's Network. According to this site's introduction, Sawnet "is a Forum for those interested in South Asian women's issues." The term South Asia includes India, Nepal, Pakistan, Sri Lanka, Burma, Bhutan, and Bangladesh. This site has many interesting links, including South Asian women's organizations, articles, News about South Asian Women, and domestic violence, as well as careers, grants, and funding.

OTHER

Organizations

◆ **Asian American Journalists Association**

http://www.aaja.org/

The Asian American Journalists Association exists to support and promote Asian American journalists, and to work for fair representation of Asian Americans in the media. The site for the nationwide organization lists the regional chapters, linking to those which have Web sites, but also on its own describes the national initiatives it and its chapters have taken, the programs and benefits available to members of the organization, the newsletter from the annual convention, and several current events articles on subjects of interest to Asian Americans.

◆ **Asian Americans United Homepage**

http://www.libertynet.org:80/~asianau/index.html

This Philadelphia-based community organization has interesting photographs of Asian American life and a history of their organization. In 1997, they published a very useful Asian/Pacific American calendar, featuring a historical event concerning Asian/Pacific Americans for nearly every day, and photographs of the lives of Asian/Pacific Americans.

◆ **Asian Community Online Network**

http://www.igc.apc.org/acon/

This site is intended as a resource for local Asian American community groups, allowing them to learn from one another's work via the ACON mailing list and find Internet resources that will help them reach their objectives. It is also useful for single users looking for resources, and the material hosted on their site is, conveniently, keyword-searchable.

◆ **Council on East Asian Libraries**

http://darkwing.uoregon.edu/~felsing/ceal/welcome.html

The Council on East Asian Libraries maintains a large amount of information on their organization and on general East Asian Web resources, broken down by country and then by subject. The site has extensive information on and links to primarily Chinese, Japanese, and Korean collections both inside and outside Asia. There is also library-related material on such topics as library technology.

◆ **National Asian and Pacific American Bar Association**

http://www.napaba.org/

This organization for Asian and Pacific American lawyers provides information about the organization, the scholarships and other benefits they offer, and the table of contents plus selected excerpts from their monthly newsletter.

Travel and Tourism

◆ **Bali Online**

http://www.indo.com

Information is provided concerning hotels, food, money, events, and resources.

◆ **Indonesian Homepage**

http://indonesia.elga.net.id

This site claims to be the first and most comprehensive Indonesian Web site. Its Traveling to Indonesia portion offers information on the islands, such as Bali, Java and Sumatra, as well as providing links to related travel sites.

◆ **Siam Guide to Thailand**

http://www.hotels.siam.net

Provides information regarding hotels.

◆ **Vietgate**

http://www.vietgate.net

This self-proclaimed "Yahoo of the Vietnamese online community" carries Internet news from Vietnam in English and links to Vietnam travel Web sites. Otherwise, it is mainly for the international expatriate Vietnamese community.

7

Chinese American Resources
SUZANNE M. SAUNDERS

INTRODUCTION

The sites in this chapter were located in several different ways. First, the categories of various Internet directories such as Yahoo, which pre-organize the sites they index, were checked. Then, in search engines such as Altavista, the keywords "Chinese American" were searched. This tended to bring up far too many sites, many of which only happened to mention the words in some different context, so it had to be narrowed down to searches such as "Chinese NEAR American AND NOT Restaurant"; such searches brought up many more relevant sites. Since nearly every site found had a document which lists and links to other sites on related subjects, it was then useful to follow the choices of others. Some other sites were found through announcements on discussion groups such as **soc.culture.asian.american**, and in one case a new site was reviewed in the general review mailing list entitled Netsurfer Digest, which was under review for reasons having nothing to do with this project. After finding this starting list, the search engines and directories were re-consulted to find out more about specific topics that had not shown up to any significant degree in the original searches (for example, martial arts, which is not usually indexed under its countries of origin). All in all, there is far from a shortage of information about China and Chinese Americans on the Internet—choosing which sites to include was the time-consuming part (along with weeding out the ones which no longer work or are not in English), and many others may have been missed or updated sufficiently so that they are now as good as any of the sites listed here.

Certain types of sites are excluded because there were simply too many of them and they were not of use outside a certain locality. The Web pages of Chinese American student organizations of colleges and universities cannot be listed individually without taking up a disproportionate amount of space; neither can Chinese restaurant sites. Student associations can generally be found through the main page of the university concerned (or viewing the directory of Chinese student associations at **http://www.cnd.org:8028/CSSA/**); restaurants with Web pages are usually found under the local area in a directory such as Yahoo.

Despite the general use of the term Chinese American, many of these sites are also concerned with Chinese Canadians and other people of Chinese ancestry living outside China. Within the United States, the states of New York, California and Hawaii are relatively over-represented because of their relatively high populations of Chinese Americans, but the sites based in these areas (and other specific regions) that are included seem to have relevance to people living in many different areas.

For people accessing the World Wide Web from the United States, the pages hosted on servers based in China, Taiwan, Hong Kong and Macau seem to load extremely slowly compared to similar pages on servers physically located in North America. Unfortunately, distance does seem to make a difference in the speed of a page's loading process.

GENERAL INFORMATION

◆ **The Asian Studies World Wide Web Virtual Library**

http://coombs.anu.edu.au:80/WWWVL-AsianStudies.html

The World Wide Web Virtual Library is a giant network of linked World Wide Web sites, all on different servers and maintained by different people. This particular site in Australia is only the directory for the Asian Studies portion of it, although it links to a few sites one level up and on the same level of specificity in the hierarchy. Here are listed the official WWW Virtual Library sites for every country in Asia, including mainland China, Taiwan, Hong Kong and Macau, as well as everything else from the Pacific to the borders of European countries. There are also official sites for regions, such as East Asia and Southeast Asia. Each site that is listed here is checked for quality of resources, so although they are hosted by sites from Taiwan to Austria, there is little risk of unreliable information.

◆ **Big China**

http://www.bigchina.com/

This organization provides links to information on many subjects related to China as well as its own services. Big China runs a translation service where one can, for a fee, e-mail English text directly from the Web page and have it translated into Chinese. (There was no indication on the page of what to do for translation into English from Chinese.) They also have an online shopping area which sells Chinese spices, herbal medicines, and handicrafts, and a Friendship and Romance Club. The pages of links to other resources cover every topic from paintings to martial arts to business. Several of their pages also have Yahoo search blanks at the bottom so that if the resources of their links pages don't have what you are seeking, a search can be made without the intermediate step of going to a separate search engine. The Books page also has a link to the search page of Amazon.com, one of the largest Internet booksellers, so that one can search for books on any subject that is not represented in the links page. This is a very useful general resource.

◆ **China Window**

http://www.china-window.com/window.html

This Web site index allows you to look at resources by geographic area as well as by subject area. It is also more business and science oriented than many of the lists.

◆ **Chinese Culture**

http://www.hk.super.net/~hsuricky/hk/chinese.html

This page is billed as "Chinese Culture—a general listing of Chinese culture related links," but the resources to which it links cover more areas than those most people might consider culture-related. The URL above is for the table of contents page, where you can select categories of information. Universities, maps, language-learning centers, art, literature, Internet discussion groups and many more are all included. Not every link is entirely in English, but enough are for it to be useful. Also included is a link to the same author's Hong Kong culture Web page, though the main page announces links to resources for mainland China, Taiwan, Hong Kong, Singapore, Macau and those of Chinese descent in other places.

◆ **Hong Kong World Wide Web Database**

http://www.cuhk.hk/hkwww.html

A search engine, maintained at the Chinese University of Hong Kong, allowing searching for Web sites that are in Hong Kong and those that are not in Hong Kong but have content related to Hong Kong. Users can browse through the categories or search by keyword. The 70 main categories make it much easier for the new user to find something without having to figure out the main category under which their subject has been classified.

◆ **Nihao**

http://www.nihao.com/

This index of China-related sites has the convenient feature of listing the language of each resource to which a link may lead. It also covers a wide range of resources.

◆ **Taiwan Government Information Office**

http://www.gio.gov.tw/

A site with everything, from an exhaustive site on traditional Chinese culture in Taiwan to information on radio stations there, and contact information for the branches of the GIO outside of Taiwan.

Current Events

◆ China Guide
http://www.waltontech.com/ch/

A keyword-searchable guide to China-related Internet resources, including politics, computers, education, culture, business, entertainment, travel, news and people on the Web. Each category is subdivided, and some subcategories have substantially fewer resources in them than others. The site covers mainland China, Taiwan, Hong Kong and Macao.

◆ Chinascape—Chinese Web Index
http://www.chinascape.org/

News, sports, travel, education, culture, and other information on all sorts of subjects relating to China and surrounding territories, some specifically about China itself and separate categories about more local resources for overseas Chinese. Available in text-only version, and includes a What's New page to check out periodically.

◆ Chinese Community Information Center
ftp://ftp.ifcss.org/

This site, maintained by the Independent Federation of Chinese Scholars and Students, contains all sorts of information—how to read Chinese characters in any of several encoding formats, software that users can download and install on their own computers, newsletters of various China-related organizations, and information on the IFCSS itself. The FTP format is quick to load on even the slowest Web-browsing equipment, but difficult to use for those who are only accustomed to the World Wide Web because there is little to indicate what is in the various files or directories except for the filename. Yet, because of this format, the site is accessible to those who do not even have a WWW browser installed yet, since a simple FTP program can make a connection to **ftp.ifcss.org**.

◆ Finding News About China
http://freenet.buffalo.edu/~cb863/china.html

An exhaustive list of news sources having anything to do with China, which even tells you in what language each source is available. Searchable.

◆ Little Asia on the Net
http://www.aracnet.com/~lotus21/tooasian.html

This URL leads to resources for China, Korea, Vietnam, and Japan, and some general East Asian resources (for example, humor, recipes subdivided by country of origin, popular musicians and actors). The graphics and image maps on this page make it difficult to navigate without the very latest browsers; if one wants readable text without graphics, the best option is to go directly to the

China page (**http://www.teleport.com/~lotus21/china.shtml**) for a long text list of links to other China-related Internet resources.

◆ **Protests against NBC's Bob Costas's Remarks at the Olympics**
http://mechatro2.me.berkeley.edu/BCSSA/NBC/

During the Summer 1996 Olympics, sports commentator Bob Costas made remarks on the air alleging that in the past, Olympic athletes from China had used illegal drugs to enhance their athletic ability. Many Chinese Americans were offended by these remarks, and made protests publicly, including advertisements in several large newspapers. This site has transcripts of NBC spokespeoples' and Costas's remarks during the protests; it also makes available articles on the issue from English- and Chinese-language papers, and a list of organizations and people who have supported the protests. At the time of the advertisements there was also information on how to send a donation toward one of them, and on how the donated money was to be used, but a note on the page now says donations are no longer being accepted.

◆ **Rochester Chinese Association Homepage**
http://www.ggw.org/freenet/r/
   RochesterChineseAssociation/index.html

The Rochester Chinese Association exists to promote "understanding and fellowship between the Chinese-American community and the Rochester community." They have membership information and a calendar of local events, as well as a Frequently Asked Question list on immigration issues and how they affect Chinese Americans in their area, especially those who may need public aid of some kind. Their Hot News link includes stories that would not directly affect Chinese Americans, but would interest those trying to keep up with current events in China.

◆ **SinaNet**
http://www.sinanet.com/

This site is so graphic-oriented that it's nearly impossible to use with a text-only Web browser, largely because almost every word in English text on the page is duplicated with a graphic of Chinese characters, and a few things are labeled only in Chinese. English-speaking users have to guess from the accompanying pictures what a link leads to. Other than that, this "WWW-based electronic plaza dedicated to the overseas Chinese community from Taiwan" has some really interesting resources, most of which are available in both English and Chinese. There are news and magazines (including current and back issues of *Sinorama*, to which a print subscription can be ordered online), an event calendar for events of interest all over the world, up-to-date financial information, and job postings (mostly for positions in Taiwan, but some other areas as well). Also, one can shop online, or chat with people of Taiwanese ancestry on their Webchat forums. The subjects range from How to Survive an American University to Taiwan vs. Mainland and seem to be more on-topic than many social chat rooms.

Newsgroups and Listservs

- **The soc.culture.asian.american Frequently Asked Questions List**

http://www.panix.com/~bwu/aa.shtml

This page lists the Frequently Asked Questions (with answers) from the Usenet newsgroup **soc.culture.asian.american,** which is dedicated to discussion of just about anything relating to Americans of Asian descent. The questions reflect this, and definitely should be read over by anyone interested in participating in the discussion. Even if one has no interest in the discussion, the FAQ has valuable information about the way Asian Americans deal with both Asian and American cultures. There are also links to the Asian American Literature and Music FAQs, as well as other links likely to be of interest to Asian Americans.

soc.culture.asian.american

This Usenet newsgroup has a higher level of discussion on the prescribed topic of the newsgroup than do many groups. There are arguments, often started on purpose by people who are just passing through the newsgroup, but with a good killfile/message filter, there is valuable information on whatever issue related to Asian Americans you or anyone else feels like starting a conversation about.

soc.culture.china

soc.culture.taiwan

soc.culture.hongkong

These three Usenet newsgroups offer a place for anyone with Internet access to discuss the culture of the country named. Unfortunately, they often includes vicious racial slurs and totally off-topic messages from people who are trying to start a fight. There can be good discussion in these newsgroups, but finding one requires weeding through an awful lot of junk.

Newspapers, Magazines, and Newsletters

- **China News Digest**

http://www.cnd.org/

China News Digest seems to be the most-recommended source for Chinese current events by almost all of the other sites which review China-related Internet resources. The organization runs five English-language e-mail newsletters, geared toward those living outside China in any region of the world, and a Chinese-language online magazine, all of which come out weekly or more often. The Web site, the FTP site which mirrors it, and the newsletters are all run by volunteers, and they attempt to be non-political in their reporting of current events. One can read both the current and past newsletters on the Web site, or subscribe to any of them on the Web site, to be sent to an e-mail address. In addition, the organization maintains several other informational sites. Gorgeous pictures of China are found at **http://www.cnd.org:8013/Scenery**.

BUSINESS

- ◆ **Asia Online, Inc. Directory—China**

http://www.asia-inc.com/aid/OR-china.html

A directory list of mostly business-related Internet resources having to do with China, as supplied by the online magazine *Asia, Inc.* One can also select the link to the main directory page and find resources on other Asian countries, or go back to the magazine's main homepage.

- ◆ **AsiaWind**

http://www.asiawind.com/

This subsidiary of InTechTra Co. lives up to its slogan "Bridging the East and the West in Business, Culture, and Technology," mixing business-related and other information to provide a tremendous amount of information, albeit only on selected subjects. Despite its name, the focus is on Hong Kong and China. There is information on the Hong Kong stock market, some portion of which is fee-based but much of which, including fourteen-day performance charts and lists of the top ten stocks to gain or lose position, is free; the site also includes links to other resources useful to an investor in Hong Kong stocks. There is also an electronic journal on Chinese chemical and pharmaceutical developments— it requires a subscription, but one issue is available for free, and all the tables of contents are there to allow users to evaluate the magazine. In addition to the business-related areas, AsiaWind maintains the Hong Kong portion of the World Wide Web Virtual Library, and the Hakku Homepage.

- ◆ **The Chinese Finance Association Page**

http://www.aimhi.com/VC/tcfa/cfa.html

The Chinese Finance Association is dedicated to encouraging commerce and investment between the U.S. and China. (Among their sponsors are the World Bank and the Asian Development Bank.) The page tells you about the organization in much greater detail than do many organization Web pages (down to their bylaws) and also links to its sponsors, media coverage in both English and Chinese of business events involving both countries, and related resources about business in general and China in general.

CULTURE AND HUMANITIES, GENERAL

◆ **Art of China Homepage**

**http://pasture.ecn.purdue.edu/~agenhtml/agenmc/china/
china.html**

This is not just the visual arts, although they are well represented here; the site also includes audio files of Chinese music and comedy, Chinese recipes, Chinese astrology, and scenic pictures.

◆ **Chinese Culture—Texts**

http://acc6.its.brooklyn.cuny.edu/~phalsall/texts.html

This is a complete bibliography of apparently everything the students in Paul Halsall's Chinese Culture class at CUNY Brooklyn may read. Confucian, Taoist, and Buddhist texts, down to articles on what a visiting Spaniard thought of Chinese food, are all listed, and all available online just by clicking on the title, with cited sources clearly listed for each document. Another page, called Chinese Cultural Studies: Bibliographic Guide (**http://acc6.its.brooklyn.cuny.edu/~phalsall/chinbib.html**), lists other, non-Web-based resources. The rest of the information for the class is also online, but it is of much less interest to the user from outside the class.

◆ **The Chinese Culture Center of San Francisco**

http://www.c-c-c.org/

This organization promotes Chinese culture and history on their page and elsewhere. Even if you don't live in San Francisco, there are some beautiful online preview tours of several of the exhibits the group has held and information on the In Search of Roots Chinese genealogy workshops and trips.

◆ **Shen's Teahouse**

http://www.geocities.com/Tokyo/Towers/3955/

Shen's Teahouse is a sort of online magazine on culture, generally traditional Chinese/Taiwanese but some articles on modern Western culture, with a current issue being put up periodically. All the past articles are organized by subject category. Most of the short commentary-style articles are written by the page maintainer, **shenjee@geocities.com**, although a few have been submitted by readers of the page and correspondents of the maintainer. There are categories for culture, food, sex (no graphic description), medicine, romantic relations, and Buddhism, and the articles are easy to read, often informative, and quite entertaining. There are both frames and text-only versions available.

◆ **Thuan Thi Do**

http://www.ics.uci.edu/~tdo/index.html

This is a personal homepage of Thuan Thi Do. Although she is Vietnamese, several of her documents here are about Chinese (and other Asians) in the U.S. There are two essays on the culture shock Asians experience upon coming to the U.S.—one as her elderly mother sees it and one as college students see it, and there is also a piece of literary criticism of Amy Tan's *The Joy Luck Club* and how a part of it is illustrative of the cultural conflict Asian American women experience. There is also an interesting piece on The Man I Most Admire, who is Buddha, although the author is a Christian. This page also links to the author's page which has Web resources on aikido and vegetarianism, among other interests.

◆ **Welcome to TeeCow—Chinese American Experience**

http://www.artsci.wustl.edu/~trkau/chinese.html

Tweeny "TeeCow" Kau's experiences with interracial dating against the wishes of her Chinese parents, and a thesis on the subject of interracial marriage. There is also a bibliography of materials of interest to Chinese and Asian Americans.

Philosophy

◆ **The Abode of the Eternal Tao**

http://www.abodetao.com/

According to its author, this site promotes "non-religious" Taoism; there is a document on What is Tao as well as excerpts from the journal *The Empty Vessel* and order information on Tools for Living the Tao. The site also maintains a Qigong page and sponsors an annual trip to China.

◆ **Chinese Philosophy Page**

http://www-personal.monash.edu.au/~sab/

This site, from Monash University in Australia, seems to be a resource page for a course in Chinese Philosophy, although no specific information about a course is given. Be sure to click on the Old Chinese Philosophy Page link and explore more resources there.

◆ **I Ching**

http://www1.power-press.com/wuwei/home.html

This site includes information about the philosophy and history of the I Ching, the ancient Chinese method of divination, its use and interpretation and about the site author Wu Wei's several books on the subject (which one can order online).

◆ **The I Ching**

http://www.teleport.com/~bioching/iching.html

Another site with basic information about the I Ching, including information on Instant I Ching that you can do yourself while reading the page.

◆ **I Ching Hexagrams**

http://www.ptf.com/ching/index.html

An online listing of the commentary/descriptions relating to each hexagram. This version is text only, but there is a link to the graphic version at **http://www.ptf.com/ching/square.html** and a "select a random hexagram" function.

◆ **I Ching Readings Online**

http://www.facade.com/attraction/i_ching

Exactly as the title states—one thinks of a question, types some relevant words in the blank on the page, and clicks on either the "cast the coins" or the "divide the yarrow" button to get a hexagram and some mystical commentary on what it means.

◆ **Intro to I Ching**

http://www1.shore.net/~rdl/iching/IChing.html

This site explains the I Ching a little more briefly, goes into each trigram individually and has a very nice table allowing a person to find the number of a hexagram from its trigrams. (Unfortunately, all the related remote links listed are outdated.)

◆ **Taoist Resource Center**

http://members.aol.com/gr8tao/index.html

This site promotes a more religious version of Taoism, with some interesting documents on comparative religions, how to live by Taoist principles in the Western World, and links to sites on the various schools of Taoism. It also has links to Chinese medicine pages and an opportunity to order books on the Tao.

EDUCATION

◆ **Education in the Republic of China**

http://www.edu.tw/english/e-index.html

Here, one can find out just about anything one could possibly want to know about any level of education in Taiwan. The color scheme is, in some sections, quite difficult to read, and it is obviously a translation of the Chinese version of the page (available at **http://www.edu.tw/**)—the English phrasing is odd at times. Nonetheless, this page is tremendously informational and should not be missed by anyone with an interest in education, from preschool to university level. It concentrates on projects to get Internet access into the schools of the country.

◆ **A Geography of Chinese Peoples**

**http://www.easc.indiana.edu/pages/easc/curriculum/
china/1995/geography/chnzhmpg.htp**

This project, done by Paul Haakenson, a graduate student in social studies instruction, is a ten-lesson unit for secondary students, including handouts and bibliographic references to the sources of the information in them. It seems to be a very good resource for social studies (or Chinese language) instructors who want to do a unit on the country and those descended from its peoples, or who would just like some basic information on the Chinese Diaspora, the population of China, or the Chinese populations in Southeast Asia and the U.S. especially.

◆ **UCLA Asian American Studies Center**

http://www.sscnet.ucla.edu/aasc/

This site gives a great amount of information on the University of California at Los Angeles' program in Asian American studies, enough for any student interested in the subject to see what the program is like. There are links to various projects in progress by students in the program, to the faculty members' work, student scholarships, events and conferences, and an online table of contents for *Amerasia Journal.* They also maintain some news pages, with issues of interest to Asian Americans, especially those in California.

FINE ARTS

Architecture and Design

◆ **Feng Shui: The Chinese Art of Design and Placement**

http://www.cwo.com/~ashlin/homepage.html

This enterprise has quite a lot of its own online information on Feng Shui (including success stories of previous customers), as well as a home video people can order, and a list of consultants in various parts of the U.S. who will help your home or business achieve the perfect placement and design for harmony and productiveness.

◆ **Searching for "China-Americana"**

http://www.sfgate.com/~chaos/asam1.htm

This site focuses on Chinatowns and Chinese styles of architecture. It contains many pictures of buildings in San Francisco's Chinatown, along with descriptions of their histories, and invites others to contribute similar information on other cities' Chinatowns. An article on Feng Shui, the Chinese art of placement, helps one understand the styles of architecture seen in these buildings, and how there could be cultural clashes even in building styles.

Art

Visual Art

◆ **Cathay Arts**

http://www.maui.net/~cthyarts/cathay_arts_home.html

Cathay Arts is a gallery where one can view or buy contemporary Chinese art and a few antique items. The owner says most of the works available are from the Shanxi province. Available are paintings and prints, embroidery, folk art, ceramics and sculpture, rubbings and calligraphy. The site includes biographical notes on the artists and a very good introductory history of twentieth century Chinese art taken from the program of an exhibition. There is also a very interesting and complete list of links to other Asian art resources.

◆ **Photographs and Artifacts from China**

http://splavc.spjc.cc.fl.us/hooks/china.html

This is a simple collection of art and artifacts from China, maintained by two community college professors. There is a thumbnail image of each picture on the main page, so it loads relatively quickly and the viewer can decide which pictures to view at their larger size.

Music

◆ **Chinese Music Page**

http://vizlab.rutgers.edu/~jaray/sounds/chinese_music/ chinese_music.html

This site is the gateway to an archive of downloadable audio clips of every type of Chinese music, from traditional folk music to the modern pop hits there, organized by time period. Other than a basic time/style category and a title for each piece, there is not much description to help the user choose between different works, but the archive is nonetheless interesting.

◆ **Musical Instruments of China**

http://www.mhs.mendocino.k12.ca.us/MenComNet/ Business/Retail/Larknet/china

This instrument seller, Lark in the Morning, describes many traditional Chinese instruments, including pictures and sound samples of each one, and gives ordering information for each.

◆ **RealAudio Marco Polo Chinese Music Clips**

http://www.hnh.com/rahome/rampc.htm

An online jukebox of Chinese music clips which can be played with RealAudio software—even available in mono or stereo depending on your computer's sound system.

GOVERNMENT, LAW, AND POLITICS

◆ **The Diaoyutai Page**

http://www.geocities.com/Tokyo/4381/

A page on the dispute between China and Japan over the Diaoyutai/Senkaku islands, which presents some articles with views from both sides of the argument.

Organizations

◆ **The Chinese American Political Association**

http://www.capa-news.org/intro.html

A nonprofit, nonpartisan political association dedicated to political education, CAPA serves primarily the Chinese American community of the San Francisco Bay Area. They promote racial unity among all people of Asian or Pacific Island descent, in order to produce a strong minority voice rather than fragmentation of their political strength. The Web site includes an introduction to the organization, back copies of their newsletters, lists of summer internship opportunities, and information on current issues affecting the community. The site could be useful even for those outside the San Francisco area, serving as a model for a local organization or providing examples of the issues that concern Chinese Americans.

HISTORY

Chinese American History

◆ **American Anti-Chinese History Timeline**

http://nova.stanford.edu/~mou/anti_chinese.html

This is a chronological account of anti-Chinese laws, court cases and other incidents in American history, with a short paragraph summarizing most of the events listed. Many of the incidents link back to a site called Chinese American History 121 for more detail, but the author also used other sources, and this short format is easier to read without having to jump between documents in a large site, which Chinese American History 121 sometimes forces one to do.

◆ **Chinese American History 121**

http://www.itp.berkeley.edu/~asam121/

This is the homepage for a class in Chinese American History at the University of California at Berkeley. Much of the information the students are to learn is available to anyone through the Web page, including an online timeline of the Chinese in America, outlines of areas of Chinese American history, articles on the stereotyping of the Chinese as the model minority, and links to all the students' papers on What Being Chinese American Means to Me. A very good way to learn for free.

◆ **Chinese Historical and Cultural Project**

http://www.dnai.com/~rutledge/CHCP_home.html

The Chinese Historical and Cultural Project, based in Santa Clara County, California, is "a non-profit organization to promote and preserve Chinese and Chinese-American history and culture." Their site transfers quite usefully to the World Wide Web much of the local work they've done. Their Golden Legacy curriculum unit on the history of Chinese in America, using Santa Clara County as a focus, listed as having units useful from third grade to eighth, has lesson plans available online and accompanying slides and a video documentary which can be ordered. The organization puts on an annual Summer Festival, of which pictures are available on the site to explain this tradition; there are also historical pictures of San Jose's Chinatown and the people who lived in it at the end of the nineteenth century. There is also a wonderfully detailed explanation of traditional Chinese wedding customs.

◆ **Chinese Women in Hawaii: A Woman of Taoist Medicine**

http://www.soc.hawaii.edu/hwhp/china/china.html

Master Chang, Dr. Lily Siou, is described as being one of very few people, perhaps the only woman in Hawaii, practicing Chinese medicine based on Taoist philosophy. There is an essay on her, one on the history of Chinese women in Hawaii, links to various resources about Taoist medicine, and links back to the general history of women in Hawaii.

◆ **(Fool's) Gold Mountain—Jeff Ow's Pages**

http://www.saber.net/~paperson/index.html

Jeff Ow maintains a page on Chinese American topics called (Fool's) Gold Mountain after the Chinese immigrant nickname for the United States, Gold Mountain. From his main page, which at the time this was written had just been moved from America Online, one can access a list of links to other sites with resources for Chinese Americans and Asian Americans in general. His best personal work is the page for Angel Island, the Ellis Island of the West, which served as a detention camp for many prospective immigrants after the passage of the Chinese Exclusion Act.

◆ **The Promise of Gold Mountain—Tucson's Chinese Heritage**

**http://www.library.arizona.edu/images/chamer/
chinese.html**

This joint project of the University of Arizona Library and the Arizona Historical Society includes many good pictures of the history of Chinese Americans in Tucson, as well as several articles on Chinese American businesses and agriculture, the Chinatown of Tucson and biographies of prominent Chinese American citizens of Tucson. Additions are made occasionally and listed as new, so that checking back for changes as they are added is easy.

◆ **Resistance to the Anti-Chinese Movement, 1852–1905: The Chinese
American Perspective**

http://uts.cc.utexas.edu/~lpaj144/tk/thesis/

This is Wei-Min Wang's senior Honors Thesis, and it is a tremendously well-documented essay on how Chinese living in the U.S. reacted to the mounting anti-Chinese movement in the U.S. during the latter half of the nineteenth century. There are quotations from both the leaders of the movement and those who fought against it, links to Web sites on subjects and of organizations mentioned in the paper, and a complete bibliography of print sources.

Chinese History

◆ **Alliance for Preserving the Truth of the Sino-Japanese War**

http://www.cnd.org:8016/njmassacre/aptsjw.html

The Alliance offers a lot of information often forgotten by Americans about the conflicts in Asia immediately before World War II. The site links to a great number of online articles and other information about Japanese imperialism in Asia (though the front page makes it clear that the Alliance does not bear any ill-will toward the Japanese people in general, only toward some national leaders of Japan from the era). The organization sponsors awareness events and photo exhibits in the U.S. They also offer links to information on more recent events.

◆ **Condensed China**

http://asterius.com/china/

All of Chinese history in very condensed format; this is a very well-organized page which allows users to pick the chronological range in which they are interested or read whole documents. The author, Paul Frankenstein, is making a good effort to keep the modern section updated in light of recent developments in the country. He is also a very readable writer.

◆ **Exploring Ancient World Cultures: China**

http://eawc.evansville.edu/chpage.htm

A searchable page on ancient China, with quizzes, maps, essays, chronologies, print resources and other Web sites. Part of the EAWC complex which includes several other ancient cultures and even an educator's page.

◆ **The Silk Road Page**

http://essl.ps.uci.edu/~oliver/silk.html

The Silk Road once ran as the only trade conduit between China and Europe. Oliver Wild's work explains the complete history of this road and includes pictures taken on his trips to China. Wild also maintains a very good list of links to other China-related sources, especially ones on traveling in China, and even (mixed in with his other scientific work on the atmosphere) some data on China's atmosphere. Yet the Silk Road page seems to be the most popular.

LANGUAGE ARTS AND LITERATURE

Language Arts

◆ **Chinese Language Related Page**

http://www.webcom.com/bamboo/chinese/

This page has links that cover just about anything related to Chinese written or spoken languages. One can find information on how to view and listen to Chinese on the World Wide Web, how to learn to speak and read Chinese either online or at one of the many institutions that offer courses in it, where to find text files in Chinese, scholarly and linguistic resources on Chinese, how to program computers in Chinese, or where to find Chinese-language radio broadcasts. There is even a section on East Asian librarianship and library collections, and a search blank, which searches for Chinese Language in any of several search engines and directories, is available on the introductory page.

Literature

◆ **Anagram Asian American Literary Journal**

http://www.jhu.edu/~anagram

This annual magazine devoted to Asian American-related concerns is mostly made up of submissions from Johns Hopkins students, as that is where it is based, but submissions are invited from anyone. The current and back issues are all on the site, and include some interesting fiction, nonfiction, poetry and photography.

◆ **China Books and Periodicals, Inc.**

http://www.chinabooks.com/

China Books and Periodicals is a firm that since 1960 has provided books and periodicals about China to patrons in the U.S. Books on all subjects are included.

◆ **Lu Xun, Father of Modern Chinese Literature**

http://www-hsc.usc.edu/~gallaher/luxun/luxun.html

An interesting page on a Chinese author not well known in the U.S. Some history of his work, and commentary on the various translations of it, are included in this page, as well as pictures of Lu Xun, links to some of his short stories translated into English as well as to the Chinese versions, and even some suggestions as to where to obtain print copies in the United States.

◆ **Novelty Publishers Limited**

http://www.558.com/novelty/

This publisher specializes in Chinese-English dictionaries and learning tools to help people speak various dialects of Chinese. Lengthy excerpts from several books are available online, allowing users to test the effectiveness of the work in helping them learn before buying. Translation services are also offered.

POPULAR CULTURE

Radio

◆ **KAZN—Radio Chinese**

http://www.radiochinese.com/html/emenu.html

This station, broadcasting 24 hours a day in Mandarin Chinese, is based in Southern California but available to anyone with satellite TV access to the GE–1 satellite. They also have sister stations broadcasting (only on the radio) in other Asian languages in their home area. The Web site gives further instructions on how to hear the station, as well as KAZN news, sports, and advertising (all in English).

Sports

◆ **China Olympics**

http://www.chinaolympics.com/

A government-run site on the Chinese Olympic athletes, which during the 1996 Games was updated every day with a medal count and still has a reasonable amount of information on the teams from 1996, and will probably continue being updated as the next Olympics draw nearer. Also has general information under China Today.

- ◆ **The China Soccer Homepage**

http://www.usc.edu/dept/CGIT/IMAGE/news/soccer.html

This site has the most comprehensive listing of Chinese soccer information that was found, though it is unusable without a frames-capable browser. It is kept very well updated with the latest game scores, and has pictures and video clips of players and games, an archive of past versions of the news page, and a comment forum. Note: As this is written, the author of this page has just graduated and while job-hunting he does not expect to be able to update the page as frequently as before. However, he expects to return to frequent updates as soon as possible.

Martial Arts

- ◆ **Chinese Styles of Martial Arts—Resources**

http://members.aol.com/taoart/amwa/amwalink.htm#MCA

This is part of a longer list, but this section deals specifically with Chinese styles of martial arts, as practiced all over the world. There are links to both general and regional resources.

- ◆ **Han Wei**

http://hanwei.com

Han Wei describes itself as a nonprofit organization dedicated to promoting Chinese culture and martial arts. The culture references on their pages are interesting but rather jumbled; the martial arts pages are just as informative, but easier to navigate. They host a martial arts newsletter, *Wushu!,* which is archived on the site, and also host several Asian-oriented presses' sites. Note: Click on the buttons by the page titles, even if they do not look like active links. (Unfortunately, the front page of the site is unusable in a text-only browser; the links do not appear.)

Television and Film

- ◆ **The Hong Kong Movie Page**

http://www.jyu.fi/~tjko/hkmovie

One of the most impressive of the many, many Hong Kong movie sites available, this includes informational documents, a database of movies, some pictures and movie clips, and what is claimed to be a comprehensive archive of postings to the Usenet newsgroup **alt.asian-movies**.

RELIGION

◆ **Chinese American Christians**

http://www.aamdomain.com/cac/

listserv@emwave.net

This site announces that it serves as a central information clearinghouse for issues related to Chinese American Christians. It is associated with an electronic mailing list, to which one can subscribe from their Web site (or by sending the message **subscribe CAC your name** to the address above), and has some of the digests of the mailing list online. There are also other articles of interest to their readers, both on religious and cultural subjects. The list of Asian American ministries announces that it includes mostly churches of Evangelical Christian convictions, and other portions of the site seem to have similar leanings.

SCIENCE AND TECHNOLOGY

◆ **China Homepage**

http://solar.rtd.utk.edu/~china/china.html

Maintained by the Institute of High Energy Physics in Beijing, this site mostly focuses on scientific, technical, and business-related information about China, but with some other areas as well, including a directory of personal homepages of people of Chinese descent. The English is occasionally broken, but never so much that it hampers use of the site.

◆ **History of Mathematics: China**

http://aleph0.clarku.edu/~djoyce/mathhist/china.html

This site details the history of mathematics in China in text and with a timeline setting the progress of mathematics against other events which took place in China's history, up to about the beginning of the 20th century. This includes a very good print bibliography of primary works in Chinese mathematics.

◆ **Mount Jade Science and Technology Association**

http://www.mtjade.org/

This organization, originally formed in San Francisco but now with chapters U.S.-wide, exists to encourage a flow of information and cooperation between U.S. and Taiwan technology professionals. They mount an annual trip of American professionals aged 23 to 35 to Taiwan for meetings, seminars and visits to Taiwanese businesses (all conducted in Mandarin Chinese), as well as some tourist opportunities. Also listed are monthly professional and social activities in the U.S. and links to U.S. business-related sites.

Health

+ **Acupuncture.com**

http://www.acupuncture.com/

Despite its name, this site has not only acupuncture resources but information on Chinese diagnosis practices, nutrition, herbology, Qi Gong, and massage. All of it is very conveniently divided into three levels: information for consumers, for students of any of the practices, and for practitioners.

+ **Acupuncture Homepage**

http://www.demon.co.uk/acupuncture/index.html

This site, put up by the British organization Foundation for Traditional Chinese Medicine, looks at acupuncture in a scientific manner, with information on the studies that have been done on the practice, uses to which it is put, and lists of many resources, print and online, on the subject.

+ **Acupuncture.html**

http://galen.med.virginia.edu/~pjb3s/Acupuncture.html

The most complete index of acupuncture resources on the Web I have seen anywhere, although there is no information other than the page titles to help the user pick and choose. Part of Dr. Peter J. Bauer's Complementary and Alternative Medicine homepage.

+ **American College of Traditional Chinese Medicine**

http://www.actcm.org/

This College of Traditional Chinese Medicine is located in San Francisco, but prospective students or people who want to know what it takes to get a master's degree in traditional Chinese medicine can find out a lot of information on this Web site.

+ **Chinese Medicine**

http://www.sirius.com/~pbarts/PBA/ChineseMedicine.html

This subsite of Pacific Bridge Arts discusses traditional Chinese medicine with Dr. Martin Inn, who advocates several aspects such as the use of Tai Chi and herbal medicines.

+ **CMNews**

http://www.dmu.ac.uk/ln/cmn/

A searchable archive of the *Chinese Medical News* e-mail newsletter. The newsletter focuses on Chinese medical and pharmaceutical research, medical statistics from China, and the functions of traditional Chinese medicine. There is also information on how to subscribe to the newsletter here.

◆ **Qi: The Journal of Traditional Chinese Medicine**

http://www.qi-journal.com/

This site has selected articles from the journal online, as well as an index to back issues and many other resources not taken from the print journal, such as animations of Tai Chi movements and a map listing professionals in Chinese medicine in the United States.

◆ **Qigong Association of America**

http://www.qi.org/

This site explains the two main styles of Qi Gong (Soaring Crane and Fragrant Qi Gong) and includes a short registry of Qi Gong teachers who have signed up to be listed, some message areas, order information for some aids to the study of Qi Gong, and other resources on this energy-balancing health practice.

Information Technology and Telecommunications

◆ **Taiwan Master Index**

http://peacock.tnjc.edu.tw/ROC_sites.html

A search engine for finding any of Taiwan's Web servers, or just a complete list of all of them. Only the actual Web servers and who maintains them are listed, rather than individual sites on each machine, but it can be useful if you are looking for a specific type of business, educational institution, or government server.

◆ **Who Uses the Internet in China?**

http://www.redfish.com/USEmbassy-China/sandt/ WEBNET.HTM

This report from the U.S. Embassy in Beijing, was written in November 1996.

OTHER

Exhibits

◆ **Kwan's Jade—Exhibit from the Chinese University of Hong Kong**

http://humanum.arts.cuhk.edu.hk/KwansJade/Kwans.html

This online exhibit gives a brief history of ancient jade carving in China and then displays many jade carvings, with identification by each. The pieces in this exhibit are all from the private collection of Dr. Simon Kwan, who has great luck in being able to own all these pieces.

◆ **The National Palace Museum—Taiwan, R.O.C.**

http://www.npm.gov.tw/english/

This government-run museum currently has three online exhibits available, but they announce that the site is still under contruction (see Archive as well as Main Page). The material that can be viewed online, however, is largely prints and other objects so old and delicate that they are not subjected to the lights of exhibition for more than a few months out of the year, so even a visitor to the physical museum itself might not be able to view them.

Organizations

◆ **Chinese American Librarians Association**

http://library.fgcu.edu/cala/

This page is the umbrella page for the Chinese American Librarians Association (which, despite its name, has chapters in Canada and other countries). Here one can find information about the organization, its officers, programs and conferences, and its chapters, each of which has its own page. On the Publications page, one can subscribe to their electronic journal and to their electronic mailing list. and there is even a membership form online (although you do have to print it out and mail it).

◆ **Chinese Organizations List (USA)**

http://www.idis.com/ChouOnline/chinese_org.html

A list of offline contact addresses for various Chinese organizations in the United States, including a separate list of those in Hawaii.

◆ **Chou Online 1997**

http://www.idis.com/ChouOnline

This site is for the Chou Clansmen of America, a fraternal, cultural, and educational organization for descendants of members of the Chou dynasty. A Welcome page for the organization is found at **http://www.lookup.com/Homepages/ 76274/home.html**, but the link to the Chou Online 1997 page is about the only useful information on it. The organization is centered in Hawaii. Chou Online 1997 is grand in its aims, although as of December 1997, it was far from finished. As of this writing, it has membership and genealogical registration forms to print out and mail in, eligibility information for membership, notices to members calling for help for Chinese flood victims and other needy people, and information about relocation from Hong Kong to Hawaii for those who do not wish to live under the rule of mainland China. At the bottom of the page, there is an outline of intended links. If all the intended information is added, this will be a detailed resource on Chinese history, culture, people and politics, the various sub-chapters of the Chou Clansmen of America, and information on Internet access and Web site hosting for organization members. An interesting subsite is found at **http://www.idis.com/ChouOnline/chechnya.html**, which utilizes Judeo-Christian lore to show how the different clans of China descend from different sons of Noah.

◆ **Detroit Chinese Network**
http://www.detroitchinese.com/

This site exists for the Chinese American community of southern Michigan. They list area organizations for Chinese Americans, businesses run by or serving Chinese Americans, Chinese restaurants in the area, and resources pertaining to China on the Web, as well as some purely fun sites.

◆ **Horizon Flash (OCA-DC)**
http://www.tiac.net/users/rdolores/oca/index.html

This is the homepage of the District of Columbia chapter of the Organization of Chinese Americans. On this page, one can find information on the organization (and its sub-chapter the Young Professionals Association), along with the complete newsletter for the organization, which includes a lot of articles of interest to all Americans of Asian or Pacific Islander descent. The homepage for the national Organization of Chinese Americans is listed on the next page.

◆ **Houston Chinese Christian Career Caring Network**
http://web-hou.iapc.net/~ccccn/

This organization covers all sorts of subjects. It is a coalition of Houston churches, but there are many non-religious resources here, as the full name suggests. There are several documents to help with finding a job, and a page of links to quite a lot of other Houston-area organizations for Chinese Americans in specific careers.

◆ **Internet Chinese Librarians Club**
http://library.fgcu.edu/iclc/

This site offers many resources for librarians working with Chinese collections, including several online publications and other services.

◆ **Organization of Chinese Americans**
http://www2.ari.net/oca/

The Organization of Chinese Americans is a group working toward equal legal and social rights for Chinese Americans, often in concert with other groups representing Asians and Pacific Islanders in the U.S. The group is headquartered in Washington, D.C., but there is a separate Web site for the D.C. Chapter, reviewed below. This is the umbrella site for the whole organization. It has information on the history and accomplishments of the organization, news on current events affecting Chinese Americans, and listings of scholarships and grants available from the organization.

◆ **Taiwanese American Foundation**

http://members.aol.com/tafinfo/index.htm

The nationwide page for the TAF has information on their annual summer conference, directories of members, a lot of links to personal homepages, and even a birthday list. Some parts are more up-to-date than others.

Travel and Tourism

◆ **China Business World**

http://www.cbw.com/tourism

China travel guide that includes an online hotel directory, air travel guide, visa application and guide, useful Chinese terms for travelers, and sightseeing tips.

◆ **China Tour**

http://www.chinatour.com

Updated frequently, this site provides China-related travel and tour information, including airlines flying to China, hotels and resorts, tourist hot spots, and more.

◆ **Chinese Cyber City**

http://www1.ccchome.com/

Chinese Cyber City offers all sorts of information of interest to Chinese Americans. Tourist information, newspaper and magazine access, investment information, entertainment and recreation, all of which is available for users anywhere. There are separate pages for San Francisco Bay, New York City, Dallas/ Fort Worth, and Los Angeles. Note: Although the FAQ on the Help page says that all information is available in English, this does not seem to be true. There seems to be a curious mixture of English and Chinese.

◆ **Following Ancient Footsteps: Exploring the Northern Silk Road**

http://www-personal.monash.edu.au/~sab/cpother.html

This site stems from an article first published in *Asia* magazine in 1994. It describes what one can see on this still-accessible part of the old Silk Road. Included are pictures, travel tips and resources.

◆ **The Homepage of Shanghai Tourism**

http://www.fudan.sh.cn/shnet/ddd/english.html

Who else to tell you what there is to do in Shanghai than people who are there? This site lists, in great detail, all the things one can spend time doing there, and other things a visitor might need to know—sightseeing, entertainment, shopping, food, transportation, and accommodations.

◆ **San Francisco Chinatown**

http://www.sfchinatown.com/

This online guide to San Francisco's Chinatown gives lots of information about the area. Restaurants, of course, but also museums, statistics, an interactive timeline of Chinatown's history, a directory of businesses and organizations, descriptions of events, and some tales by local people can all be found here.

◆ **Shanghai-ed**

http://www.shanghai-ed.com

Online city magazine of Shanghai is a source for local listing of restaurants, hotels, art galleries as well as additional tourist information. The site provides links to newspapers.

◆ **Virtual China Tour**

http://math.uc.edu/~xiongjo/chinatour.html

A map of mainland China and a province-by-province description (of what is in each province), with a few pictures.

◆ **Wacky Seester in China**

http://www.seester.com/china/chinaindx.htm

The amusing experiences of some Asian Americans taking a tour of China and encountering everything from a beautiful Chinese wedding to braised dog meat on a restaurant menu.

8

Japanese American Resources

D. RUSSELL BAILEY AND VICKI L. GREGORY

INTRODUCTION

This chapter focuses on Internet/World Wide Web resources, highlighting Japanese-United States issues. An attempt has been made to exclude sources that are primarily Japanese or primarily American, but some will naturally be predominantly one or the other. Sites covering broader areas of Asia are included in chapter 6 entitled Asian American Resources. The reader should also see related chapters in this volume (Chinese American Resources and Asian Indian American Resources).

While we have attempted to avoid sites of less substance and only general interest, there is naturally tremendous variety in the type and quality of sites included. Section headings should serve the reader in selecting sites for specific purposes. Japanese American sites vary extensively in subject matter. The historical sites look at early Japanese American relations and continue through modern times. There are sites on martial arts, militarism and World War II, the graphic arts, business, government and politics, the many Japanese American societies, and many other topics.

Where possible we have indicated those sites with text only, those with some links, and those with extensive links. Depending on the reader's interests, the most valuable resource may be a specific text, graphic images, or simply the possibility of linking to related resources, as the reader moves from site to site.

Many of the sites are updated regularly, while some remain the same over longer periods of time. A particular site can often be located by deleting a section/domain of the URL and simply searching for the site "manually."

While several search services or search engines were used in the compilation of this chapter, Infoseek yielded the highest quality results. Three Infoseek searches proved most productive: Japan, America; Japan, U.S.; and Japanese, American. All sites included in this chapter were selected from the top 100 graded and prioritized sites in each of the three searches. Additional searches using simply the terms Japan, Japanese, Asia, Asian, East Asia, East Asian, Orient, or Oriental will yield additional sites, albeit sites with less likelihood of being Japanese American. Still, as is often true of Web searches, nuggets appear on surprising and often unexpected strands.

GENERAL INFORMATION

- **NACSIS Homepage**

http://www.nacsis.ac.jp/

The National Center for Science Information Centers (NACSIS) is the information systems wing of the Japanese Ministry of Education, Science, and Culture. NACSIS has enormous electronic databases of sci/tech and humanities research gray literature that is gradually being moved over to the Web.

- **U.S.-Japan International Cooperation and Interchange**

http://www.libertynet.org/jitmt/

This site has information about opportunities for U.S. scientists, managers, and students for research, work, and study periods in Japan. The University City Science Center (UCSC) acts as the coordinating body. The page has excellent links to related information.

Current Events

- **Global Reporting Network on Japan**

http://solar.rtd.utk.edu/~aboyle/grn/japan.html

This site includes extensive news analysis and analysis concerning Japan with text but no graphics. It does have a URL bibliography and some links to similar sites.

- **Nikkei Net**

http://www.nikkei.co.jp/enews/index.html

Nikkei Publications provides this impressive site. English-language information includes front page summaries and the full text of the cover story from *The Nikkei Weekly,* as well as headlines and top stories updated three times daily from the *Nihon Keizai Shimbun,* including market data. The Japanese version of the site contains an even larger range of content. More than just an advertisement for the printed editions, Nikkei Net is a serious conduit of Japan news.

- **Tokyo Kaleidoscope**

http://www.smn.co.jp/

In-depth analysis on a weekly basis of news and commentary with current events in Japan.

Newsgroups and Listservs

clari.world.asia.japan: Clarinet Japan News

If your Usenet news provider subscribes to this commercial service, it carries Japan-related news from the major newswire services such as Reuters, AP, and Kyodo.

◆ H-Japan

Subscription address: listserv@h-net.msu.edu

H-Japan is a bilingual, moderated electronic mailing list for scholarly discussions of Japanese history, culture, religion, and society. To subscribe send the message **subscribe H-JAPAN your name** to the above address.

◆ SSJ-Forum

Subscription address: ssj-forum-request@iss.u-tokyp.ac.jp

This moderated electronic mailing list serves as an extension of the Institute's publication *Social Science Japan,* which focuses on the political economy, social science, and history of Japan with an academic emphasis. To subscribe send an e-mail message contining the word **subscribe** in the subject header to the above address.

◆ U.S.-Japan Links—Listservs

http://www.us-japan.org/resources-listserv.html

Electronic mailing lists have become one of the most popular forms of Internet communication. This site provides information about a number of lists related to general Japanese information, language, and studies.

Newspapers, Magazines, and Newsletters

◆ Asahi.com: English News

http://www.asahi.com/english/english.html

Newspaper from Tokyo. Japanese and English versions (URL above for English edition). Good mix of text and graphics.

◆ The Chubu Weekly Online Newspaper

http://www.eal.or.jp/CW/

The homepage for this newspaper claims that it is the top English bi-weekly news source for the Chubu region. One can read it in html format or download it as a PDF document.

◆ Connections: The Newsletter of U.S.-Japan Links

http://www.us-japan.org/about.html

U.S.-Japan links is a collaborative media project whose goals include providing access to and disseminating Japan-related information. The current issue of this newsletter is available here under the section entitled Publications. Articles in the current issue are linked via a table of articles. The archive of back issues is directly available at **http://www.us-japan.org/pubs/connections/connectionsarchive.html.**

◆ **Jam Jam: The Mainichi Newspapers**

http://www.mainichi.co.jp/index-e.html

This is an impressive offering that has generated a lot of interest within Japan as the first of the big three newspapers to publish on the Web. Beneath the colorful user interface, Mainichi is providing high quality content.

◆ **Japan-America Journal Index**

http://planet-hawaii.com/jash/journal.html

Index of Japan-America journals from 1995 to the present; an excellent site.

◆ **Japan Echo**

http://www.japanecho.com

Quarterly journal that presents English translations of significant articles from the Japanese media about politics, business and the economy, society, culture, and other topics of current interest within Japan.

◆ **Japan Times Online**

http://www.japantimes.co.jp/

Weekly news roundup; includes domestic and international news, features, and political cartoons.

BUSINESS

◆ **Anime & Manga Mall of North America and Japan**

http://www.lookup.com/Homepages/49845/anime-mall.html

Directory of Japanese animation and comic stores. The Japanese animation (anime) and comic (manga) mall provides the anime or manga you are looking for. Come see; an excellent site.

◆ **Japan Is a Major Export Market for U.S. Manufactured Goods**

http://www.jetro.go.jp/3what/FACTS/UA-HANDBOOK/ 6.html

This site provides economic data about the importation of U.S. manufactured goods, including cars and electronic technology, into Japan. There are clear and well-presented charts and graphics to supplement the text.

◆ **Submission by the Government of the United States to the Government of Japan Regarding Deregulation, Competition Policy, and Transparency and Other Government Practices in Japan**

http://www.ita.doc.gov/industry/basic/usjfinal.html

This site has the text of the agreement and copies of the related letters exchanged by the United States and Japan regarding this trade agreement.

EDUCATION

◆ **International Journal of Educational Management: The Deming Approach to Education: A Comparative Study of the USA and Japan**

http://www.mcb.co.uk/services/articles/documents/ijem/ yoshida.htm

Extensive text with graphs and bibliography.

◆ **National Clearinghouse for U.S.-Japan Studies**

http://www.indiana.edu/~japan/

An adjunct-ERIC clearinghouse, the National Clearinghouse for U.S.-Japan Studies specializes in providing educational information about Japan. The audience is K–12 students, teachers, specialists, and curriculum developers. The site features an easy-to-use lesson plan database that utilizes a powerful full-text search engine.

◆ **U.S.-Japan Links—Japan Resources: Education and Research**

http://www.us-japan.org/resources.html

When this page loads, look for the links to various subsections and select Education and Research. The site provides annotations and links to current information on such topics as research libraries, fellowships, and research institutes.

FINE ARTS

Art

◆ **Daruma: Japanese Art & Antiques Magazine**

http://www.darumamagazine.com/

Daruma, the only English-language magazine devoted solely to Japanese art and antiques, is a quarterly publication featuring articles covering a wide range of topics related to these subjects. Of special note is *Daruma*'s Print Corner, which features an article on Japanese woodblock prints in every issue.

◆ **The History of Ikebana**

http://www.tni.co.jp/sogetsu/history-e.html

This site provides a brief narrative of the 600-year-old art of Ikebana, flower arrangement.

◆ **Japanese Calligraphy**

http://japanese.miningco.com/msub6.htm

The features of this site include What Is Calligraphy?, What Distinguishes Good Calligraphy from Bad?, A Brief History of Japanese Calligraphy (sho), and Notes on Japanese Poetry. This is a good site for the beginner.

◆ **Japanese Woodblock Printing**

http://www.geocities.com/Tokyo/Flats/3503/index.html

Jason Lew gives a succinct explanation of the woodblock printing process. His page contains information on the history, materials, and techniques of woodblock printing as well as information on his own first experiences in creating woodblock prints.

◆ **The Origin and Development of Netsuke: Chapter 3 of the "The Netsuke Handbook"**

http://rrnet.com/~nakamura/ap/netsuke/handbook.html

This site has an excellent narrative history of netsuke, which originated from the custom of attaching a toggle to one end of a cord that passed between the obi (the sash or cummerbund of the kimono) and the hip that had at its other end a suspended object such as a bunch of keys, a tobacco pouch, or some other type of hanging object.

◆ **What Is Ikebana Homepage**

http://www.tni.co.jp/sogetsu/ikebana-e.html

This site explains the fine art of Ikebana arrangement, art in a vase with plant material.

◆ **What's Washi**

http://www.com.rd.pref.gifu.jp/e-main2/kamiwasi/ what1.html

This site is a guide to the history and production of Japanese paper.

Visual Art

◆ **Ohararyu Ikebana Sempo**

http://pweb.aix.or.jp/~satosi-k/esenhou.htm

This site has graphical reproductions of the Ohararyu Ikebanas flower art of Sempo Kobayashi. There is a monthly Ikebana art work, which is archived for a year, as well as other exhibitions of her work.

◆ **Ukiyo-e: The Pictures of the Floating World**

http://www.bahnhof.se/%7Esecutor/ukiyo-e/

A definitive collection of Ukiyo-e related material on the Web. The gallery is arranged by artists and by categories, such as actors and theatrical performances, animals and flowers, festivals and processions, landscapes and street scenes, and sumo wrestlers. The site is highly graphical but loads quickly because the images are not full screen unless you choose to click on one of the small images to bring it up to half-screen size.

Drama

◆ **Kabuki for Everyone**

http://www.fix.co.jp/kabuki/kabuki.html

This highly graphical site explores the world of Kabuki through an online theater and the experiences of a present day onnagata (actor specializing in the role of females), Ichimura Manjiro. One section of the site deals with the instruments used in Kabuki, such as the taiko drum and the three-stringed shamisen, and gives the user the opportunity to actually hear their sounds.

GOVERNMENT, LAW, AND POLITICS

◆ **The Dead Fukuzawa Society**

Subscription address: listserv@ucsd.edu

An unmoderated electronic mailing list devoted to the discussion of Japan-United States relations with an emphasis on policy. To subscribe send the message **add fukuzawa** to the above address.

◆ **Issho Kikaku**

Subscription address: listproc@ishiilab.dnj.yntu.ac.jp

A moderated electronic mailing list run by Tokyo-based foreign nationals to facilitate the internationalization of Japan. To subscribe send the message **subscribe issho your name** to the above address.

◆ **Japan Policy Research Institute**

http://www.nmjc.org/jpri/

JPRI is an attempt to bring a variety of critical academic voices to the U.S.-Japan relations policy debate through conferences, public lectures, and research. The site provides access to the Institute's periodical, *JPRI Critique* (**http://www.nmjc.org:80/jpri/publications.html**).

Civil Rights

◆ **U.S. Department of Justice, Civil Rights Division, Office of Redress Administration**

http://www.teleport.com/~macphers/ora.htm

This is a federal government site set up to deal with the Civil Liberties Act of 1988, which authorized payments of $20,000 to any Japanese American who suffered as a result of internment during World War II. The Office of Redress Administration (ORA) was established to identify, locate, and pay these individuals. The site has information about eligibility, an application form, and more.

HISTORY

◆ **The Japanese American Internment**

http://www.geocities.com/Athens/8420/main.html

This site is dedicated to the victims of the Japanese American Internment, with the intention that it will serve as "a constant reminder of our past so that Americans in the future will never again be denied their constitutional rights." The site has excellent photographs and contains extensive links to other relevant sites.

◆ **Japanese Farmers in California**

http://www.uwec.edu/Academic/Geography/Ivogeler/ w188/j1.htm

This site contains information about the Japanese American farmers in California who were interned during World War II.

◆ **Japanese War Crime Trials**

http://www.thehistorynet.com/WorldWarII/articles/ 0996_text.htm

This is Robert Barr Smith's account of the events of the trial of General Tomoyuki Yamashita before the International Military tribunal for the Far East and his execution in 1946.

- ◆ **Manzanar Relocation Camp**

http://members.aol.com/EARTHSUN/Manzanar.html

This site contains information about the Manzanar Relocation or, as the site describes it, Concentration Camp, located in Owens Valley, California. There are excellent pictures and posters from the era to give the reader a view of the time and the nature of the camp.

- ◆ **National Japanese American Historical Projects**

http://www.nikkeiheritage.org/projects.html

Sample projects included here are the MIS (Military Intelligence Service) Biography Project, Japanese Peruvian Oral History Project (which deals with Japanese Peruvians who were forcibly deported to the United States to be interned during World War II), and the Nikkei Music History Project.

- ◆ **Some Files Relevant to the Japanese Attack on Pearl Harbor**

http://sunsite.unc.edu/pub/academic/history/marshall/
  military/wwii/pearl.harbor/pearl_harbor.txt

This site has files that contain the following documents, among others: U.S. Note to Japan, November 26, 1941, and Message from the President to the Emperor.

LANGUAGE ARTS AND LITERATURE

Language Arts

- ◆ **Gakusei-L Series**

Subscription address: listproc@hawaii.edu

An electronic mailing list that serves as a forum for learners of Japanese to communicate in Japanese with other learners of the language worldwide. There are currently five separate lists:

- Gakusei-L (beginning level, all mail is in romanized Japanese)
- Gakusei–2L (intermediate level, romanized)
- Gakusei–3L (advanced, romanized)
- Gakusei-KL (beginning, all mail must be JIS-encoded)
- Bunpou-L (a grammar discussion forum for the Gakusei-L lists)

To subscribe, send an e-mail message to the above address, containing the following message in the body: **SUBSCRIBE name_of_listabove yourfirstname yourlastname**.

◆ **Japanese Language**

http://japanese.miningco.com/blank.htm

This site has lessons in the Japanese language for the beginner.

Literature

◆ **Flowering Haiku**

http://www.thunkek.net/abqpoet/haiku/

A streaming slideshow of Haiku. Recommended for frames-capable browsers, but the Haiku are accessible without one.

POPULAR CULTURE

Games

◆ **Pachinko Homepage**

http://www.pachinko.co.jp/eng/eindex.html

Select What Is Pachinko? from the welcome screen for this site to obtain a history and description of the game, with color graphics.

Music

◆ **CBP Totally Japanese: Karaoke**

http://www.cyber-bp.or.jp/japan/living/karaoke.html

Karaoke is a form of entertainment that has recently become so popular in Japan that regulations have had to be passed to control the noise it creates. The word Karaoke comes from "kara," meaning empty, plus "oke," short for orchestra. Tapes are played with backing music but no words, and people sing the words with the music, using a microphone.

◆ **Japan Related Web Links: Music**

http://www.panix.com/~tn/j-music.html

This site contains links for concert information, the Weekly Top 100, information about television and radio stations as well as record shops, agents, and brokers, and links to sites with information about Japanese musicians.

Sports

◆ **History of Shotokan Karate of America**

http://www.gwu.edu/~ska/history.htm

This site opens with a lineage tree graphic of karate history, which can be traced back some 1,400 years, to Daruma, founder of Zen Buddhism in Western India.

- ◆ **International Golf: Japan**

http://sport-hq.com/spectate/golf/japan.shtml

Everything you want to know about playing golf in Japan.

- ◆ **Shotokai's Karate-do and Japanese Martial Arts Encyclopedia**

http://www.pmuc.udec.cl/~shotokai/ingles/indice2.html

There are two versions of this page: one is basically text with only a few graphics and the other is a full graphical version. The index provides access to articles, biographies, and pictures dealing with the Japanese martial arts. There are numerous animated gif files that demonstrate different karate techniques.

- ◆ **Shotokan Karate Magazine**

http://www.zee.com/skm

This site provides access to the current issue of *Shotokan Karate Magazine.* Selected articles from previous issues are also available.

- ◆ **SumoWeb!**

http://www.sumoweb.com/

Features of this site include basic information about Sumo wrestling, a glossary, statistics, essays from fans, and extensive links to other Sumo sites on the Web.

- ◆ **Sumo World Homepage**

http://iac.co.jp/~sumowrld/

This site provides access to current and back issues of *Sumo World,* a bimonthly English magazine devoted to Sumo wrestling.

RELIGION

- ◆ **Japanese Buddhism**

http://www.japan-guide.com/e/e2055.html

This site includes information about both historical and current practices. In 1175, the Jodo sect (Pure Land Sect) was founded. It was the first sect to find followers among all different social classes because its theories were very simple. It remains the largest sect today. In 1191, the Zen sect was introduced into Japan. Its complicated theories were popular particularly among members of the military class. In Zen Buddhism, one should achieve enlightenment through meditation and self discipline. The site provides a good overview for anyone who is not familiar with the religious history and practices of Buddhism.

◆ **Journal of Buddhist Ethics**

http:/japaneseculture.miningco.com/msub12.htm

An extremely well-produced online Buddhist journal and guide to the religion, with a strong Japanese orientation.

◆ **Shinto**

http://www.webcom.com/jinja/english/s-0.html

Shinto (the way of the gods) is the traditional Japanese religion. It originated as a religion of the farmers in Japan during the sixth century.

SCIENCE AND TECHNOLOGY

◆ **U.S.-Japan Links: Science and Technology**

http://www.us-japan.org/resources-scitech.html

This site is managed by the Japan Information Access Project (JIAP), which is a nonprofit educational organization. There are links from this site to current information and project initiatives in the areas of science and technology.

Information Technology and Telecommunications

◆ **Japan Information Access Project**

http://www.nmjc.org/jiap/pubs.html

This site includes publications and information on Trade and Technology, S&T Information, Patents, Electronic Information, and Public Policy. Links are provided to newsletters and other publications in these areas.

◆ **U.S.-Japan Center for Technology Management, Vanderbilt School of Engineering**

http://shogun.vuse.vanderbilt.edu/usjapan

The purpose of the U.S.-Japan Center for Technology Management is to create a corps of American scientists, engineers, and managers with significant experience in Japanese industrial and technology management practices. This site contains information about the Center, its staff, and events.

OTHER

Exhibits

◆ **The Japanese American National Museum**
http://www.lausd.k12.ca.us/janm/

The Japanese American National Museum is the first museum in the United States expressly dedicated to sharing the experience of Americans of Japanese ancestry. The site states that the mission of the museum is to make known the Japanese American experience as an integral part of our nation's heritage in order to improve understanding and appreciation for the ethnic and cultural diveristy of the United States. Sections of this site include general information about the museum, current exhibits and museum events, different departments of the museum, the National School Project, and the museum store. There are numerous color graphics of items in the museum's exhibits.

Organizations

◆ **Japan-America Society of Washington, D.C. Calendar of Events**
http://www.us-japan.org/dc/calendar.html

The JASW calendar includes events of interest to Japanese Americans in the Washington, D.C., area.

◆ **U.S.-Japan Links: Text-Based Site Map**
http://www.us-japan.org/text-welcome.html

This site provides links to the national electronic network of Japan America Societies. Excellent site.

Travel and Tourism

◆ **TokyoQ**
http://www.so-net.or.jp/tokyoq

A weekly guide to happenings in Tokyo, including lists of events, a restaurant guide, a list of izayaka (Japanese-style pubs), bars, baths, and available tours of unusual places.

9

Asian Indian American Resources

CYNTHIA A. NUHN

INTRODUCTION

India has been portrayed in film and literature as a magical land full of exotic animals and people clothed in colorful and ornately decorated saris. The air in India has been described as being thick with the scent of spices and the sounds of strange, yet sweet-sounding musical instruments. Hindu mythology describes many tales of immortals successfully performing heroic tasks. Many individuals have come to associate India with the country's famous cuisine. The words "Indian cuisine" bring to mind a variety of dishes that are wildly tempting and deliciously hot. Although these varying images of India have fascinated people for many years, the statistical facts associated with modern India are equally fantastic. The country of India has a population of over 950 million people and possesses an extremely diverse population base. The *World Almanac and Book of Facts* for 1997 explains that Hindi is the official language, English is the associate official language and seventeen other regional languages are spoken. According to *Background Notes* of the Department of State, the principal religions of India are Hindu (82.6 percent), Muslim (11.4 percent), Christian (2.4 percent), Sikh (2 percent), Jain (0.5 percent), Buddhist (0.7 percent), and Parsi (0.2 percent). Ethnic groups residing in India include Indo-Aryan (72 percent), Dravidian (25 percent), Mongoloid (2 percent) and others. Since the infancy of Indian civilization around 2500 B.C.E., the country has been invaded by many different groups of people. These invasions in the past, from the Iranian plateau, Central Asia, Arabia, Afghanistan and the West have produced a unique blend of races, religions, and culture in the modern country of India.

India is a country of many contrasts. The geography of India ranges from the extraordinary heights of the Himalayan mountains to low-lying beaches. The climate varies from tropical temperatures in the southern part of the country to the chill of close-to-Arctic temperatures in the north, but with other areas of

India enjoying a temperate climate. Cities and towns of India offer a variety of living styles. The city of Bombay has a large population and is the financial, as well as the film-making capital of India. However, many individuals live in rural and remote villages or communities. Different regions of India differ not only in climate, geography, and population, but also in culture as well. Customs and languages may vary from region to region. It can be said that culture and customs can vary every two miles down the road! Eating customs vary greatly and Indian cuisine is a combination of the beliefs of many different religious groups. Hindu believers do not eat beef and those that practice Islam do not eat pork. In food preparation or any other activity of daily living, Buddhists do not believe in taking any life at all. Many people in India of different religions are vegetarians.

Because of India's great diversity, India has stirred the imagination of its visitors for hundreds of years and it is hard to imagine a person who has not at one time dreamed of visiting India. Not everyone has the financial resources to travel to India, but through the Internet there are many opportunities to visit India-related sites and explore the country through a home computer.

Asian Indians living in the United States are faced with many unique problems. Of course, they wish to communicate with individuals from India. However, they may be seeking communications with people from a specific region of India or from a specific ethnic group or from a specific religious background. All people who leave their country of origin try to keep their culture alive in their new country, and Asian Indians are no different in that respect. However, Asian Indians may have specific informational needs and be seeking information about their specific region of India.

The Internet provides many useful sources of information for the Asian Indian living in the United States. Usenet newsgroups and electronic mailing lists offer individuals opportunities to ask questions, post information, or share ideas on a variety of subjects related to India. Many Usenet groups serve individuals from one specific geographic area, such as Teluga or Kerala.

There is a large and growing number of Web sites maintained by Asian Indians living in the United States. These sites provide a wide variety of information ranging from the correct postures of Yoga to the cast of the latest movie release in Bombay. Individuals can locate India's daily stock information or cricket scores. The Internet provides many excellent sources of information for both Asian Indians living in the United States and individuals interested in the study of India.

Techniques used to locate resources on India for this chapter included printed Internet reference guides as well as recommendations posted on India-related Usenet groups and listservs. Many different search engines were employed to locate useful and unusual India sites, including AltaVista, LooksSmart, AOL Net Find, InfoSeek, Yahoo, LYCOS, Web Browser, Web Crawler, HotBot, and Excite.

Some pleasant experiences resulted with the use of HotBot, as this search engine allows more sophisticated searching in the advanced searching selection. Not only can the researcher perform a Boolean search, this search engine also allows the searcher to select the date panel. This will assure more recent sites will be obtained in the final search. The user also has the option of specifying the geographic location as well as the media type. Excite is fun to use, as this search engine recommends related words to add to your search.

In exploring the subject of India on the Internet, search terms must be specific or the user will be overwhelmed with the number of sites that will be listed. For example, a Yahoo search in the Arts and Humanities division using the search expression "India" yields 4,388 hits! My beginning searches were primitive, using search expressions such as "India states and regions." As I learned more about the culture, religion, and regions of India, I was able to perform more sophisticated searches, using words and expressions learned from earlier searches.

As mentioned earlier, India is a country of great cultural and geographical diversity. Equally diverse is the information on India available on the Internet. The Internet user may locate traditional information on India, such as travel hints or background facts on the country. On the other extreme, one may also discover a new form of dance music with its roots based in India and Pakistan.

Individuals looking for traditional information on India should visit Discover India at **http://jan.ucc.nau.edu/~vdk/india/indianew.html**. This site is useful to both Asian Indians, as well as others seeking background and travel information on India. The site offers comprehensive information on the country of India. The topics covered are extensive, and include health and education, country information, travel and immigration, religion, newsgroups, and the Internet in India. Vipul Kapadia, the creator of this site, manages a large collection of well-maintained and visually pleasing Web sites.

All music lovers, as well as anyone seeking the new and unusual should visit the Desi Dance Music Page at **http://www.uwm.edu/~qazi/dance.html**. Desi Dance Music was created in the 1980s and is influenced by American and European dance music, as well as the music of India and Pakistan. Young South Asians living in England, Canada, and the United States who wished to return to the music of their country began forming their own Bhangra bands. Desi Dance Music was born when the traditional musical instruments of South Asia, such as the tabla, dhol, dholak, and the sitar were combined with the Western styles of R&B, hip hop, house, Euro, techno, and jungle. This new sound is enjoyed by people all over the world, and its faithful fans reside in Canada, the United States, Australia, and India. Internet users can experience this unique music form by downloading and listening to the WAV audiosamples offered on this site.

As mentioned earlier, the Internet provides the Asian Indian with extensive sources of information reflecting all aspects of Indian life. The non-Asian Indian can learn much about the country of India through the use of the Internet. The Internet offers facts about India for the serious scholar, as well as information for individuals interested in traveling to India. More importantly, the Internet offered me the opportunity to learn about another country and communicate with people I would have never met otherwise. I would like to thank Ann M. Lieberman for her help in the initial research of this project.

GENERAL INFORMATION

- ◆ **Best of India—Bala & Rangarajan**

http://www.people.memphis.edu/~sganpthy/india.html

Although the introduction states that this homepage is oriented towards South India, there seems to be something available for everyone through this site. Links include India News, Sports India, Indian Music, Indian Dances, and Madras News. There are links dealing with education in India, as well as Indian cultural programs in the United States. The Hindu religion, Cuisine of India and Tourist Attractions of India are also represented. Interesting graphics are employed.

- ◆ **Bhaarat Ek Khoj: Discovery of India**

http://www.mahesh.com/india/

This site is filled with much information on arts and drama, entertainment, business and employment, engineering and technology, government and law, health and medicine, news and publishing, and regional information. The first page discusses India's history. This Web site also has links to baby names, astronomy, yoga, matrimonial, meditation, seminars that are related to India, as well as companies and corporations in India.

- ◆ **Discover India**

http://jan.ucc.nau.edu/~vdk/india/indianew.html

This site offers a wealth of information on the country of India. As well as the general country information discussed in the introduction, there are links to Yoga and meditation, newsgroups, humor, electronic journals, health and education, computers and the Internet, art and culture, business, matrimonial, and sports. Site is updated frequently.

- ◆ **General Information on India**

http://www.dallas.net/~noel/gen-info.html

This site offers a diverse collection of links to many different resources on India. Some of the links include Silk Threads Indian Fashion Page, the music of India, Desi Web pages, Internet Servers in India, India Online, Web India, the India Homepage, India World (for News and Information on India), as well as *IndoLink* (The Online Magazine of India). General country information is included in the link to the CIA Factbook on India. Interesting links include the Latest New Headlines in India, Indian film, and the Indian National Anthem.

- ◆ **India**

http://www.goodnet.com/~sunsjv/India.html

This site, which also calls itself The Indian Connection HomePage, offers extensive information on the country of India. It has a huge number of links representing all aspects of Indian life. The user can connect to India Abroad

News-Paper, All India Radio, or More Indian Restaurants. Areas of interests covered are diverse. There are links to humor, Indian movies, Indian Matrimonial, names and their meanings, Indian cuisine and recipes, and much more.

◆ **India—The Land of the Indus**

http://www.cen.uiuc.edu/~jvshah/bharat.html

There is much unusual information at this site, including links to Indian scientists and the history of traditional Indian medicine. There is an interesting link to the ancient city of Harappa, which offers a ninety slide tour with commentary from experts. There are links to information on the Indus valley, major religions of India, the Taj Mahal, and Indian sculpture.

◆ **Information on India**

http://sbmp32.ess.sunysb.edu/akhilesh percent20images/ india.html

Tourism and general country information is featured on this Web site. Many of the links are related to culture and the fine arts. The site also includes links to Indian music, tourism, Indian states, Indian cities, and many other India-related sites. There is a mirror site at India Institute of Science. The initial concept was created by Sridhar Venkataraman and the site is maintained by Dinesh Venkatesh.

◆ **Know about India**

http://www.cs.buffalo.edu/~skumar/india.html

This is a Web site specializing in gopher sites. It provides useful factual information about India that is in text form only. The information can be downloaded very quickly. Know about India provides links to gopher sites about news, language, music, literature, agriculture, finance, commerce, culture, industry, defense, national symbols, news, and religion.

◆ **Links to India Information**

http://webhead.com/WWWVL/India/india2.html

A great source for general country information. Links represent art and culture, events and festivals in or about India, humor, languages, literature, education, movies, music, businesses, newsgroups, and much more. This site has its own India search engine. All subjects are subdivided many times. It is part of the WWW Virtual Library with information categorized by subject (India). Site is updated frequently.

◆ **Yahoo!: Regional: Countries: India**

http://www.yahoo.com/regional/Countries/India

This is a wonderful resource for general country information on India. There are links to Usenet groups, business and services, sculpture, education, entertainment, news, travel, Internet in India, maps, events and festivals, and real estate information. Other links include the India WWW Virtual Library, the useful India search engine, and many other links.

Current Events

◆ **IndiaConnect—Connect India to the World**

http://www.indiaconnect.com/

This is a gigantic collection of India related news items. The news related links range from the fun to the serious, and every aspect of life seems to have a link. There are links to fashion and style, movie reviews, music charts, arts, dance, and culture. Business and investment, real estate and property, health and medicine, and government are also represented. This site also has its own search engine that allows the user to search for India-related sites.

◆ **Indiaserver**

http://www.indiaserver.com/ilink.html

This is a wonderful resource for news related to the country of India. Users can link to *The Hindu,* which is updated daily, or to *The Business Line.* Other links include news, music reviews, sports, government, and business. Directions are given on hosting a Web site with Indiaserver.

◆ **INDIAWORLD: India on the Internet**

http://www.indiaworld.co.in/open/rec/index.html

This site contains a huge collection of links related to the news of India. There are too many links to mention all of them. However, some of the areas covered included business, news, market trends, Hindi films, cricket, astrology, art, food, and India world headlines.

◆ **Indozone: The Complete Indian Website**

http://www.indozone.com/index.html

This site offers a variety of news information related to the country of India. There are links to business pages, travel, fashion, Indian movies, sports, and recipes. For the investor, there are weekly and monthly financial reports on the Indian industry and stock markets.

◆ **Welcome to INDOlink**

http://www.indolink.com/

This site offers a huge collection of news-related information of interest to the Indian community. Some of the links include India news, health and fitness, film reviewer, book reviews, poetry, humor, astrology, movies, law forum, and Travelog. There is also a global directory of businesses, products, and services. Information on the Indian Consulate, regional listings, and classifieds are also available from this site.

Newsgroups and Listservs

alt.culture.us.asian-indian

Discussions in this Usenet newsgroup cover all aspects of Indian culture and life. Topics covered include history, films, music, politics, customs, dietary habits, and religion.

alt.politics.india.progressive

This electronic mailing list has discussions of politics relating to India, as well as discussions on other topics relating to the country of India.

- ◆ **The India News Network (India-L)**

Subscription address: listserv@indnet.bgsu.edu

The India News Network is an electronic mailing list located at Bowling Green State University in Kentucky. Topics of discussion are related to current events in India and topics of interest to Asian Indians living in the United States. To join, send the message **sub INDIA-L your name** to the above address.

- ◆ **Looking**

Subscription address: listserv@indnet.bgsu.edu

This electronic mailing list is the "e-mail network of the Asian Indian Community." The list carries three digests per week. One digest is a jobs bazaar, one a matrimonial digest, and the third is for general information. Digests are posted on Tuesdays, Wednesdays, and Thursdays, in random order. To join, send the message **sub LOOKING your name** to the above address.

soc.culture.indian

Discussions in this Usenet newsgroup cover all aspects of Indian culture and life. Topics covered include art, religion, dietary habits, politics, social customs, and films.

soc.culture.indian.kerala

This Usenet newsgroup has discussions on topics relating to Kerala, but also general discussions on Indian life and culture.

soc.culture.indian.teluga

Discussions in this Usenet newsgroup are on topics relating to Teluga, but also general discussions on Indian life and culture.

Newspapers, Magazines, and Newsletters

- ◆ **The Hindu**

http://www.webpage.com/hindu/index.html

The Hindu is the daily online edition of India's national newspaper. It is an excellent source of current information. The news coverage is extensive and includes international news, national news, state and regional news, the arts, biographies, business, cuisine, education, the environment, information science and technology, medicine, religion, sports, and tourism. It includes classified advertisements and employment opportunities. National and international stock quotes are also available from this site.

BUSINESS

◆ **The India Type: Economic Forum at BGSU (INDIA-E)**
Subscription address: listserv@indnet.bgsu.edu

This electronic mailing list is part of the India Network maintained at Bowling Green State University in Kentucky. Discussions are related to issues pertaining to economics, such as investments, banking, and company information. Individuals may join by approval only. To join, send the message **sub INDIA-E your name** to the above address.

◆ **IndiaExpress: Welcome to India on the Net**
http://www.indiaexpress.com/

This site offers information on business services. There is a hypertext Business Directory to the left of the homepage. The user can simply click on the selected type of service. The services range from construction, moving companies, clothing, health care and much more. The site includes links to jobs, India Express Yellow Pages, and directions on how to publish your Web site on India Express.

◆ **Invest—India**
http://quark.kode.net/india/

This site offers free quotes from the Bombay Stock Exchange. Investment services information, the latest business news, investment resources, and Business India Links are all available from this site. For individuals who have investments in India or are considering such transactions, this site can be a valuable resource. India's online newspaper, *The Hindu,* is also available from this site. It is possible to connect to All India Radio from this site.

◆ **South Asia Milan**
http://www.samilan.com/

This site was once titled "India Related Links." Now titled the South Asia Milan, it provides services, information, and business opportunities for South Asians in North America and lists information pertaining to those topics. It still has hyperlinks to business, regions of India, food, arts, education, and languages and much more India related information. Entertainment links include the Best of Bollywood and Horoscope links.

◆ **The World Business Center, India**

http://indiaonline.com/wbc/

This site provides information on a variety of business services in India, including courier service and locating office and industrial facilities. Marketing and legal services are explained, and joint ventures are described. Real estate development opportunities are also discussed.

CULTURE AND HUMANITIES, GENERAL

◆ **Culture of India**

http://www.meadev.gov.in/culture/overback.htm

This is a very good resource for the historical background on the dance forms of India, Indian cuisine, music, and the religions of India. There are also links to art, music, and dance schools and museums of India. Images employed are visually pleasing.

◆ **Links about India: Art and Culture**

http://www.iac.co.jp/~daccordo/i-culture.html

This is a huge collection of links related to the art and culture of India. Links are too numerous to mention by name. Some of the subject categories include the different forms of Indian dance, sculpture, Asian art, Indian culture and life, architecture, mats and basketry, as well as American galleries and museums exhibiting the art of India.

◆ **Manushi**

http://www.arbornet.org/~manushi/

Manushi, A Journal about Women and Society was founded in 1978. The journal states that one of its goals is "to build an information-gathering process about the life situations of the people of different communities within India." Articles include interviews, historical pieces, book and film reviews, and civil liberties and human rights issues. It is a nonprofit organization that does not accept advertisements in its publication. The visitor to this site can explore select articles from the issues of this journal. Many interesting related links to women are included.

◆ **Sourashtras**

http://www2.dtc.net/~rtirukon/history.html

Clicking on the "wall of links" gives the history and other information about the Sourashtraians or silk weavers and silk thread merchants of India. There are links to the Sourashtra Directory, Sourashtra language, events and functions, Tamil pages, matrimonial pages, and other India and non-India related links.

FINE ARTS

◆ **Arts of South Asia**

http://www.wisc.edu/southasia/arts.html

This site has something for everyone. There are links to classical forms of Indian music, Hindu poetry, classical dance forms of different regions of India, and the Asian Art Gallery. Clicking on the Indian Music Site allows the user to download samples of hindustani, carnatic, and classical music as well as articles related to these topics. For those seeking unusual art forms, clicking on Buses, Trucks, and Tankers of Pakistan is a must. This is a link filled with many photographs of ornately decorated vehicles.

Dance

◆ **Dances of India**

http://people.unt.edu/~sga0001/dance.html

This is a huge site filled with information on Indian dance forms. There are too many links to mention all of them by name. The classical dances of India are divided by region. There is also a link to Folk and Tribal Dances. Links include many beautiful photographs of dancers in elegant costumes. Each link to a dance style has an extensive explanation of that particular dance form. There are also links to lists of dance schools and names of famous dancers. Related links for Indian dance are included.

◆ **Kathak Classical Indian Dance**

http://www.cs.nott.ac.uk/Department/Staff/ef/kathak.html

This site has no links or graphics, but it offers very good explanations of the different forms of Indian classical dance. Each main heading is subdivided with an explanation of the type of dance, the type of costume employed, and which sex would perform the dance.

◆ **Mary Varghese's Introduction to Kuchipudi**

http://wwwpks.atnf.csiro.au/~plintel/MENON/ kuchipudi_mary_varghese.html

This site offers a wonderful description of Kuchipudi, a classical dance form of India. The introduction explains that, like other forms of Indian Art, dance has its roots in religion. A classical Indian dancer not only had to excel in dance, but also had to have a good knowledge of religion, literature, art, and music as there is a relationship between all these fields of study. The classical Indian dancer also had to be an excellent vocalist. All links are related to Kuchipudi.

Music

◆ **Carnatic Beginner's List**

http://www.medieval.org/music/world/carnatic/cbl.html

This site is directed to the person who is just starting to research Carnatic music. Extensive information is available from this site. Some of the links include discussions of instruments used, vocalists living and deceased who contributed to this form of music, as well as lists of recordings of Carnatic music.

◆ **Carnatic Homepage: N. S. Sundar**

http://www.cis.ohio-state.edu/~sundar/carnatic

The Carnatic Homepage's introduction describes what Carnatic music is. The user can link to frequently asked questions about Indian classical music or to the newsgroup **rec.music.indian.classical**. Other links include lyrics for compositions, transliteration schemes for lyrics, lyrics for Bhajans, and biographies of great musicians and composers. A link to Indian classical arts is also provided.

◆ **Cyberports of Indian Classical Music**

http://www.cs.tamu.edu/people/badari/.spic/icmlinks.html

This is a very extensive list of Indian Classical music sites on the Internet. It is a fabulous resource for explanations of the different forms of Indian classical music. Many links offer historical background of the different musical forms. There are also links to the Hindu Newspaper Arts Section, which also allows the user to view back issues. Many Carnatic homepages are listed, as well as information about Hindustani music.

rec.music.indian.classical

This Usenet newsgroup includes discussion of classical music. Requests for song lyrics can be made.

◆ **Indian Classical Arts Homepage: N. S. Sundar**

http://www.cis.ohio-state.edu/~sundar/

This is a fun site to visit. I have included it under the heading of music, as it has links to the Carnatic Homepage, Hindustani Music, and Classical Dance forms of India. However, my favorite link is Alternative Images. This link provides biographies and images of famous classical Indian singers and dancers, past and present. There is also a link called Other Information about India, which gives cultural information about this nation.

HISTORY

- ◆ **Indian Rulers**

http://www.cnct.com/home/bhaskar/INDIA/people.html

India's rulers from the fourth century B.C.E. to the nineteenth century are described in brief summaries on this site. The site connects to other India-related links.

LANGUAGE ARTS AND LITERATURE

Language Arts

- ◆ **INDOLOGY**

http://www.ucl.ac.uk/~ucgadkw/indology.html

This is a fabulous resource for Sanskritists, MIA and NIA language specialists, historians, and Dravidologists, and other university level scholars interested in Indological studies. This organization offers extensive information on its Web site. There is a virtual archive of Indic e-texts, learned societies, digital art and manuscript images, conference announcements, online dictionaries, library catalogues, and important position or review papers on Indological topics. There is even an experimental system for ordering copies of Sanskrit manuscripts.

LITERATURE

- ◆ **SAWNET: South Asian Books for Kids**

**http://www.umiacs.umd.edu/users/sawweb/sawnet/
    kidsbooks.html**

Sponsored by the South Asian Women's NETwork, this is a fabulous site for parents, librarians, and everyone that loves children's books. The site lists books for or about South Asian children. Most of the books were written in English, but a few have been translated. There are some wonderful descriptions of children's fiction, as well as books of a factual nature. The hypertext "generally recommended" list includes books with strong female characters. At the end of this page, other children's books recommendations are made; however, they are not related to Asia (for example, *A Wrinkle in Time* by Madeleine L'Engle). There are links related to children's books as well.

POPULAR CULTURE

Clothing

- ◆ **Chantal Boulanger: Indian Saris—Research**
http://www.devi.net/sari.html

This is a fascinating site discussing the saris of India. Chantal Boulanger has spent over six years studying the draping styles of saris and has noted more than one hundred different ways to drape a sari. Unfortunately, many individuals have adopted a "modern" draping style and many of these traditional tying techniques will be lost forever. Many of the draping styles have already been forgotten. This was a valuable social study, as sari draping told a story about the history and social hierarchy in India. The links show the families of drapes, photos, more pictures of saris, books, and favorite Web sites. There is also a link to connect to an En Français version.

Food and Drink

- ◆ **Cuisine of India**
http://www.incore.com/india/cuisine.html

This site gives the history of Indian cuisine. There are links to the Indian Recipe Index, Dishes from Other Asian Countries Adapted to Indian Tastes, vegetarian links, and links to Indian restaurants around the world. This is a source for many Indian recipes.

- ◆ **Links about India: Recipes and Cooking**
http://www.bayarea.net/~emerald/i-recipes.html

Although some of the links sell books or spices, this site is still one of the most diverse homepages on the cooking of India. The links divide the country by region. Links include explanations of spices, as well as a history of Indian cooking. There are many links to tasty recipes. For the individual on a restricted diet, there is even a link to a fat-free Indian recipe site.

- ◆ **Recipes: Indian Collection**
http://george.ee.washington.edu/~desika/recipes.html

This is an excellent resource as it contains a huge collection of Indian recipes. Links include cuisine of different regions of India. There are many interesting food links, including Graduate Student's Guide (Cookbook of Indian Recipes), World Guide to Vegetarian Restaurants, Vegetarian Stuff WWW Server, and much more. Everyone should click on Recipes from the Beyond to view a mouth-watering photograph.

◆ **Vegetarianism: The Higher Taste**

http://www.webcom.com/~ara/col/books/VEG

This site is also somewhat commercial, as it offers to sell *The Higher Taste* cookbook for $1.00. However, there are some worthwhile links to the Hare Krishna Vegetarian Society, Hare Krishna's Food for Life, and Vegetarianism.

Music

◆ **Desi Dance Music Page**

http://www.uwm.edu/~qazi/dance.html

As mentioned in the introduction, Desi Dance Music is a relatively new form of music that is a marriage between the traditional music of India and Pakistan and Western pop music. This site features a different Hindi remix and Bhangra album every month. The Internet user simply downloads and listens to the WAV audio sample on this site to preview the album. A list is kept of every album that was featured in the past along with ordering information. Links from this site offer the newest of the new.

rec.music.indian.misc

Discussions in this Usenet newsgroup concern Indian music that is not classical in nature. Lyrics are discussed and songs are queried.

◆ **Sami's Urdu/Hindi Film Music Page**

http://www.lehigh.edu/~sm0e/sami.html

This is a wonderful site for the lover of Urdu/Hindi film music. It is evident that the creator of this site holds this music in his heart, as he has created a huge document filled with interesting links. The introduction gives an historical background of Urdu/Hindi music. There is a Hindi MIDI page which includes midi files, karaoke, and chords for film songs. Another link describes how to order Hindi cassettes or CDs by mail. The site visitor can link to **rec.music.indian.misc**. This site has many more great links, but space does not allow a discussion of all of them!

Sports

◆ **100+ India Links—Sports**

http://member.aol.com/indialinks/sport.htm

This site offers everything imaginable for the lover of the game of cricket. Links include Laws of Cricket, Cricket Explained Simply, Cricket World Monthly and many more cricket-in-India related links. There are links relating to sports in general, such as Sports in Ancient India, National Sports Federation/ Associations of India, and other sports homepages. The user can also click on links to movies, music, pictures, and humor.

◆ **Links to India Information: Sport**

http://www.webhead.com/WWWVL/India/india223.html

This site is part of the WWW Virtual Library: India. The site offers extensive information on the sports of India. There are many links relating to Cricket in India, which include Women's Cricket Association, CricInfo (Gopher), Indian Cricket page and much more. There are also links to information about Indian Field Hockey and general sports information. From this site, the user can link to general country information about India as well as link to newsgroups information.

Television and Film

◆ **Bollywood**

http://www.mahesh.com/india/bollywood.html

This site has links to new Hindi movies, Teluga movies, the Tamil Film Music Page, Archive of Hindi movie songs, Tamil songs, reviews of Hindi movies, theaters in the U.S. showing Indian movies, and the Hindi song archive. Read the top ten rules of filmmaking in Bollywood, which offers a humorous view of story lines in Indian films.

◆ **Indian Movies**

http://webhead.com/WWWVL/India/india213.html

This site features all aspects of Indian movies. It has links to films of India, movie music, photographs of film stars, film reviews, movie recommendations, and many other links to Indian movie information. This site is part of the WWW Virtual Library.

◆ **The Indian Movies Index**

http://www.gadnet.com/movies.htm

This is a huge collection of links related to Indian films. The visitor to this site can connect to the Review Page, and give his or her rating to the Film of the Week. The top of the page lists the names of Indian actors, actresses, and directors in hypertext. The user can click on a name and read about the individual's film career. The links include pictures of film personalities, links to film magazines, and the U.S. Library of Congress selected list of Indian films and videos, to name a few.

◆ **IndiaPlus—EntertainmentPlus—All about Indian Movies**

http://www.indiaplus.com/Entert/index.htm

This site give biographies on contemporary Indian actors, actresses, singers, film directors, and music directors. The names appear in hypertext form, and one can simply select a name and click upon it to learn more about that particular person.

◆ Yahoo!: Regional: Countries: India: Entertainment:
   Movies: Bollywood

**http://msn.yahoo.com/Regional/Countries/India/
Entertainment/Movies/Bollywood/**

Bombay or Bollywood produces huge numbers of films. This site is all Bollywood links and they represent all aspects of Bollywood. There are links to pictures of stars, movie music, Bollywood tour, gossip, and even an online chat board.

RELIGION

◆ India's Spice'N Flavor (Religion)

http://www.indias.com/religion.html

This site does have one link to recipes for Masala, but all the other links have nothing to do with the cuisine of India. Instead they relate to food for the soul, as they are all religion of India links! Links include information on Buddhism, Hinduism, Islam, and Christianity in India.

◆ Religion in India

http://webhead.com/WWWVL/India/india222.html

This site is a great resource for information on the religions of India, as it has a huge number of links. The religions discussed include the Bhagavat Gita, the Baha'i, Buddhist, Christian, Hare Krishna, Hindu, Islamic, Jewish and Sikh faiths in India, and the Jain World Wide Web Page. Information on Sufism, Vedic Astrology, Zoroastrianism, and Yoga are also provided. This site is part of the WWW Virtual Library.

Baha'i

◆ The Baha'i Faith Page

http://oneworld.wa.com/bahai/magazine/homepage.html

This site offers much information about the Baha'i faith. The introduction includes links to the teachings of Baha'i, early and recent history, and the current status of the religion, as well as references. The user can search the sacred writings via using key words. There are also links to FTP archives of a Baha'i discussion group Usenet newsgroups archive, as well as links to other Baha'i related sites.

◆ Baha'i Resources on the Internet

http://www.bcca.org/services/srb/resources.html

This is a wonderful resource for the study of the Baha'i faith. This site contains a huge number of links relating to this religion. Links include Sacred Scriptures and other texts, Baha'i Related Images, Regular Net Events, Newsgroups/Mailing Lists, and Baha'i Organizations. Some of the introductory material links are in French, and Italian, as well as English. The link to German News online is in German.

Christianity

◆ **The Indian Orthodox Church Homepage**
http://www.indian-orthodox.org/

This site explains the history of Christianity in India and the forming of the Indian Orthodox Church. Some of the links are a Brief Overview of the Church, News from India, and Our Parishes on the WWW. Questions or comments can be submitted to the link titled The Indian Orthodox Church Discussion Board.

◆ **Religions—Christianity**
http://www.meadev.gov.in/culture/religion/christ.htm

The beginnings of Christianity in India are described in this site. This site offers numerous links to many different aspects of India. Links include foreign relations, social issues, and culture.

Hare Krishna

◆ **Hare Krishna Homepage**
http://www.iskcon.net/hkindex/

This homepage includes links to books, the magazine *Back to Godhead Online*, founder information, the centers around the world, as well the philosophy of the religion Hare Krishna. The link Krishna Art displays colorful reproductions of art relating to Hare Krishna.

◆ **A Hare Krishna Index**
http://www-ece.rice.edu/~vijaypai/hkindex.html

This is a gigantic site and resource for the study of Hare Krishna. Links are too numerous to mention, but include periodicals, Krishna conscious philosophy and lifestyle, temples and farms communities, vegetarianism, education, arts and culture, the Bhagavad Gita, and much more. Regional or national homepages on Hare Krishna link the user to general information about the movement. These pages are in French, Spanish, Russian, German, Italian, Swedish, Czech, Slovenian, and English.

Hindu

◆ **Bhagavat Gita**
http://www.iconsoftec.com/gita/

The eighteen chapters of the *Bhagavat Gita* (Sanskrit Verses) can be downloaded, as well as a free copy of Adobe Acrobat. This site offers links to an

English translation, as well as a complete verse-by-verse transliteration from a book on the Gita.

◆ **GHEN: Hindu Scripture Reference Center**

http://www.hindunet.org/scriptures/

Sponsored by the Hindu Students Council, this site has links to the Bhagawad Gita and related sites, Hindu Community Event Calendar, and other Hindu related sites. There is a link to a glossary, in which the user can type in a word to perform a search. The Hindu Universe Chat is available as a link from this site as well.

◆ **Global Hindu Electronic Network: The Hindu Universe**

http://www.hindunet.org/

This site is sponsored by the Hindu Students Council. The links offered including information on Scriptures, as well as the Jain, Buddhist, and Sikh religions. There are also links to a Hindu calendar and Hindu history. If a nonprofit Hindu organization wants some Web space, the creators of this site will, at their discretion, offer assistance.

◆ **Hindu Gods & Goddesses Photographs Download Page**

http://www.lifcobooks.com/vrangan/Gods.htm

This site has no text, but it does display colorful images of Hindu gods and goddesses. These images can be downloaded.

◆ **Hinduism**

http://jan.ucc.nau.edu/~vdk/india/hinduism.html

This site explores the Hindu religion extensively. A thorough description of Hinduism is included, as well as numerous links relating to this religion. Links include Hindu related newsgroups, Indian festivals, Hindu scriptures, and explanations of Hindu customs. The colorful graphs employed are visually pleasing.

◆ **Hinduism Today**

http://www.HinduismToday.kauai.hi.us/ashram/htoday.html

This site is a full color Macintosh-generated magazine. It has a page of cartoon and humorous quotes. The user can click on the link to find online current and back issues of the magazine. Other links include a 700-word glossary of terms, the teachings of Sage Yogaswami, Health and the Healing Homepage. Links to vegetarianism; nonviolence; and current news articles from newspapers, magazines, and the World Wide Web that are of interest to followers of the Hindu religion are included. There is also an archive and resource search engine.

◆ **Spirituality/Yoga/Hinduism Homepage**
http://www.geocities.com/RodeoDrive/1415/

This site has a clever design and the information is presented well. The site includes extensive links to Biographies on Indian Saints, Sanskrit Books and Documents, Symbolism in Hinduism, Yoga, and Meditation. There is even a link to Kipling's famous poem "If"!

Islam

◆ **Religions—Islam**
http://www.meadev.gov.in/culture/religion/islam.htm

This site describes how the religion of Islam was brought to India in the eighth century C.E. by Arab traders. The site offers links to other religions of India, such as Buddhism, Jainism, Sikhism, and Hinduism. There are also links to Indian culture, sports, and much more.

Jain

◆ **Global Hindu Electronic Network (GHEN) The Hindu Universe**
http://www.hindunet.org/jain_info/

This site is sponsored by the Hindu Students Council and offers information on the Jains. Some of the links include Jain Web Site, Jainist Texts, to be searched (from UNC), and the Young Jains of America. There are also links to temples, scripture, the latest news, and the newsgroup **alt.Hindu**.

◆ **Jain Database**
http://sunsite.unc.edu/jainism/

This site gives an overview of the Jain religion. Clicking on Jain Database Current Information allows the user to select such links as Jain education quotes, rituals, articles, books, stories for youth, youth essays, and world religion. If the user clicks on Jain BBS e-mail Bulletins, lists of related e-mail bulletins appear.

◆ **Jain Studies**
http://www.dmu.ac.uk/~pka/guides/jain.html

A very comprehensive site on the Jain religion. Sponsored by De Monfort University, this Web site calls itself a "starting point for people looking for resources on the religion and culture of the Jains available over the Internet." Links are too numerous to mention all of them. Links include libraries housing Jain collections, to be searched index of Jain texts on the Sunsite gopher at UNC, Jain lists of homepages, as well as Internet resources in related areas.

◆ **Jainism**

http://dolphin.upenn.edu/~alok

The introduction explains the main teachings of the Jain religion and offers links to other Jain resources on the Internet. Links include Jain-list information, Jain-list archives, as well as World Wide Web Jain sites. The user can do a Lycos or Gopher search via one of the many links. One link is to Jain FTP sites.

◆ **Jainism: The Religion of the Jains**

http://www.cen.uiuc.edu/~jvshah/Jina/

This site explains that Jainism began in the sixth century B.C.E.. There are many interesting links such as Places of Jaina Pilgrimage in India, Jain Art From India, Concepts of God in Jainism, Jain Festivals, Jain Scholars and Research Center, and Jain Virtues. The Jain Database is also available from this site.

Sanskrit

◆ **Sanskrit Religions Institute**

http://www.sanskrit.org/

This homepage was developed by the Sanskrit Religions Institute of California. They are a nonprofit organization begun in 1995 to promote the development of Sanskritic-based religious organizations in the United States. They offer many services, such as Sanskrit language education and Hindu temple development. This site includes many Hindu-related sites, as well as links to Hare Krishna. Clicking on India: Languages and Scripts allows the user to choose from the many languages of this country. After clicking on a selected language, a history and description of the language is given.

◆ **WWW Sanskrit Directory**

http://www.lehigh.edu/~ksn2/sanskrit.html

This resource is a wonderful collection of Sanskrit related sites. The link, The ISB Sanskrit Index, contains eighteen Sanskrit documents including the *Bhagavad Gita*. Other links include *The Ramayana, The Mahabharata, Shrimad Bhagavad Geeta,* Other Scriptures, *Sanskrit Subhashit Sangraha,* the Sanskrit Homepage, and More Interesting Sanskrit Links. Electronic journals related to the study of Sanskrit and the Indology homepage can also be accessed through this site.

Sikh

◆ **Sikh Religion**

http://www.sikhs.org/

This site has a very unique design with visually pleasing graphics. There are no lists of links. Instead, the user clicks on icons to obtain further information about the Sikh religion. This site is constantly evolving. There are links to the Sikh alphabet, glossary, essays on Sikhism, Sikh bibliography, Sikh way of life, and the philosophy and scriptures of the Sikh religion. One interesting link shows Sikh photographs from the nineteenth century.

Yoga

◆ **Sivananda Yoga Vendanta Center**
http://www.sivananda.org/

This site features the Sivananda Yoga Vendanta Center, a nonprofit organization founded to spread the teachings of Vendanta and Yoga worldwide. The introduction promises "a wealth of Yoga information." The site offers links to information of proper exercise, proper breathing, proper diet, proper relaxation, meditation, karma and reincarnation, spiritual links, vegetarian Yogic recipes and much more. The user can click on French, Spanish, or German links to receive the information in other languages.

Zoroastrianism

◆ **Information About Zoroastrianism**
http://coulomb.ecn.purdue.edu/~bulsara/ZOROASTRIAN/
  zoroastrian.html

This is a very compressive site on Zoroastrianism. The introduction explains that Zoroastrianism is one of the oldest monotheistic world religions, tracing its beginnings between 1500 B.C.E. and 1000 B.C.E. Images of the prophet Zarathustra are presented in the introduction. Abundant links further describe this religion and include links to the Zoroastrian calendar, homepages of Zoroastrians, Zoroastrian mailing list, and much more information on Zoroastrianism.

SCIENCE AND TECHNOLOGY

Health

◆ **Ayurveda: National Institute of Ayurvedic Medicine**
http://www.niam.com/index1.html

The NIAM or National Institute of Ayurvedic Medicine sponsors this site. It is an interesting site about the goals and current research of this organization. There are links to information on medicinal plants as well as books related to the subject. NIAM is located in Brewster, New York. The research library of NIAM holds one of the largest collections of Ayurvedic literature in the United States. The collection is in Hindi, Sanskrit, English, Malayalam, Tamil and several more dialects. This site has a disclaimer that the information provided here is for historical note only. Individuals should not try to diagnose or treat themselves without the guidance of a licensed health professional. Many of these plants are poisonous and can be dangerous if not used properly.

OTHER

◆ **Visit India via Stamps**

http://www.cerc.wvu.edu/~rahul/stamps.html

This site is very unusual and for that reason does not fit well under any category. However, it is a site worth exploring. As the title suggests, the user can visit India via postage stamps. The visitor can click on a major season of the year, cricket legends, or classical dances to view beautiful stamps from India. Other links represent locomotives, famous people, and flora and fauna. There is also a link to news about stamps. A wonderful site for the stamp collector or anyone interested in viewing colorful images related to India.

Travel and Tourism

◆ **Bharat Samachar—Travel to India, Information**

http://www.bharatsamachar.com/tguide.htm

An excellent resource for the individual traveling to India. All aspects of travel are explained. Links include customs, passports, visas, airports, departure from India, health regulations, India by rail, and India by road. The Travel Guide link serves as an introduction and explains the major seasons of India and the weather conditions for the seasons are discussed. This site offers useful links to other travel related sites, such as business travel, golf, and wildlife.

◆ **India—The Country I Love the Most (Travel and Immigration)**

http://jan.ucc.nau.edu/~vdk/india/indtravel.html

This site offers helpful hints for traveling in India. Topics covered include hotels and resorts, customs and baggage, transportation information, tourism, and travel agent surveys and maps. Proper clothing selection for different weather conditions and hints on maintaining health while traveling are discussed. Immigration links are numerous and include the listings of the Indian Embassy and Indian Consulate in different countries. The site is updated frequently.

◆ **India Tourist Information**

http://www.qqq.com/india/

A very complete listing of information for anyone considering travel to India. The site gives information on hotels and accommodations, conference and convention facilities, wildlife sanctuaries and national parks, fairs and festivals, as well as travel connections to neighboring countries. The site covers general travel information, such as temperature and rainfall, as well as an explanation of different regions. This homepage is provided by the India Tourist Office located in Amsterdam, The Netherlands.

◆ **Wildlife in India**
http://www.meadev.gov.in/tourism/wildlifewildlife.htm

Children and anyone who enjoys viewing beautiful photographs of exotic animals will love this site. There are links to eleven of India's national parks as well as the Sarisha Tiger Reserve. There are 70 national parks and 411 sanctuaries established by the Indian government to protect this nation's valuable wildlife population. This site offers a taste of these sanctuaries and parks to the cyber-visitor.

10

Jewish American Resources
EMILY K. DUNSKAR

INTRODUCTION

The area of Jewish American information resources and organizations, cultural events, history, and the like is very broad, and the practice of Judaism is not the focus of this discussion, but it should be noted that while Jewish persons in the United States are not considered a race, but rather a group of people who possess a common religious heritage, and Jewish religious customs and rituals vary according to level of affiliation, be it Reform, Conservative, Orthodox, or Reconstructionist (to name a few). The diversity of Jewish religious observance leads to a wide variety of information sources and styles. For example, if one wished to access discussion groups on the role of Jewish women in America, the tenor and content of information from a traditionalist perspective, for example, from an Orthodox or Hasidic community, would differ from that derived from a liberal Reform or Reconstructionist perspective.

The highlight of this chapter is, naturally enough, the Religion section, which contains a short description of the major divisions of religious practice among Jewish Americans and their governing bodies and a section on holidays so that the reader may gain an overview of the Jewish calendar and how information relevant to all sites, regardless of level of observance, including information pertinent to culture, stories, songs, foods, and the like, center around the lunar calendar and observance of the Jewish holidays.

Perhaps the most comprehensive and well managed site for information on Jewish practice and culture is authored by Andrew Tannenbaum from Brookline, Massachusetts (Tannenbaum, 1997). This comprehensive subject directory is titled Andrew Tannenbaum's Judaism and Jewish Resources (**http://shamash.org/trb/judaism.html**). I began research on Jewish American resources via this page and added information by using several search engines and Jewish subject directories as well as links from Tannenbaum's original page. Comprehensive Jewish/Israeli subject directories that were used for further research include:

Virtual Jerusalem: The Jewish World from the Heart of Israel; **http://www.virtual.co.il/**.

Maven; **http://www.maven.co.il/**. More than 5,000 Jewish/Israel Links!

The Ultimate Jewish/Israel Link Launcher; **http://ucsu.colorado.edu/~jsu/ launcher.html**. Authored by Steve Ruttenberg from the University of Colorado.

IdeaNet Links; **http://www.geocities.com/Athens/Acropolis/2232/ idealink.htm#per**. By Avi Frierl; contains subject related links from the Geocities Web site.

The Jewish World Homepage; **http://www.thejewishworld.com/**. Includes links to family and women's centers.

GENERAL INFORMATION

◆ **Andrew Tannenbaum's Judaism and Jewish Resources**
http://shamash.org/trb/judaism.html

A project of the Hebrew College, this is a comprehensive listing of Jewish resources and links.

◆ **The Ultimate Jewish/Israel Link Launcher**
http://ucsu.colorado.edu/~jsu/launcher.html

Compiled by Steve Ruttenberg, this massive collection of over 4,650 Jewish and Israeli links also contains many interactible features.

Current Events

◆ **A. Engler's Jewish News Links**
http://www.libertynet.org/~anderson/newslist.html

Engler's page is an excellent source for daily or near daily news including links to Israeli newspapers, election results from the Israel Embassy in Washington, and the Israel Broadcasting Authority. There is also a section for Non-Daily Jewish News, Right-of-Center News, and Other Jewish News Sources.

◆ **Boston's Yiddish Voice on WUNR 1600**
http://world.std.com/~yv/

Boston's Yiddish Voice maintains a Web site for those primarily Orthodox Jews who still wish to receive Jewish news in Yiddish. If one has access to RealAudio, the Internet traveler may receive news in audio format from this site.

◆ **Israel Internet News Service**

http://www.iinsnews.com/

The Israel Internet News Service (IINS), also from the Virtual Jerusalem site, includes links to daily news headlines, as well as Science and Medicine, Computers and Hi-Tech, Weather, Special Reports, and Travel Israel. IINS offers a free subscription service to provide the latest breaking headlines directly to the subscriber's e-mail account.

◆ **JTA Page**

http://www.virtual.co.il/news/jta/

Virtual Jerusalem sponsors a JTA (Jewish Telegraphic Agency) page with a frames version of News at a Glance and a sidebar of links to Latest Stories, Mideast, Washington, International, American Jewry, Community News, Holiday Features, and the Full Daily Edition.

◆ **Southern Shofar**

http://www.bham.net/shofar/

The Southern Shofar boasts that it is the only southern on-line source of local and national Jewish news on the Internet. The latest edition at the time of this writing was June 1997 (vol. 7, issue 7). It contains an archives search engine and subscription information.

Newsgroups and Listservs

◆ **CyberCaje Online Discussions**

http://www.caje.org/discuss.htm

The Coalition for the Advancement of Jewish Education has compiled a list of online discussion groups on a variety of topics from B'nai Mitzvah, Tzedakah, and Yiddish to discussion of a Jewish perspective on sexual orientation.

◆ **Jerusalem One e-mail Lists**

http://www.jer1.co.il/city_services/lists/cat.htm

Jerusalem One has compiled an index of topic-related e-mail listservs. Topics include the following: Aliyah, Arts and Entertainment, Classifieds, Education and Students, Foreign Language and Culture, Jewish Organizations, News and Media, Politics, Policy and Government, Science and Technology, Torah and Judaism, Virtual Jerusalem, Virtual Sounds, and World Communities.

◆ **Jewishnet Global Jewish Information Network**

**http://mofetsrv.mofet.macam98.ac.il/~dovw//jw/1/
mail4.html**

Jewishnet publishes an unannotated list of listservs in alphabetical order from A–Z. This is a very comprehensive list of discussion groups. Lists are categorized alphabetically by topic on a preceding page (**http://jewishnet/lis.html**).

◆ **Liszt: Culture/Jewish**

http://www.liszt.com/select/Culture/Jewish/

The Liszt site categorizes sets of e-mail discussion groups by type and topic. Under Jewish/Culture, there are approximately seventeen listservs that cover topics such as parenting, music, travel, Jewish scouting, disease, and Holocaust sub-topics.

◆ **UAHC Other Resources**

http://shamash.org/reform/uahc/resc.html#grps

The Union of American Hebrew Congregations provides a listing of Internet discussion groups from their Web site. These discussions are focused on liberal practices and philosophies regarding the practice of Judaism.

◆ **USCJ Archives**

http://www.uscj.org/scripts/uscj/uscjarchive/

As Reform Jews have access to discussion groups aimed at liberal audiences, the United Synagogue of Conservative Judaism also maintains an archival site with discussion groups surrounding the practice of Conservative Judaism.

Newspapers, Magazines, and Newsletters

◆ **B'Tzedek's Online Journal/Magazine**

http://btzedek.co.il/

This online journal is devoted to Responsible Jewish Commentary. This is a liberal periodical that features rather outspoken writers on issues of Law, Philosophy and Theory, International Law, Natural Law and World History, The Value of Words, and Dialogue Between Arabs and Jews. This journal also includes an Art and Fiction section. Some of the articles that appear in the online edition may refer to the print version of the magazine.

◆ **The Forward**

http://www.forward.com/index.html

The Forward is an award-winning American-Jewish paper published in New York City devoted to Israeli and American-Jewish interests of all philosophical persuasions. Originally published in Yiddish, the paper credits itself for assisting thousands of Jews to escape from the Nazi holocaust, and having premiered dozens of award-winning Jewish authors such as Saul Bellow, Chaim Potok, Philip Roth, Elie Weisel, and Isaac Bashevis Singer.

- **Jerusalem Post Daily Internet Edition**

http://www.jpost.com/

The *Jerusalem Post Daily* provides a mirror site for the United States. Internet travelers may purchase back orders (last five years) on a CD-ROM disc for $39.95. Additionally, there is a search engine included on the page to search for articles from past editions. Sections include News, Business, Columns, Opinion, Tourism, Features, and Sports. The Internet version of the *Post* is supported by Pineapple out of San Francisco and Tel Aviv, located at **http://www.pineapple.net/**.

- **Jewish Bulletin Homepage**

http://www.jewish.com/

The *Jewish Bulletin Homepage, a Guide to Jewish Life in the San Francisco Bay Area,* is a weekly periodical published in hard copy and electronic form. The Bulletin covers issues relevant to national concerns and those topics pertinent to residents of Northern California. Articles cover relevant news (international, national, and local), Editorial and Opinion, Entertainment, Torah Thoughts, Cooking, and Life-Cycle Events, to name a few.

- **Jewish Family and Life: Homepage**

http://jewishfamily.com/

Jewish Family and Life is an online magazine devoted to issues relevant to Jewish American families of the 1990s. Articles of interest include how to pick a Hebrew day school, methods of dealing with attention deficit children, celebrations and holidays with family, recipes, and Bar and Bat Mitzvah planning and budgets. This is similar to a Jewish *Good Housekeeping* but slightly more substantive in content.

- **Jewish Post of New York Online**

http://www.melizo.com/jewishpost/

The *Jewish Post of New York* maintains this Web site that includes a Jewish Web Network News as well as a pull-down menu with selections of articles on Home, JWNN News, Features, News Articles, Business, Editorial, Judaica Online, and subscription and contact information. The site is published every two months.

EDUCATION

This section covers sites of interest to parents and children, then includes learning sources for adults and sites for Rabbinical Institutes. The reader should note that three languages are used in modern Jewish education: Hebrew, Yiddish, and English. The first may be studied as part of religious education, in preparation for Bar and Bat Mitzvah, and for training in modern conversational classes in anticipation of a trip to Israel. Yiddish is now predominantly used only in Orthodox communities; however, a sprinkling of the language is used as part of humor and modern colloquialisms.

◆ **Jewish/Israel Index**

http://www.maven.co.il/subjects/idx174.htm

Contains serveral screens listing Jewish education sites and Jewish studies sites. A related index from Maven involves study programs mostly from university environments (**http://www.maven.co.il/subjects/idx177.htm**).

Children's Learning/Teacher Resources

◆ **The CyberCaje—Homepage**

http://www.caje.org/

CAJE, The Coalition for the Advancement of Jewish Education, has always been known as one of the premier Jewish Educators organizations. The organization lists curriculum materials that may be e-mailed or faxed online. Pricing for the materials is nominal and CAJE members are entitled to eight lessons free of charge. Topics include Family Life, Arts, History, Prayer, Resources, Holidays, Bible, Early Childhood Education, Israel, School Leadership, Special Education, Jewish Living, Hebrew, and Jewish Values.

◆ **Holocaust Studies**

http://www.socialstudies.com/holo.html

An excellent source for a social studies curriculum and Web teaching sources on this topic. Developed by the Social Study School Service, this is an extensive site that includes materials appropriate to children and teens. Curricular materials relevant to this subject are accessible from prominent links on the homepage for this site.

◆ **Nurit Reshef's Funland**

http://www.bus.ualberta.ca/yreshef/funland/funland.html

Reshef's Funland is an interactive Web site that includes sound files and games for primary school age children. The author hails from the Talmud Torah School in Edmonton, Alberta, Canada. There are Word Match, Holiday Scramble, Alef Bet Puzzle, Wordsearch, Hebrew picture games, and Hangman games on Jewish concepts for kids ages kindergarten to sixth grade.

◆ **The Pedagogic Center**

http://www.jajz-ed.org.il/

The Pedagogic Center is the joint authority for Jewish Zionist Education. Their main menu includes links to Hebrew resources, Education Departments, Festivals, Study in Israel, Torah Education Department, as well as a list of important links to Jewish Education resources. The Education page located at **http://www.jajz-ed.org.il/jewdpt.html** is committed to Jewish Education and Culture in the Diaspora (locations outside of the state of Israel). Departments include an early childhood division, Zionist Century Timeline, IvritNet (Hebrew Net), The Hebrew Corner, and a Book Catalog.

◆   **Uncle Eli's Haggadah**

http://www.ucalgary.ca/~elsegal/Uncle_Eli/Eli.html

Uncle Eli's Haggadah is a hypertext interactive Passover Haggadah in rhyme for children. The narrative is a tongue in cheek depiction of a family's modern seder experience but still conveys the message of the holiday. The most recent version of the work requires a plug-in for a midi file. The author, Eliezer Lorne Segal, is a professor from the University of Calgary.

◆   **Virtual Jerusalem's Education**

http://virtual.co.il/education/education/

A rich resource for teachers and students alike is Virtual Jerusalem's Education page. Resources include Religious Study Centers, Resource Room, Theme Room, Education from a Jewish Perspective, Innovations, and Higher Education in Israel. A pull-down menu permits the user to select Sites in this Neighborhood where one can travel to various areas throughout Israel (using transliterated Hebrew names). This is an excellent resource for teachers. An excellent link for technology innovations is **http://www.virtual.co.il/education/education/4.htm** under the Innovations link.

◆   **World ORT Network**

http://www.ort.org/edu/edu.htm

World ORT Network sponsors an Education Division. ORT is an organization that promotes technology education and currently supports more than 260,000 students in over 60 nations. The International headquarters for ORT is located in London, England. This site contains the Education Page, featuring projects such as Navigating the Bible, an interactive tutor for Bar and Bat Mitzvah students, Computer Training Links, ORT Schools Curricula, and the Penpals project. There are additional links for Teachers, Kids, Question Services, Educational Conferences, and Schools On-line.

Resources for Adults

◆   **Aish HaTorah Discovery Page**

**http://www.discoveryseminar.org/cgibin/var/aishdisc/
    index2.htm**

http://www.aish.edu/cgibin/var/aish/welcome.htm

Aish HaTorah Discovery Page is written by a team of scholars, scientists, mathematicians, lawyers, physicians, and other professionals, and includes Rabbinical input. The founder, Rabbi Noah Weinberg, has compiled a series of online and weekend seminars on a diverse set of adult education and Jewish topics. The site sponsors project Shabbat Shalom, a listserv that will send you updates weekly with commentary on the Torah portion of the week (**listproc@shamash.org**). Potential subscribers may sign on to the service by writing to the above address and typing

subscribe shabbatshalom [Your Full Name]. The International Aish HaTorah: The Jewish Educational Experience page (the second Web address) provides a series of online classes somewhat different from the first address.

◆ **Bat Kol**

http://home.sprynet.com/sprynet/batkol/

Bat Kol is a feminist seminar program offered in Israel. Unaffiliated with any branch of Jewish studies, it is a multi-level study program that examines facets of social action, feminism, and traditional practice and recontextualizes the experience for seminar participants.

◆ **Jewish Learning**

http://www.maven.co.il/subjects/idx117.htm

Focuses on continuing education for adult students.

◆ **Judaism 101**

http://members.aol.com/jewfaq/index3.htm

Tracey Rich has created this basic guide to Judaism. This page is extremely user friendly and offers basic information on Jewish beliefs, languages, practices, people, places, and things. Very helpful in the frames version of this work, Ms. Rich has included a glossary of terminology that one can use as different sections of the material are accessed.

Rabbinical Colleges / Seminaries

◆ **Gratz College**

http://www.geocities.com/CollegePark/Quad/4177/

Gratz College is the oldest non-denominational graduate school of Jewish studies in the Western Hemisphere. Located in Melrose Park, Pennsylvania, the school offers graduate programs in Jewish education, Jewish librarianship, a Hebrew teacher's diploma, and a program in Jewish music in coordination with the Reconstructionist Rabbinical College.

◆ **Hebrew Union College**

http://www.huc.edu/

Hebrew Union College (HUC) is the Reform Rabbinical College affiliated with the Union of American Hebrew Congregations. With four branches, in Cincinnati, New York, Jerusalem, and Los Angeles, the school offers programs for Jewish educators, graduate degrees in religious studies, biblical archeology, a school for sacred music, and rabbinical degrees.

◆ **The Jewish Theological Seminary of America**
http://www.jtsa.edu/

This institution is the Rabbinical College for the Conservative movement. Located in New York, the graduate school offers rabbinical programs for ordination, cantorial programs and Jewish music, a College of Jewish studies, a joint program with Columbia University, and other listings. The site uses the Excite search engine to assist users in finding information available through this Web page.

FINE ARTS

◆ **American-Israeli Cultural Foundation**
http://aicf.webnet.org/

The American-Israeli Cultural Foundation is an organization committed to the promotion of Israeli arts and artists. This organization does not limit itself to the visual arts but includes music, theater, television and film media, dance, and the visual arts. AICF provides sponsorship and membership information as well as a calendar of events of upcoming concerts and shows throughout the United States.

Art

Visual Art

An excellent compilation of visual art sites can be found at Maven under the topic of Arts and Humanities. This site, Maven-Jewish/Israel Index (Art), includes approximately 51 links to galleries, individual artists' works, Ketubot (Jewish marriage certificates), exhibits, and museums. This site may be accessed at **http://www.maven.co.il/subjects/idx192.htm.**

◆ **Art Judaica**
http://www.artjudaica.com/vend/svend

Art Judaica is perhaps the largest virtual gallery available on the Internet. The gallery is organized alphabetically by artist, and e-mail and order information is available from this site.

◆ **Jewish Portraits**
http://www.jewish-portraits.com/

This is a gallery of portraits by European artists. The user may click directly on a portrait to access information on the price of a work, the artist, and the subject of the portrait. Less costly reproductions are also available; price and order information are provided on the page.

◆ **On-Line Holy Days Exhibition**

http://www.ort.org/community/benuri/holydays/tour_3.htm

The Illustrated Tour of Ben Uri Gallery is not one the Internet traveler should miss. The exhibit is located in London's West End and contains over 800 works by Jewish artists. Public domain reproductions in GIF format and organized by holiday can be downloaded.

◆ **VJ Feature: Artists' Showcase**

http://www.virtual.co.il/depts/artists/index.htm

Virtual Jerusalem features this Web page, VJ Feature: Artists' Showcase. These pages are organized into five galleries: Bible Series Covers, AVIV GEFEN Magazine, Campaign Ads, United Middle East, and All Sorts.

Dance

◆ **Avodah Dance Ensemble/Homepage**

http://www.artswire.org/avodah/

Avodah, whose name means "work" or "service," is a modern dance repertory dance-performance arts group rooted in Jewish tradition that presents repertory for Sabbath services, concerts, arts festivals, and educational programs out of Hebrew Union College in New York.

◆ **Israeli Folk Dancing**

http://www.israelidance.com/

Israeli Folk Dance is a site devoted to folk dance information including workshop and camp information, Online Dance Session Database, and links to other Israeli dance sites. The online database permits searchers to locate dance groups or sessions within their local vicinity.

◆ **Kesher LeMachol**

http://orion.webspan.net/~hgpklm/#Index

Kesher is a wonderful resource for those interested in Israeli folk dance. It features a compilation of Israeli dance resources. Included in this site is an index of dances listed alphabetically as well as instructions, song lyrics, discography of dance music, contact lists, and announcements of workshops, special events, and parties.

Music

For a general overview, The Jewish Music Homepage, sponsored by Tara Publications, is available at **http://www.jewishmusic.com/**. Included is a music store and RealAudio files of music samples. Additional links to related music sources are available that contain sources for Klezmer music, common prayer chants (Niggunim), a music list, and an entertainment page. A comprehensive list of music sites, much too numerous to list separately, is located at the following Virtual Jerusalem site: Maven, Jewish/Israel Index (**http://www.maven.co.il/subjects/idx196.htm**).

Klezmer Music

Klezmer music (sometimes spelled Klezamir) is based on traditional instrumental music from Yiddish-speaking Jewry in Eastern Europe. This music was especially popular at the turn of the last century in Romania and the Ukraine and was played extensively at weddings where Jewish musicians were unavailable or unaffordable. In the latter half of the 1970s and 1980s there was a revival of this music in the United States, and its popularity as an ethnic tradition continues to increase in the 1990s. Several bands have taken up residence on the Web. A list of Klezmer resources with concert information, comprehensive lists of Klezmer groups, and the like are posted at **http://www.maven.co.il/subjects/idx137.htm**.

◆ **The Hot Latkes**

http://www.execulink.com/~mstowe/klez.html

This band hails from London, Ontario and was formed in 1993. They claim to specialize in Klezmer and Yiddish theater music. The site has included links to learn more about the band and a means of contacting them directly.

◆ **Israel Zohar**

http://www.klezmer.co.il/

This site features a concert at the Philharmonic of Israel Zohar's music, performed by him with Itzhak Perlman and Zubin Mehta, and a quote from Good Morning Israel. Two buttons appear on this site; one to order a multimedia show or videotape of Zohar's performances, the other to order any number of compact disks of the artist's work.

◆ **Klezamir**

http://www.saturn.net/~dschrag/klezamir.html

This band originates from Massachusetts and specializes in Klezmer and Yiddish theater music. Additionally, they incorporate jazz, pop, and Israeli dances and other musical genres in their performances. They offer a school program in multicultural music lectures/performances. An audio clip is available from the site.

Sephardic Music

◆ **Shakshuka**

http://ourworld.compuserve.com/homepages/Shakshuka/

The Shakshuka Web page is one that advertises a Chicago-based group dedicated to the traditions of Sephardic music. The music features a blend of guitars, drums, and voice and a Landino sound that is slightly primitive.

HISTORY

Because this topic is so broad, I have included comprehensive links to indexes related to global world history for the Jewish people. The majority of listings are confined to American Jewish history, with a separate section on the Holocaust. For more extensive resources relating to the Holocaust and Jewish history, consult Maven's Index on the Holocaust and Anti-Semitism, at **http://www.maven.co.il/ subjects/idx178.htm**. Ruttenberg's Link Launcher has a complete index with five subcategories related to the Holocaust, Neo-Fascism, Black Anti-Semitism, and Anti-Zionism at **http://ucsu.colorado.edu/~jsu/antisemitism.html**.

◆ **American Jewish Historical Society**

http://www.ajhs.org/

Headquartered at Brandeis University in Waltham, Massachusetts, the Society's mission is to "foster awareness and appreciation of the American Jewish heritage and to serve as a national scholarly resource for research through the collection, preservation and dissemination of materials relating to American Jewish history" (**http://www.ajhs.org/mission.htm**). The site includes Genealogy Reference Services, Library and Archives, a Museum, and History Department. The Society publishes an online journal available at **http://control.press.jhu.edu/ press/tocs/ajh.html**.

◆ **Bloom Southwest Jewish Archives**

http://dizzy.library.arizona.edu/images/swja/swjalist.html

The Bloom Southwest Jewish Archives, from the University of Arizona, contains links to the history of Crypto Jewish Life. Crypto refers to people of the Southwest, in this case focusing on Jewish pioneer contributions to southwestern American history. An exhibit of Crypto Jewish life may be found at **http:// dizzy.library.arizona.edu/images/swja/crypto.html**.

◆ **Introduction/General Reading List: General Jewish History**

http://www.shamash.org/lists/scj-faq/HTML/rl/ gen-history.html

This is a bibliography of general history sources. The information is compiled from a series of citations from the Usenet newsgroup **soc.culture.Jewish reading list**.

◆ **The Jewish Genealogy Page**

http://www.genhomepage.com/jewish.html

The Jewish Genealogy Page lists various access points to genealogy societies around the United States and around the world. One can also subscribe to a list-serv related to Jewish genealogy via the following e-mail address: **listserv@mail. eworld.com**. To subscribe type in **subscribe jewishgen firstname lastname** to receive mail from the Jewish genealogy group. An archival list is also available from the newsgroup **soc.genealogy.jewish**.

◆ **Jewish Identity Link Launcher—Diaspora History**

http://ucsu.colorado.edu/~jsu/history.html#diahis

Steve Ruttenberg at the University of Colorado maintains a history page that contains general, American, and ancient and modern Israeli historical resources. The General History link is located at **http://ucsu.colorado.edu/~jsu/ history.html**. Look for American under the heading Diaspora History.

◆ **Jewish People in Winona**

http://wms.luminet.net/demographics/jewish/index.html

This site chronicles the history of the Jews in Minnesota. Linked sections for this site include The First Jewish Americans, First Jews in Minnesota, Why Did They Come?, The Jewish Religion and Culture in Winona in 1950, and the Jewish Religion in Winona today.

◆ **Jewish Studies, Tulane Manuscript Department**

http://www.tulane.edu/~lmiller/JewishStudiesIntro.html

Tulane University maintains a page devoted to Jewish Studies, including information relevant to a Southern United States perspective. The site is committed to historical contributions of Jewish men and women from the south, particularly New Orleans.

◆ **New York Public Library**

http://www.nypl.org/research/chss/jws/jewish.html

The New York Public Library has a section devoted to Judaism and Jewish history worldwide. Begun in 1897 by Jacob Schiff, by early in the 20th century, the library began to rival those of Jewish libraries throughout Europe. Menu selections from the NYPL include History, Collections, Rare Books and Periodicals, Preservation of a Legacy, Oral History, and the Years Ahead.

◆ **Project Judaica—American Jewish Projects**
http://www.newc.com/pj/global/usa.html
http://www.newc.com/pj/default.html

Project Judaica is a source committed to preservation of Jewish history on a worldwide basis. Projects include The Dead Sea Scrolls, Precious Legacy Exhibit, and Judaica Renaissance Exhibit, to name only a few. The section on American Jewish projects includes the Washington, D.C. project, the Washington Haggadah, West Point Torah Dedication, and Judaic Treasures of the Library of Congress.

Holocaust

◆ **The Holocaust: Background, Tragedy, and Aftermath**
http://www.csuchico.edu/~sedelman/

A course offering is available on the Holocaust from California State University, Chico. The authors, Dr. Carol Edelman and Dr. Sam Edelman, have provided an extensive set of links on Genocide, the Holocaust, Survivors, Resistors, Anne Frank, Auschwitz, and Teaching and Jewish resources.

◆ **March of the Living Homepage**
http://www.bonder.com/march.html

This is a "must see" page devoted to youths who tour various sites such as Warsaw, Cracow and Lublin. The tour begins with a march from various camp locations in Eastern Europe, Auschwitz to Birkenau on Holocaust Memorial Day and culminates in Israel on Israeli Independence Day and Holocaust Memorial Day.

◆ **Simon Wiesenthal Center—Homepage**
http://www.wiesenthal.com/

The homepage for the Simon Wiesenthal Center headquartered from Los Angeles is a wealth of information relating to the Holocaust and other discrimination issues.

◆ **Survivors of the Shoah Visual History Foundation**
http://www.vhf.org/

Founded by Steven Spielberg in 1994, Survivors of the Shoah Visual History Foundation is a nonprofit organization dedicated to videotaping and archiving interviews of Holocaust survivors all over the world. This site is a "must see" for all people interested in the abolishment of bigotry and prejudice.

LANGUAGE ARTS AND LITERATURE

Literature

◆ **Israel Judaica Children's Book Department**

http://www.macom.co.il/emporium/book_video/books.html

The Israel Judaica Children's Book Department online provides a reader's advisory of literature for children via its Web page.

◆ **J. Brill Publishers**

gopher://ns1.infor.com:4900/1.browse

J. Brill Publishers, Leyden, The Netherlands, presents their large catalog of Jewish and other theology books via Gopher resources at the address shown above.

◆ **Jewish American Literature Research Homepage**

http://omni.cc.purdue.edu/~royald/jewish.htm

Derek Royal, located at Purdue University, has compiled a Web page devoted to research in Jewish American literature. The site includes such authors as Woody Allen, Philip Roth, Grace Paley, E. L. Doctorow, E. M. Broner, Stanley Elkin, Cynthia Ozick, Art Spiegelman, and Joseph Heller.

◆ **Jewish Book News and Review**

http://www.ort.org/communit/jbook/start.htm

Jewish Book News and Review chronicles booksellers, libraries and readers of contemporary Jewish literature sources. The site is sponsored by the World ORT Union. Senior editors are Stephen Massil and Michael Daniels.

◆ **Jewish Folklore in Israel-Main Page**

http://www.tau.ac.il/~gila1/folklore/

This site is authored by Gila Gutenberg of Tel Aviv University and provides a number of links including books, periodicals, and folktale archives. Links to related sites at the top of the page include Folklore at the University of Haifa, Jewish Short Stories from Eastern Europe and Beyond, SHTETL-Yiddish Language and Culture Homepage, A Guide to Chabad Literature, and a variety of other Sephardic chants, music and literature links.

◆ **Jewish Short Stories from Eastern Europe and Beyond**

http://www.kcrw.org/b/jss.html

Jewish Short Stories from Eastern Europe and Beyond on the Web is available with celebrity actors such as Leonard Nimoy reading stories. One can listen to the stories with use of an audio plug-in program for either Windows or Macintosh formats. The entire audiocassette set is also available for purchase on nine cassettes from station KCRW.

◆ **Noah's Window—Welcome**

http://www.noahswindow.com/

Noah's Window is authored by Noah benShea, a poet, philosopher, columnist, scholar, and the author of *Jacob the Baker.* More information may be accessed about this talented author at the following: **http://www.noahswindow.com/noahbio.htm**. The Children's Broadcasting Corporation now features the author's column on AM radio stations listed at **http://www.noahswindow.com/noahinfo.htm#radio/**.

◆ **Notes from the Windowsill—Jewish Culture in Children's Books**

http://www.armory.com/~web/jbooks.html

This site is authored by Wendy Betts and contains a list of appropriate children's book about Judaism arranged by genre and age/grade appropriate content. This author reviews picture and chapter books on a variety of topics for Jewish children.

◆ **Stars of David**

http://www.the-stars-of-david.com/

This Web page features a Jewish science fiction series edited by D. J. Kessler, including two books in the first volume, *Can androids Be Jewish?* by Joe Sampliner, and *Miriam's World* by Sol Weiss.

POPULAR CULTURE

The Ultimate Jewish/Israel Link Launcher (**http://ucsu.colorado.edu/~jsu/cgi-bin/entertainers.cgi**) lists over 150 famous Jewish entertainers. The site conducted a poll to determine the "most noteworthy" of these and a number in brackets indicates how many votes each celebrity received. Ryan Colker's The Famous Jews Homepage (**http://grove.ufl.edu/~rmcolker/jews.html**) enables the user to access celebrities as though thumbing through an index.

Food and Drink

This topic encompasses everything from holiday recipes, traditional foods, and Jewish dietary laws to restaurants. For purposes of brevity, I have included general sites that contain lists of categorized links of resources. Maven's Food and Drink category can be found at **http://www.maven.co.il/subjects/idx186.htm**. This page lists 44 resources under this category. Three subsets of food and drink include Kosher-Kashrut, Recipes, and Restaurants. Virtual Jerusalem lists a set of recipes on their Kosher Kitchen page (**http://www.virtual.co.il.city_services/kitchen/index.htm**. Recipes are arranged by soups, meats, kugels and other side dishes, dairy dishes, salads, and desserts. A few of the sites are listed in this section.

◆ **The Chocolate Emporium**

http://www.choclat.com/

The Chocolate Emporium produces parve (contains no milk or meat product) chocolates and other kosher confections. The site features information to place special orders, view their online catalog, place an order, and the like.

◆ **Empire Kosher Chicken**

http://www.empirekosher.com/

Empire, one of the best-selling kosher products on the market, sponsors a visually elaborate Web page. A site map includes buttons for information regarding What makes chicken kosher?, a tour of the Empire facility, recipes, new products, and What is Kosher?

◆ **Foods of the Bible**

http://www.ariga.com/visions/biblfood/wheat.htm

Written by Phyllis Glazer, this site includes such recipes as The Seven Species: Wheat for butter, flat bread, unyeasted breads, wheat and chickpea salads and many more biblically derived recipes. Updated weekly from Tel Aviv, the reader may subscribe to an electronic mailing list for updates.

◆ **Gan Eden Wines Homepage**

http://www.ganeden.com/

Gan Eden Wines Homepage, a kosher California winery, has this beautiful Web site with order information, and background, as well as a photograph of the winery in Sonoma County's Green Valley.

◆ **A Great Miracle Happened There**

http://www.foodwine.com/food/egg/egg1296/eggsalad.html

Steve Holzinger has compiled a comprehensive Web page with Chanukkah recipes and background stories on the holiday.

◆ **Hagafen Wines**

http://www.nauticom.net/users/judaica/Hagafen/

Hagafen, whose name means "vine," is another California-based kosher winery located in the Napa Valley, owned by vintner Ernie Weir. His Web site features information on the company, a list of the wines they produce, Hagafen recipes, critical acclaim, and an ordering site.

◆ **Jewish Food Recipe Archives**

http://www.eskimo.com/~jefffree/recipes/

The Jewish Food Archives is written by Jeff Freedman from University Place, Washington and Linda Shapiro from Naples, Florida, and contains a compilation of kosher recipes, including a master index. Recipes are arranged according to Jewish classics such as briskets, bagels, blintzes, chopped liver and the like, holiday favorites, other goodies, and desserts.

◆ **Jewish Holiday Kitchen**

http://www.epicurious.com/e_eating/e06_jewish_cooking/ nathan_home.html

The Jewish Holiday Kitchen from Joan Nathan and Epicurious Foods was a challenge to find in the Epicurious index. This comprehensive site on traditional recipes and cooking from the author Joan Nathan is an excellent source of holiday recipes. Nathan has posted excerpts from her many books, including an introduction to the Jewish holidays, a Meet the Author section, and Holiday Recipes broken down by individual celebration.

◆ **Jewish/Kosher Foods**

http://www.cyber-kitchen.com/pgjewish.htm

Another comprehensive site for Jewish food and recipes including international Jewish foods and holiday cooking may be found at Mimi's Cyber-Kitchen Web site. Mimi may be contacted at the following e-mail address: **mimi@cyber-kitchen.com**. Included on her index of recipes titled Jewish/Kosher Foods, are California Cooks Kosher links, Ethiopian Jewish Cooking links, Foods of the Bible, Israeli recipes, *Kashrus Magazine,* as well as a special Passover section with lists of Usenet archived recipes.

◆ **Kosher Restaurant Database**

http://shamash.org/kosher/krestquery.html

Kosher Restaurant Database is maintained by the Shamash Project. The database uses a form for name, city, metropolitan area, state or province, country, and category including meat, dairy, or vegetarian.

◆ **Maven-Jewish/Israel Index—Recipes**

http://www.maven.co.il/subjects/idx187.htm

Included on Maven's Index are Chanukkah recipes, traditional Israeli recipes, kosher recipes from Asia, traditional foods for Passover and Rosh Hashana, and Yiddish recipes.

◆ **Old Jerusalem Trading Company**

http://www.oldjerusalem.com/

Old Jerusalem Trading Company is a kosher food emporium that targets upscale clientele interested in obtaining kosher gourmet foods. The company furnishes coffee, cookies, biscuits, salmon, and dressings as well as order information and related links.

- ◆ **Rokeach Food Distributors**

http://www.rokeach.com/

Rokeach, another popular distributor of convenience, frozen, and packaged kosher foods, has this Web site that contains a Product List, Company History, On-line Shopping, and New Product site maps.

- ◆ **Wines in Israel**

http://www.agmonet.co.il/wines/

Wines in Israel is a Web page devoted to lists of Israeli wineries compiled by Sasha Cooklin. Links include wine facts, wineries in Israel, wine review, vineyards, and wine and liquor stores.

Humor

- ◆ **Israelisms, the Lighter Side of an Intense Country**

http://israelisms.simplenet.com/index.htm

This site offers an Israeli humor magazine written in English. Menu options include Home, Photo Gallery, Jokes, Charley's Notebook, Articles, and Form. This author recommends the photo gallery for a very funny look at current political leaders in Israel and elsewhere.

- ◆ **The Jewish Humor List Homepage**

**http://www.jer1.co.il/city_services/lists/jewish-humor/
    index.htm**

The Jewish Humor List Homepage contains information about and a subscription form for this moderated discussion group intended to share Jewish humor with its members on a monthly basis. The moderator is Marty Weiss (**mweiss@virtual.co.il**) and a description of the listserv contains the following, "This list is published monthly, usually on the first of the month. It contains the best (and maybe the worst) of the jokes, riddles, anecdotes and funny stories about Jews, Jewish subjects and Israel that you, the reader, has submitted." A footnote reminds the potential subscriber that materials submitted must be clean and appeal to a family oriented group of subscribers.

- ◆ **The Joke a Day**

http://www.jer1.co.il/city_services/lists/joke-day/

This homepage is a link to a humor listserv moderated by Yaacov Weiss. The author will drop a Jewish joke per day into your mailbox should you wish to subscribe. Should the reader wish to subscribe, as in the previous list, one can click the mailbox on the page to subscribe easily to this list.

Music

Jewish pop music sites are found at **http://www.maven.co.il/subjects/ idx298.htm**.

Sports

- ◆ **Famous Jews—Competitors**

http://ucsu.colorado.edu/~jsu/cgi-bin/competitors.cgi

The Jewish Identity Link Launcher lists a page entitled Famous Jews— Competitors with a list of over 100 names of famous Jewish sports figures.

- ◆ **Jewish Communications Network (JCN)**

http://www.jcn18.com/scripts/jcn18/paper/ Index.asp?ColumnID=91

The Jewish Communications Network authors a complete listing of sports related articles, including Jewish participation in a variety sports such as boxing, baseball, basketball, hall of fame Jewish winners, horse racing, and football.

- ◆ **Maccabiah Games**

http://www.maccabiusa.com/

Each year the United States sends a team of Jewish athletes to Israel for athletic competition in the Maccabiah Games for two weeks. Athletic competition covers Master Sports, including Badminton, Basketball, Beach Volleyball, Fencing, Field Hockey, Golf, Gymnastics, Ice Hockey, Judo, Karate, Rowing, Rugby, Sailing, Soccer, Softball, Squash, Swimming, Table Tennis, Taekwando, Track and Field, Triathalon, Volleyball, and Wrestling. Updates on the winners may be accessed at **http://www.maccabiusa.com/final.HTM#masters**. Other events and participants include special Physically Challenged, Open, and Junior Sports competitions.

- ◆ **Maven-Jewish/Israel Index (Sports & Hobbies)**

http://www.maven.co.il/subjects/idx188.htm

Maven's Sports Index lists a comprehensive collection of sites related to this topic. Selections include the Israeli team at the Atlanta 1996 Olympics, Grand Slam Baseball Camp, International Jewish Sports Hall of Fame, and the Unofficial Israeli Athletics Homepage.

- ◆ **Mosaic Outdoor Clubs of America**

http://www.mosaics.org/

While not visually stunning, this page is still full of worthwhile information regarding outdoor activities, such as boating, backpacking, camping, running, tennis, and a variety of outdoor sports and recreational activities, that the Mosaic Outdoor Clubs of America offers for the American Jew. Events and camps are organized geographically, and the site is a must for families and singles who wish to participate in Jewish outdoor natural activities.

Television and Film

◆ **Films, Videos and TV Programs of Jewish Interest**
http://www.uidaho.edu/~mschreck/j-film-a.html

Though an older source (November 2, 1995), this is a good starting place to access a list of Jewish oriented films, videos, and television programs. Authored by Myron Schreck out of the University of Idaho, the index is arranged in alphabetical groupings.

◆ **Jerusalem On Line**
http://www.cyberscribe.com/jol/

This site features previews of shows of American-Israeli interest including information concerning cultural events in Israel, human interest stories, archeological finds and the like. The shows are broadcast across North America on a number of cable television stations. To view a list of coming attractions, click the map titled Latest Jerusalem On Line, then go back to the previous page to access a list of locations via the search engine for Where to View Jerusalem On Line.

◆ **Jewish Film Archive Online**
http://members.aol.com/jewfilm/index.html

The Jewish Film Archive Online provides an excellent resource on entertainment and educational films sorted by category or those released as of a particular year. The reader should first sort the films by category before proceeding on a full scale hunt for titles.

◆ **Kochavim36**
http://www.virtual.co.il/arts/kochavim/index.htm

Kochavim, which in Hebrew means "stars," is maintained by Virtual Jerusalem (**http://www.virtual.co.il**) and provides weekly updates on Jewish celebrities, television shows, and movies forthcoming. The author is Steve Walz, a member of TV Critics Association of America.

◆ **Maven-Jewish/Israel Index (Film)**
http://www.maven.co.il/subjects/idx199.htm

An extensive list of sites related to Jewish American films may be found at Maven's index of Jewish films. At the time of this writing, 25 sites were listed under this category.

RELIGION

Parsing out the relevant religion information sources and sites requires a brief overview of the four major Jewish philosophical schools of practice, that is, the Reform, Conservative, Orthodox, and Reconstructionist schools of religious practice. Each varies in its level of religious observance and interpretation of biblical and Talmudic law. One example of how philosophical orientation affects content pertains to the practice of Kosher laws. *Kashrut* or *Kosher* refers to the observance of Jewish dietary laws and may entail the use of separate dairy and meat dishes, the exclusion of pork and shellfish, and the separation of dairy products and meat-based recipes. Conservative, Orthodox, Hasidic, and some Reconstructionist groups still adhere as a group to the practice of kosher dietary laws. Reform Jews as a whole do not subscribe to kosher practice, and therefore Reform Jewish American sites that list traditional foods for the holidays may differ significantly from Orthodox or Hasidic Jewish American sites.

For those interested in basic Judaism resources, these may be found along with a subset of menus on Conservative, Orthodox, Reform, Reconstructionist, Hasidic and other resources from the Jewish/Israel Index (Judaism) (**http://www.maven.co.il/subjects/idx111.htm**).

◆ **Conversion to Judaism**

http://www.convert.org/

Larry Epstein, Ph.D., has written this Web page for those interested in becoming a Jew by choice. Because this process involves so much study about basic Judaism, this proves an excellent site for introduction to various Jewish levels of practice and the basic differences between Judaism and Christianity. Includes a guide to Jewish books and videos.

◆ **The Learner's Minyan**

http://members.aol.com/judaism/lm/index.htm

The Learner's Minyan provides very good introductory material as well as transliterated Hebrew prayers and songs for the neophyte synagogue member or those with little formal training in Hebrew or the order of the service. Written by Jordan Wagner, an active synagogue member in Newton, Massachusetts, and administrator of his shul, The Synagogue Survival Kit walks the reader through every aspect of introduction in the synagogue. Information pertaining to his book may be found at **http://members.aol.com/jordanleew/ssk/ssk.htm**.

◆ **The Torahnet Page**

http://shamash.org/reform/uahc/torahnet/

The Torahnet Page provides a wealth of opportunities to study weekly readings and Rabbinical commentary online. The page, authored by Eric Simon, draws from a cross-representation of levels of religious observance. Links include a variety of moderated listserv discussion groups, resources in Hebrew and

English, Talmud resources, Virtual Jerusalem sites, Chabad sites (ultra-Orthodox Eastern European, Hasidic practice), and sites for learning to read Hebrew and chant tropes online are listed on this comprehensive page.

Reform Judaism

Sometimes referred to as liberal Judaism, Reform Judaism differs from Orthodox practice in the assertion that Rabbinic law, which over the centuries has led to a set of firm religious practices and customs, is the result of human judgment. Reform Jews maintain that the "eternal" laws or customs and legalities are a result of cultural, historical, and geographical influences and are therefore malleable.

An excellent treatise on Reform Judaism and its guiding principles is located at the following Internet address: **http://shamash.org/reform/rj.html**. The presiding authority for Reform Jews is known as the Union of American Hebrew Congregations or UAHC, and is the official sponsor for the Reform treatise.

Conservative Judaism

The Conservative movement was founded in 1913 by Dr. Solomon Shechter, whose work evolved into the United Synagogue of Conservative Judaism. Conservative Jews adhere to the observance of a traditional Sabbath, including abstention from all work-related activities, driving, turning on and off of electrical appliances, lighting fires (cooking), and carrying, to name a few. Additionally, Conservative Jews adhere to the kosher dietary laws, encourage their children's attendance of parochial schools, and embrace an orientation towards observance of traditional Jewish laws and practices. The distinction between Reform and Conservative services rests in the latter's use of Hebrew (in contrast to Reform Judaism's adoption of the vernacular), longer services, the practice of keeping a traditional Sabbath, and adherence to Jewish dietary laws. A History page devoted to Dr. Shechter's work and the principles that guide Conservative Jews at the homepage for the United Synagogue can be located at **http://www.uscj.org/uscj01.html.**

Orthodox Judaism

The term Orthodoxy in the Jewish religious context was used by early Reform Jews to denote those who held unwavering faith that Rabbinic and biblical law and practice was unquestionably Divinely inspired. Orthodox Judaism is varied in its forms and includes the Hasidic movement and Mitnaggedim as well as those from both Ashkenazic and Sephardic traditions. One unified belief held by Orthodox Jews is that the revelation of the Law at Mount Sinai, as described biblically, is an accurate historical account and the Rabbinic laws derived through this event, from both oral and written traditions, were to be followed as the word of God. In contrast to Reform and Conservative practice, Orthodox practitioners see laws as immutable and binding throughout all times. Orthodox Jews oppose proselytizing, musical accompaniment at services, mixed seating of genders during religious services or events, and divergence from the Jewish dietary laws, and strictly adhere to the Rabbinic laws for keeping the Sabbath (abstention from cooking, driving, use of electricity, carrying, etc.).

The Orthodox Union is one of the principal presiding bodies of modern Orthodoxy in the United States. Its Internet address is **http://www.ou.org/**. A fact sheet about the number of synagogues affiliated with this organization can be found at **http://www.ou.org/about/**.

Reconstructionist Judaism

Reconstructionism was founded in the United States by Mordecai M. Kaplan and is a form of dynamic traditionalism. The Reconstructionist movement resembles that of Conservative Judaism in practice but differs from its philosophical tenets in terms of the context in which Jewish practice occurs. The nature of faith is perceived as an outcome of people's search for meaning and can only be fully attained through study and inward meditation as to the nature of God. Rooted in tolerance and respect for individual diversity, Reconstructionist Jews embrace all forms of Judaic practice. Unlike the Orthodox view that the account of the laws given at Mount Sinai is immutable, Reconstructionism views Judaism from a sociological perspective. An excellent essay on the philosophical foundations of this Jewish-American movement by Shulewitz is found at **http://shamash.org/jrf/whorrcon.html**. Another excellent treatise on Reconstructionism is presented by Or Hadash, a Reconstructionist Congregation of Fort Washington, Pennsylvania, at **http://libertynet.org/~orhadash/recon.html**.

Sephardic and Ashkenazic Jews

A distinction between Sephardic and Ashkenazic Jewish heritage has existed since the mid-ninth century. Sephardic Jews are those whose ancestry originates from Spain and the Iberian peninsula, the descendants of those ancestors being known as Sephardim. The Sephardic community has come to be associated with Jews from the Southern Mediterranean region of Europe, North Africa, and the Middle East following the expulsion of Jews from Spain during the Inquisition in 1492. Ashkenazic Jews are those whose descendants are essentially Franco-German in their heritage. The term has been generalized to represent those Jews who come from Western Europe and who subscribe to a set of unified customs, ritual, and law that differ from their Sephardic counterparts.

Glossary of Terms

An excellent Web source of Jewish terms, compiled by Robert A. Kraft of the University of Pennsylvania, is located at **http://philo.ucdavis.edu/Courses/RST23/gloss.html**. Indicated on the page are sets of tags that refer the reader to a bibliographic reference and derivation of the language, and the appropriate referent to the religious term.

The Holidays and the Jewish Lunar Calendar

Hebrew Calendar

The Hebrew calendar, unlike its Western Christian counterpart, comprises 12 months with an additional 13th month added for leap year. Correspondence to the Christian calendar is a complicated process because the lunar months base the length of the month as approximately 29 days. In order to make up for the discrepancy (11 days) between 354 days on the 12 month lunar calendar and 365 days in the solar calendar, a 13th month named Second Adar or Adar II is added over the course of a 19-year cycle. To account for additional discrepancies between the solar and lunar forms of the calendar, some months are deemed "defective" and contain 29 days, while others are "full" or 30 days long.

Fortunately there is an ample supply of software and English-Hebrew calendars available through bookstores, synagogue bookshops, and Internet resources. One such conversion Internet resource, published by the Jewish Communication Network, is located at **http://www.jcn18.com/holiday/index.html**. To convert a given date, one selects a month from a pull-down menu, and a Hebrew calendar corresponding to the English one will be calculated for the user. Additionally, B'nai B'rith, an interdenominational Jewish organization, publishes a Web-based calendar with English/Hebrew dates of the holidays from 1996 through 2006. The location of this useful URL is **http://bnaibrith.org/caln.html**.

Holidays

For an excellent and concise overview of the holidays one can access the following Web site: **http://www.jewish.com/resource/ch2.htm**. Additional readings in bibliographic form may be accessed at **http://www. shamash.org/lists/scj-faq/ HTML/rl/tra-year.html**.

The following sources are relevant to Jewish holiday information.

◆ **Around the Calendar**

http://www.ucalgary.ca/~elsegal/Shokel/ Calendar_Index.html#RH

http://www.ucalgary.ca/~elsegal/Shokel/ 950330_Rest_Days.html

Eliezer Segal, a professor from the University of Calgary, has reproduced noteworthy articles on Jewish topics from two Calgary newspapers, *The Jewish Star* and *Jewish Free Press*.

◆ **Calendar of Jewish Holidays**

http://bnaibrith.org/caln.html

A calendar and description of the Jewish holidays from 1996 to 2006 is published by the B'nai B'rith Organization.

◆ **Jerusalem Post of New York: Judaica Online**

http://www.jewishpost.com/judaica.html

http://www.jewishpost.com/festivals/

A link from here provides information on a variety of Jewish American interests. Select Jewish Holidays and Festivals on the Net to access a rich array of information sources pertinent to celebrations of the holidays.

◆ **Mordechai Torczyner's WebShas**

http://www.virtual.co.il/torah/webshas/yomtov.htm

A comprehensive site that is part of the Virtual Jerusalem Web pages. Includes links organized under four major topics: The Calendar, Specific Holidays, Topics in Celebration of Holidays, and Work Forbidden on Certain Holidays.

◆ **Traditional Liturgy, Practice, Lifestyle: Holidays Reading List**

http://shamash.nysernet.org/lists/scj-faq/HTML/rl/
   tra-year.html

Good bibliography of reading material relevant to Traditional Liturgy, Practice, Lifestyle, and Holidays from the Usenet newsgroup **soc.culture.Jewish** reading list.

◆ **YomTov**

http://www.torah.org/learning/yomtov/index.html

Written by Rabbi Yehuda Prero, this site offers an Orthodox perspective on celebration of the holidays. This page is sponsored by the Global Learning Network. Good traditional source of materials about the holidays.

SCIENCE AND TECHNOLOGY

◆ **Maven-Jewish/Israel Index (Science & Technology)**

http://www.maven.co.il/subjects/idx202.htm

Maven has compiled a wealth of science and technology resources in this index. Some of the sites include: Hadassah College of Technology, Israel Arts & Science Academy, Israel National Museum of Science, Israel Science Museum, *Israel Technology Newsletter, Independent Newsletter* with information on technology investment opportunities, and Israel Technology Resources.

◆ **Virtual Jerusalem: Science and Technology Department Homepage**

http://www.virtual.co.il/depts/science/index.htm

This magnificent site includes a directory of Jewish technology resources. As of the time of this writing there was a feature article on Internet World Israel, an exhibit in Jerusalem's Convention Center under their Monthly Features Section, Mini-Feature Archives, Famous Jewish Scientists, and a set of related sites.

Health

* **Maven-Jewish/Israel Index (Hospitals & Medicine)**
http://www.maven.co.il/subjects/idx203.htm

Maven lists approximately 53 links related to medicine, physicians' cooperative services, disease control, and medical ethics, as well as hospitals across the United States, Israel, and some countries of Europe.

Information Technology and Telecommunications

* **Jewish Resources in Computer Networking**
http://jewishnet.net/jewish96.html

This site provides the following links relevant to those interested in Internet resources of a Jewish nature. The following is a list of categories of links on the homepage: The Net, Network Tools, Hebrew in the Net, Libraries, E-mail Lists, Newsgroups, Jewish Networking, The Global Jewish Information Network, Areas of Interest, Chat Modes, Across Borders, and Bibliography.

* **Maven-Jewish/Israel Index (Computers & Internet)**
http://www.maven.co.il/subjects/idx154.htm

Good set of cross-referenced materials on Internet resources, FTP sites, Gopher sites, Hebrew for Netscape, HPCU (High Performance Computing Unit), History of Jewish Internet, Jews and Computers, to name a few of these links.

OTHER

Exhibits

Many of the museums listed here are located in Israel or Europe but sections of the collections are able to be previewed via the Internet. For a more comprehensive list, see Andrew Tannenbaum's site at **http://shamash.org/trb/judaism.html#mus** and Maven's resources at **http://www.maven.co.il/subjects/idx170.htm**. Museum lists may also be found on Jewish/Israel Culture—Link Launcher at **http://ucsu.colorado.edu/~jsu/culture.html#museum**.

* **Arta Gallery, the Chagall Exhibit**
http://www.logotime.com/arta/

Arta Gallery has an exclusive contract with the estate of Marc Chagall to reproduce the artist's Judaic artifacts on the Internet. The collection includes lithographs, serigraphs, mezuzot, candle sticks, and kiddush cup, and a Gallery of Personalities.

◆ **Chagall Windows**

http://www.md.huji.ac.il/special/chagall/chagall.html

Located in Hadassah Hospital in Israel, Chagall created 12 windows, each portraying a Tribe of Israel

◆ **Chaim Goldberg Virtual Museum**

http://www.chaim-goldberg.com/

Actual museum site is in Boca Raton, Florida. This site, sponsored by the Jewish Institute for the Arts, features the works of Chaim Goldberg. Born in 1917, Goldberg is considered one of the premier Jewish-American artists of our time. One may tour the Virtual Museum by Theme or Media.

◆ **Cybrary of the Holocaust**

http://remember.org/

A comprehensive list of resources dedicated to all victims of the Shoah, both Jewish and non-Jewish. The links are too numerous to mention here. There are several sites mapped on the homepage that categorize resources by topic: Education, Witnesses, Books by Survivors, Children of Survivors, Teacher's Guide, Imagine, and Images.

◆ **Dead Sea Scrolls—An Exhibit at the Library of Congress, Washington, D.C.**

http://sunsite.unc.edu/expo/deadsea.scrolls.exhibit/ intro.html

Reproduction of Dead Sea Scrolls, information on the ancient Qumran Library, the Qumran Community, and the relationship of the Scrolls to modern scholarship.

◆ **Israel Museum & Gallery Listing**

http://www.update.co.il/gallery/gallery.html

Geographically organized exhibits include directories from Tel Aviv, Jerusalem, Haifa, Abroad, and Online.

◆ **Israel Museum, Jerusalem**

http://www.imj.org.il/

This is the official National Museum of Israel. A virtual tour complete with site map is located at **http://www.imj.org.il/main.html**. Exhibits include an art wing, archeology room, youth wing, Judaica and ethnography.

◆ **Jerusalem Mosaic**

http://www1.huji.ac.il/jeru/jerusalem.html

This site provides a tour of Jerusalem past and present. Two links are presented, the Old Jerusalem Mosaic and the New. Travel the city through the different periods, meet the people, taste the food, enjoy the special costumes and visit the sites.

◆ **Jewish Museum New York**

http://www.jewishmuseum.org/

Chronicles 4,000 years of Jewish history. This site is still under construction but previews promise informative and visually exciting Web pages.

◆ **Museum of Tolerance**

http://www.wiesenthal.com/mot/

Located at the Wiesenthal Museum, the mission of the Museum of Tolerance is to eradicate bigotry and prejudice throughout the world.

◆ **Nahum Goldman Museum of the Jewish Diaspora—Bet Hatefutsoth**

http://www.bh.org.il/

Stunning Web site that includes images of faces with visual effects within a television screen. This site features genealogy, exhibits, photographs, education, communities, music, and family names all dedicated to the history of the Jewish people in the diaspora (outside of Israel). The Virtual Exhibit features Jewish communities living presently in Arab lands and includes breathtaking photographs.

◆ **The Project Judaica**

http://www2.judaica.org/pj/

The Project Judaica is an organization devoted to the preservation of Jewish artifacts, literature, culture, and art and sponsors traveling exhibits throughout the United States. The focus of the efforts has been to restore Judaica from the Czech Republic and Poland. Projects include the Dead Sea Scrolls exhibit, a Renaissance Gallery, and a Precious Legacy Exhibit to name a few.

◆ **United States Holocaust Memorial Museum**

http://www.ushmm.org/index.html

Located in Washington, D.C., the museum attempts to reenact as much as possible the horrors of the Holocaust. An aerial view of the exhibit portrays a train that carried many to their deaths. Additional links from the homepage include Archive of Historic Photographs, Nazi Olympics 1936, Excerpts from the Official Nuremberg Trial, including doctors' reports and photographs.

Organizations

◆ **American ORT**

http://www.aort.org/

Founded over 100 years ago, ORT is an acronym for the original Russian name, Obschestvo Remeslenovo i. zemledelcheskovo Trouda. The purpose of ORT is to provide communities in industrialized countries with technological education. ORT offers instruction in such areas as agriculture, road mainte-nance, family health care, science, and technology development. This site offers links to other valuable ORT sites and Shamash, the Jewish Internet Consortium.

◆ **The Anti-Defamation League**

http://www.adl.org/

Founded in 1913 to fight anti-Semitism through programs and services that counteract hatred, prejudice and bigotry. The mission of the ADL is "to stop the defamation of the Jewish people and to secure justice and fair treatment to all citi-zens alike." The headquarters for the Anti-Defamation League is in New York City. Thirty-two regional and satellite offices provide services around the country.

◆ **B'nai B'rith**

http://bnaibrith.org/

An international organization, half a million strong, that has met the chang-ing needs of the Jewish community for over 150 years. B'nai B'rith members are dedicated to making a difference, today and tomorrow, for the family, for the community and for the Jewish people. B'nai B'rith's mission is to support Israel and community services, political activities, social groups, youth groups and senior centers.

◆ **B'nai B'rith Youth Organization**

http://bnaibrith.org/bbyo/index.html

BBYO is a youth-led, worldwide organization that provides opportunities for Jewish youth to develop their leadership potential, a positive Jewish identity and commitment to their personal development. Links to the following sites are available from this Web page: Summer Programs, BBYO University, March of the Living, International Leadership Study in Israel (ILSI), Young Leader-ship Development Program, Parent Teen Dialogue, College Ambassador Alumni Program, BBYO TASC—Teens Actively Serving Communities, Actively Concerned Teens (ACT) Network, BBYO Holocaust Expression Theatre, and Advisor Certification Program.

◆ **Hadassah**

http://www.hadassah.org/

Hadassah is a Zionist organization predominantly for women. The Youth Division sponsors camp programs and a leadership program for young women. The Young Judea program has its own Web site and summer camp programs that may be accessed via the Hadassah homepage.

◆ **Hillel**

http://hillel.org/

Founded in 1923, Hillel is the base of Jewish community on over 400 college campuses nationwide. This Jewish campus organization has foundations and affiliates in the United States, Canada, Israel, Australia, Europe and South America. This site includes information on the History of Hillel, student departments, conferences, calendar of events, accreditation and publications.

◆ **Jewish Defense League**

http://www.jdl.org/

The Jewish Defense League is the most controversial of all Jewish organizations. Founded in 1968, this activist group has been responsible for bringing such issues as Soviet Jewry, Nazi war criminals, black-and-white anti-Semitism/Jew-hatred and Jewish self-defense to the front page of every major newspaper.

◆ **Jewish Defense Organization**

http://www.jdo.org/

The stated goal of the JDO is to fight back against anti-Semitism in all of its forms. The JDO sponsors self-defense programs "to make sure the strong Jewish brain is backed by a strong Jewish body." Includes links to hate groups, Holocaust sites, other Jewish organizations, youth groups, newspapers and politics, among other topics.

◆ **The Jewish Singles Connection**

http://www.thejewishpeople.org/

This Web site provides information on Hillel groups on campuses, travel opportunities, and Jewish groups and Jewish publications. This site, designed for adults aged 20–40, is a good resource for social and political organizations and information.

◆ **The Jewish War Veterans (JWV) of the USA**

http://www.penfed.org/jwv/home.htm

The Jewish War Veterans (JWV) of the USA, organized in 1896 by Jewish Veterans of the Civil War, is the oldest active national veterans' service organization in America. The purpose of this organization is to provide historic documentation of the contributions of American Jewish men and women to the military forces throughout the history of the United States.

◆ **Mazon: A Jewish Response to Hunger**

http://www.shamash.org/soc-action/mazon/

Founded in 1985, Mazon (the Hebrew word for food) has been raising funds to provide for those who are hungry and to help alleviate the poverty that causes hunger. Mazon funds food banks/food pantries in inner cities and rural areas; kosher meals-on-wheels programs for homebound elderly people; multi-service centers that provide poor, hungry and homeless families with food, shelter and counseling; state and national organizations that conduct research and education activities and work for the kind of public policies that can bring about long-term solutions to hunger.

◆ **National Conference of Synagogue Youth**

http://www.ou.org/ncsy/

NCSY is a multi-faceted, educational Jewish youth organization in North America that fights assimilation by offering programs to bring Jewish teens back to their heritage. It is open to all Jewish youth regardless of background and affiliation and offers social and educational programming in hundreds of communities across the U.S. and Canada. This Web site is a great place to learn about NCSY's programs and projects.

◆ **North American Federation of Temple Youth**

http://shamash.org/reform/nfty/

Founded in 1939, NFTY is the branch of the Union of American Hebrew Congregations devoted to Jewish youth. NFTY "works to instill Jewish identity, foster commitment to the ideals and values of Reform Judaism, and increase synagogue participation in high school youth." Visitors to this site can explore the following areas: What Is NFTY, What Are NFTY's Purposes and Values, What NFTY Is Committed To, Local Youth Groups, The Region—Your NFTY Neighbors, The North American Office—What NFTY Has to Offer and Where Is NFTY.

◆ **United Jewish Appeal**

http://www.uja.org/

The United Jewish Appeal was created in November 1938 and represents the unity of the Jewish people and the responsibility of one Jew for another. UJA is the primary fundraising organization for the United Israel Appeal, which distributes funds to the Jewish Agency for Israel, and the American Jewish Joint Distribution Committee. UJA enhances Jewish federation and independent community campaigns with consultation services, overseas missions, solicitation opportunities, marketing and communication support, public relations, national constituent groups, leadership development, and networking among lay and professional leaders.

◆ **The United Synagogue of Conservative Judaism**

http://www.uscj.org/index.html

Founded in 1913, this Jewish organization serves as a resource to its affiliated congregations and works to devise a formula for Conservative Jewish responses to important social and religious issues. United Synagogue encompasses approximately 800 affiliated congregations, representing some 1.5 million members.

◆ **United Synagogue Youth**

http://uscj.org/usy/

USY is an affiliate of The United Synagogue of Conservative Judaism, offering Jewish high school aged teenagers a wide range of social, educational and religious activities. Includes links to USCJ homepage and the Jewish Communication Network.

◆ **Young Judea**

http://www.youngjudaea.org/

The Young Judea Web site is a visually stunning site complete with sections entitled Roadside Stories, Learn Hebrew, Souvenir Shop, Stuff to Do, and a Welcome Center.

◆ **Zionist Organization of America**

http://www.zoa.org/

Founded in 1897, the Zionist Organization of America is one of the biggest and oldest pro-Israel organizations in the United States supporting the re-establishment of a Jewish State in Israel. Today, it has over 50,000 members in active chapters throughout the U.S. and works to strengthen American-Israeli relations through educational activities, public affairs programs, support for pro-Israel legislation on Capitol Hill, and combating anti-Israel bias in the media, textbooks, travel guides, and on campuses.

11

Resources for Americans of Middle Eastern and North African Descent

ALICIA BARRAQUÉ ELLISON AND THOMAS KEENE

INTRODUCTION

The regions and countries that constitute the part of the world generally known as the Middle East and North Africa are a matter of some debate. People of diverse cultures, ethnic backgrounds, and religions or religious sects, are found throughout those parts of Eastern Europe, Southwest Asia and Africa that have from time to time been referred to as Middle Eastern, but one or both of two unifying factors bond these diverse peoples: Arabic language (or in cases where Arabic is not spoken, Arabic script) and/or Islamic religious and cultural tradition.

Reference sources, both print and electronic, vary widely in their listings of Middle Eastern and North African countries. Internet searches using terms such as Near East and Mideast yield different results from Middle East. Sometimes, these subjects are grouped under the term, Asian Studies. Other terms can be the names of specific regions, such as Levant and Maghreb, or of ethnic groups, such as Berber, Kurd, and Assyrian.

For purposes of this chapter, we have focused on the following countries: Algeria, Bahrain, Egypt, Iran, Iraq, Jordan, Kuwait, Lebanon, Libya, Morocco, Oman, Palestine, Qatar, Saudi Arabia, Syria, Tunisia, United Arab Emirates, and Yemen. Israel was not included, as this country is covered in the chapter on Jewish American resources. Certain other countries and cultures of Asia Minor and Eastern Europe, such as Turkey and that of the Kurds (of the region of Turkey, Iran, and Iraq known as Kurdistan), which are often grouped with the Middle East and North Africa, are also not covered specifically in this chapter, but readers should be aware that many of the comprehensive resources listed in this chapter contain links to sites about—or located in—countries that are not covered in this chapter.

Efforts have been made to list resources that are representative of the ethnic and religious diversity of the region. For example, religion resources cover various Islamic traditions, as well as other faiths, such as Baha'ism and various forms of Eastern Christianity. Islam, which pervades the entire region, is covered in some depth, but non-Islamic religions are covered in this section as well. Resources are included that represent non-Arab groups such as Berbers, Kurds and Assyrians.

"Authoritative" resources, that is, those supplied by U.S. and Middle Eastern governments, international organizations, and universities, are given preference. Many university-sponsored World Wide Web sites are included because, aside from offering information about their academic programs in Middle Eastern/ North African studies, they include excellent "libraries" of links. The chapter favors WWW sites that are updated frequently, contain internal and/or external search engines, and have e-mail links to the Webmaster. A number of personal homepages by nationals from the subject countries are also included. These generally provide good links to other resources about their countries, intimate views of these countries, and the opportunity to establish e-mail contact with nationals. Efforts have been made to include, when available, resources other than WWW pages, such as mailing lists and newsgroups. Gophers and ftp sites tend to be included in the best, comprehensive sites.

Where appropriate, resources have been separated into two subsections within each major topic area or category—a general or regional subsection and country-specific subsection—to provide wide subject coverage for the region as a whole, while still allowing the user to target specific countries. Under the regional subsection for each topic, comprehensive resources are listed that give broad coverage to all the countries listed above. The topics and subdivisions are consistent with the rest of the chapters in this book. The specific country subsections for each topic follow the regional subsections. Some topics do not include a specific country subsection (e.g., Religion).

The level of a country's connectivity and technological advancement, as well as cultural factors, may influence the number and type of resources provided. However, though certain countries may be less-developed overall, educated individuals from those countries, instilled with national pride, are making sure that their cultures are well-represented on the Internet. The rise of nationalism and the resurgence of Islam contribute to a growing Middle Eastern presence on the Internet. The only obstacle seems to be the lower technological level and meager connectivity within the countries themselves, a condition that is rapidly changing.

GENERAL INFORMATION

Regional

◆ **Al-Mashriq—Levant Cultural Multimedia Servers**

http://almashriq.hiof.no/

A master collection of cultural, historical, commercial and political resources relating to the region. Cinema, cosmetics, food, as well as maps and archaeological sites.

◆ **Arab.net**

http://www.arab.net/

Owned by ArabNet Technology (ANT), part of the Saudi Research and Marketing Group, publisher of Saudi newspapers and magazines. Contains Links to History, Geography, Business, Culture, Government, Transport, Tourism, and Country Pages, as well as links to many other ANT sites, mostly commercial and financial.

◆ **ArabSeek**

http://www.arabseek.net/

Sponsored by the Bahrain Promotion and Marketing Board, this is an index of Web sites located in or pertaining to Arab countries in the Middle East/North Africa and includes links to: Middle East Sites; Publishers; Chambers of Commerce; Universities; Dialing Codes; Banks; and Libraries. Each topic is subdivided by country.

◆ **Assyria On-Line**

http://www.aina.org/aol/

Modern descendants of the Semitic inhabitants of ancient Mesopotamia, today northern Iraq. Many live in Europe and America, but the majority are in Iraq, Syria, Turkey, and Lebanon. Many links to language, culture, religion (various Christian churches: Nestorian, Jacobite and Chaldean Church of Babylon), and history.

◆ **Background Notes: Middle East & North Africa, U.S. Dept. of State**

http://www.state.gov/www/background_notes/ neabgnhp.html

Contains information on geographic regions and international organizations, updated periodically. Click on Middle East and North Africa to get a list of countries. Country information includes brief entries on people, history, government, economy, foreign relations, and travel.

◆ **CIA World Factbook**

http://www.odci.gov/cia/publications/nsolo/wfb-all.htm

Contains facts, figures, and maps, per region/country. Searchable by topic, region and download selectors. Downloadable World Factbook text, flags, maps. Includes vital statistics on people, government, geography, economy, transportation, communication, and defense.

◆ **Middle Eastern Studies**

http://www.music.princeton.edu/chant_html/east.html#meg

From the Chant page of the Princeton University Music Department, this is an excellent collection of links to mostly university-sponsored or scholarly megasites.

◆ **Model League of Arab States**

http://192.203.180.62/index.html

Sponsored by the National Council on U.S.-Arab Relations, with support from the Arab League Information Center and the U.S.-Arab Chamber of Commerce, this site aims at providing links to information regarding all nations of the Arab League, Arab world, and non-Arab countries of interest. Information provided spans culture, language, politics, business, human rights, technology, travel, etc.

◆ **Saud El-Hajeri's Arab Countries WWW Sites**

http://www.liii.com/~hajeri/arab.html

This site is maintained by Saud Al-Hajeri, a Kuwaiti national, and contains lists of newspapers, Arab and Arab-American organizations, companies and commercial services in the Middle East, Arabic computing, language, calligraphy, recipes, and more. Regional and subdivided by country.

◆ **University of Durham (UK), Centre for Middle Eastern and Islamic Studies**

http://www.dur.ac.uk/~dme0www/

A launchpad to a good variety of resources, including Middle East studies Web sites provided by universities worldwide; Middle Eastern news sources on the Internet; general information about the region; the Middle East Peace Process; Middle East water; and regional and country-specific homepages.

◆ **University of Pennsylvania African Studies**

http://www.sas.upenn.edu/African_Studies/Home_Page/AS.html

This site contains individual country pages for various African countries, including Algeria, Egypt, Libya, Morocco, and Tunisia. Each country page includes maps, U.S. State Department Travel Advisories, Embassies, CIA World

Factbook entries, and many other resources covering all aspects of life in these countries. Different resources linked than from UPenn's MEC pages.

◆ **University of Pennsylvania, Middle East Center**

http://mec.sas.upenn.edu/

This excellent resource contains links to Middle East Organizations, Networks, Associations & Information, Miscellaneous Middle East Sites, and Countries. Individual pages are provided for all countries covered in this chapter. Different resources linked for countries covered by University of Pennsylvania's African Studies page.

◆ **University of Texas MENIC: Middle East Network Information Service**

http://menic.utexas.edu/menic.html

MENIC is an outstanding virtual library, organized by subject and subdivided by country. Subjects include ancient history/archaeology; arts/culture; business/finance/economics; government/country profiles; maps/travel/regional information; religion; oil; government/country profiles (from U.S. government); business/finance; and news media/newsgroups. Additional Research Resources include Middle East Centers and Institutes and Organizations/Associations. Countries include all those nations covered in this chapter.

Specific Countries

Algeria

◆ **Algeria Page—Model League of Arab States**

http://192.203.180.62/mlas/algeria.html

MLAS is sponsored by the National Council on U.S.-Arab Relations, with support from the Arab League Information Center and the U.S.-Arab Chamber of Commerce. The Web site aims at providing links to information regarding all the nations of the Arab League, of the Arab world, and within the limits of the Middle East. Information spans culture, language, politics, business, human rights, technology, travel, etc.

◆ **Algeria Page—University of Texas Middle East Network Information Service**

http://menic.utexas.edu/menic/countries/algeria.html

A virtual library and annotated guide to Web sites in and about Algeria. MENIC is one of 12 U.S. Department of Education National Resource Centers for Middle East studies.

- **Algeria WWW Sites**

http://www.liii.com/~hajeri/algeria.html

Good starting point for finding information about Algeria. Links from this site are categorized under General Information, Schools and Educational Institutes Homepages, Commercial Companies, and Personal Homepages.

Bahrain

- **Bahrain Page—Model League of Arab States**

http://192.203.180.62/mlas/bahrain.html

MLAS is sponsored by the National Council on U.S.-Arab Relations, with support from the Arab League Information Center and the U.S.-Arab Chamber of Commerce. The Web site aims at providing links to information about all nations of the Arab League, the Arab world, and other countries of interest. Information spans culture, language, politics, business, human rights, technology, travel, etc.

- **Bahrain Page—University of Texas Middle East Network Information Service**

http://menic.utexas.edu/menic/countries/bahrain.html

A virtual library and annotated guide to Web sites in and about Bahrain. MENIC is one of 12 U.S. Department of Education National Resource Centers for Middle East Studies.

- **Bahrain, The Pearl of the Gulf**

http://copper.ucs.indiana.edu/~hqasem/bahrain/

This site contains lots of images and links, from the homepage of Hussam Husain Qasem, a Bahraini student at Indiana University.

- **Bahrain WWW Sites**

http://www.liii.com/~hajeri/bahrain.html

This site is a good starting point for finding information about Bahrain. Links are categorized under General Information, Schools and Educational Institutes' Homepages, Commercial Companies, and Personal Homepages.

Egypt

- **Amr Haggag's Homepage**

http://www.cen.uiuc.edu/~haggag/

This is the personal homepage of an Egyptian graduate student at the University of Illinois. Contains many links to sites in and about Egypt.

◆ **Egypt Page—Model League of Arab States**

http://192.203.180.62/mlas/egypt.html

MLAS is sponsored by the National Council on U.S.-Arab Relations, with support from the Arab League Information Center and the U.S.-Arab Chamber of Commerce. The Web site aims at providing links to information about all nations of the Arab League, the Arab world, and other countries of interest. Information spans culture, language, politics, business, human rights, technology, travel, etc.

◆ **Egypt Page—University of Texas Middle East Network Information Service**

http://menic.utexas.edu/menic/countries/egypt.html

A virtual library and annotated guide to Web sites in and about Egypt. MENIC is one of 12 U.S. Department of Education National Resource Centers for Middle East Studies.

◆ **Egypt WWW Index**

http://pharos.bu.edu/Egypt/

This large index contains many links to art and culture, commerce, history, politics, and government.

◆ **Egypt WWW Sites**

http://www.liii.com/~hajeri/egypt.html

This site contains a great collection of Web pages relating to Egypt, including corporate and personal homepages.

◆ **Egyptology Resources—University of Cambridge**

http://www.newton.cam.ac.uk/egypt/

Here one finds abundant historical and current information about Egypt as well as links to journals and magazines, institutions, other Egyptology sites, and personal Egyptology homepages.

◆ **Egypt's Information Highway**

http://www.idsc.gov.eg

Initiated in 1995 by Egyptian Cabinet Information and Decision Support Center, this site includes links to culture, tourism, health, environment, and other subjects.

Iran

- ◆ **FarsiNet**

http://www.farsinet.com

Megasite of the Iranian Christians International, which is mostly in English, with some Farsi. Includes many links to Iranian business and culture; cities in Iran; Christianity in Iran and Persian culture; Iranian-Christian churches.

- ◆ **Iran Page—Model League of Arab States**

http://192.203.180.62/mlas/iran.html

Provides an Arab perspective on Iran, as well as many useful links about Iranian culture, politics, government, business, technology, travel, etc. MLAS is sponsored by the National Council on U.S.-Arab Relations, with support from the Arab League Information Center and the U.S. Chamber of Commerce.

- ◆ **Iran Page—University of Texas Middle East Network Information Service**

http://menic.utexas.edu/menic/countries/iran.html

A virtual library and annotated guide to Web sites in and about Iran. MENIC is one of 12 U.S. Department of Education National Resource Centers for Middle East Studies.

- ◆ **Persia Homepage**

http://www.ed.ac.uk/~bhm/persia.html

Links: art; culture; geography; history; literature; publications; religions; and personal homepages.

Iraq

- ◆ **Iraq Page—Model League of Arab States**

http://192.203.180.62/mlas/iraq.html

Sponsored by the National Council on U.S.-Arab Relations, with support from the Arab League Information Center and the U.S.-Arab Chamber of Commerce. Aims at providing links to information regarding all the nations of the Arab League, of the Arab World, and within the limits of the Middle East. Information spans culture, language, politics, business, human rights, technology, travel, etc.

- ◆ **Iraq Page—University of Texas Middle East Network Information Service**

http://menic.utexas.edu/menic/countries/iraq.html

A virtual library and annotated guide to Web sites in and about Iraq. MENIC is one of 12 U.S. Department of Education National Resource Centers for Middle East Studies.

◆ **Iraq WWW Sites**

http://www.liii.com/~hajeri/iraq.html

A good starting point for finding information about Iraq. Links are categorized under the headings General Information, Schools and Educational Institutes' Homepages, Commercial Companies, and Personal Homepages.

Jordan

◆ **Hashemite Kingdom of Jordan Page**

http://www.iiconsulting.com/jordan/

Comprehensive collection of links that include background on the country, cultural resources, tourism information, and more.

◆ **Hussein Dia's Homepage**

http://civil-www.eng.monash.edu.au/people/postgrad/dia/ jordan.htm

Maps and images of Jordan.

◆ **Jordan Page—Model League of Arab States**

http://192.203.180.62/mlas/jordan.html

Sponsored by the National Council on U.S.-Arab Relations, with support from the Arab League Information Center and the U.S.-Arab Chamber of Commerce. Aims at providing links to information regarding all the nations of the Arab League, of the Arab World, and within the limits of the Middle East. Information spans culture, language, politics, business, human rights, technology, travel, etc.

◆ **Jordan Page—University of Texas Middle East Network Information Service**

http://menic.utexas.edu/menic/countries/jordan.html

A virtual library and annotated guide to Web sites in and about Jordan. MENIC is one of 12 U.S. Department of Education National Resource Centers for Middle East Studies.

◆ **Jordan WWW Sites**

http://www.liii.com/~hajeri/jordan.html

Good starting point for finding information about Jordan. Information is categorized under the headings: General Information, Schools and Educational Institutes' Homepages, Commercial Companies, and Personal Homepages.

◆ **Web Server of the Hashemite Kingdom of Jordan**

http://iconnect.com/jordan/

Includes the constitution of the Kingdom, currency rate, Radio Jordan schedule, investment opportunities, and more.

Kuwait

◆ **Kuwait.Net**

http://www.kuwait.net

Homepage of Kuwait's Internet service provider. Links to customer information and services; homepages of individual users, and corporate/organizational clients. About Kuwait link was not functional at press time.

◆ **Kuwait Page—Model League of Arab States**

http://192.203.180.62/mlas/kuwait.html

MLAS is sponsored by the National Council on U.S.-Arab Relations, with support from the Arab League Information Center and the U.S.-Arab Chamber of Commerce. The Web site aims at providing links to information about all nations of the Arab League, the Arab world, and other countries of interest. Information spans culture, language, politics, business, human rights, technology, travel, etc.

◆ **Kuwait Page—University of Texas Middle East Network Information Service**

http://menic.utexas.edu/menic/countries/kuwait.html

A virtual library and annotated guide to Web sites in and about Kuwait. MENIC is one of 12 U.S. Department of Education National Resource Centers for Middle East Studies.

◆ **Kuwait WWW Sites**

http://www.liii.com/~hajeri/kuwait.html

Maintained by a Kuwaiti national. Excellent starting point for research on Kuwait. Information is categorized under the headings: General Information, Schools and Educational Institutes' Homepages, Commercial Companies, and Personal Homepages.

◆ **Welcome to Kuwait**

http://hsccwww.kuniv.edu.kw

This university department site (managed by the Kuwait University Health Science Computer Center) has a wide variety of links about Kuwait. Includes information from the Kuwait National Committee for Missing and POW Affairs (regarding Kuwaiti nationals held in Iraq), and a Kuwaiti perspective/chronology of the Gulf War. Also: Kuwait-At-A-Glance; History; Architecture; Wildlife;

Agriculture; Living in Kuwait; Relaxing in Kuwait; Government; and National & International Organizations in Kuwait.

Lebanon

◆ **American University in Beirut**

http://www.aub.ac.lb/

Includes many links about Lebanon in general, plus access to the University's general and medical libraries.

◆ **Lebanon Page—Model League of Arab States**

http://192.203.180.62/mlas/lebanon.html

MLAS is sponsored by the National Council on U.S.-Arab Relations, with support from the Arab League Information Center and the U.S.-Arab Chamber of Commerce. The Web site aims at providing links to information about all nations of the Arab League, the Arab world, and other countries of interest. Information spans culture, language, politics, business, human rights, technology, travel, etc.

◆ **Lebanon Page—University of Texas Middle East Network Information Service**

http://menic.utexas.edu/menic/countries/lebanon.html

A virtual library and annotated guide to Web sites in and about Lebanon. MENIC is one of 12 U.S. Department of Education National Resource Centers for Middle East Studies.

◆ **Lebanon WWW Servers**

http://www.sparc.com/lebanon.html

A large collection of links dealing with many subjects. Some of the links are to English-language sites and others are in Lebanese. Flags beside the links are an indication of the language.

◆ **Leb.Net (English, French & Arabic)**

http://www.leb.net

Software map; Arabic script software resources; many technology and culture links relating to countries of the Fertile Crescent—mostly Lebanon, but also Syria and Iraq.

Libya

◆ **Libya Page—Model League of Arab States**
http://192.203.180.62/mlas/libya.html

MLAS is sponsored by the National Council on U.S.-Arab Relations, with support from the Arab League Information Center and the U.S.-Arab Chamber of Commerce. The Web site aims at providing links to information about all nations of the Arab League, the Arab world, and other countries of interest. Information spans culture, language, politics, business, human rights, technology, travel, etc.

◆ **Libya Page—University of Texas Middle East Network Information Service**
http://menic.utexas.edu/menic/countries/libya.html

A virtual library and annotated guide to Web sites in and about Libya. MENIC is one of 12 U.S. Department of Education National Resource Centers for Middle East Studies.

◆ **Libya WWW Sites**
http://www.liii.com/~hajeri/libya.html

Excellent starting point for research on Libya. Information is categorized under the headings General Information, Schools and Educational Institutes' Homepages, Commercial Companies, and Personal Homepages.

Morocco

◆ **Morocco Page—Model League of Arab States**
http://192.203.180.62/mlas/morocco.html

MLAS is sponsored by the National Council on U.S.-Arab Relations, with support from the Arab League Information Center and the U.S.-Arab Chamber of Commerce. The Web site aims at providing links to information about all nations of the Arab League, the Arab world, and other countries of interest. Information spans culture, language, politics, business, human rights, technology, travel, etc.

◆ **Morocco Page—University of Texas Middle East Network Information Service**
http://menic.utexas.edu/menic/countries/morocco.html

A virtual library and annotated guide to Web sites in and about Morocco. MENIC is one of 12 U.S. Department of Education National Resource Centers for Middle East Studies.

◆ **The One and Only Morocco WWW Page**

http://www.dsg.ki.se/maroc

This site contains images of Morocco, Historical Events, The Lion Search, and Moroccan Cities. Also contains information on Moroccan culture, economy, practical information, cooking and sports.

Oman

◆ **Oman Page—Model League of Arab States**

http://192.203.180.62/mlas/oman.html

MLAS is sponsored by the National Council on U.S.-Arab Relations, with support from the Arab League Information Center and the U.S.-Arab Chamber of Commerce. The Web site aims at providing links to information about all nations of the Arab League, the Arab world, and other countries of interest. Information spans culture, language, politics, business, human rights, technology, travel, etc.

◆ **Oman Page—University of Texas Middle East Network Information Service**

http://menic.utexas.edu/menic/countries/oman.html

A virtual library and annotated guide to Web sites in and about Oman. MENIC is one of 12 U.S. Department of Education National Resource Centers for Middle East Studies.

◆ **Oman WWW Sites**

http://www.liii.com/~hajeri/oman.html

A good starting off point to research Oman. Information is categorized under the headings General Information, Schools and Educational Institutes' Homepages, Commercial Companies, and Personal Homepages.

Palestine

◆ **Palestine Page—Model League of Arab States**

http://192.203.180.62/mlas/palestin.html

MLAS is sponsored by the National Council on U.S.-Arab Relations, with support from the Arab League Information Center and the U.S.-Arab Chamber of Commerce. The Web site aims at providing links to information about all nations of the Arab League, the Arab world, and other countries of interest. Information spans culture, language, politics, business, human rights, technology, travel, etc.

- ▾ **Palestine Page—University of Texas Middle East Network Information Service**

http://menic.utexas.edu/menic/countries/palestine.html

A virtual library and annotated guide to Web sites in and about Palestine. MENIC is one of 12 U.S. Department of Education National Resource Centers for Middle East Studies.

Qatar

- ◆ **Abdulaziz Al-Khater's Homepage**

http://www.cs.purdue.edu/people/alkhater

Get a personal perspective on Qatar from this native student at Purdue University.

- ◆ **Qatar Page—Model League of Arab States**

http://192.203.180.62/mlas/qatar.html

MLAS is sponsored by the National Council on U.S.-Arab Relations, with support from the Arab League Information Center and the U.S.-Arab Chamber of Commerce. The Web site aims at providing links to information about all nations of the Arab League, the Arab world, and other countries of interest. Information spans culture, language, politics, business, human rights, technology, travel, etc.

- ◆ **Qatar Page—University of Texas Middle East Network Information Service**

http://menic.utexas.edu/menic/countries/qatar.html

A virtual library and annotated guide to websites in and about Qatar. MENIC is one of 12 U.S. Department of Education National Resource Centers for Middle East Studies.

- ◆ **Qatar WWW Sites**

http://www.liii.com/~hajeri/qatar.html

A good starting point for finding information about Qatar. Information is categorized under the headings: General Information, Schools and Educational Institutes' Homepages, Commercial Companies, and Personal Homepages.

Saudi Arabia

- ◆ **Saudi Arabia Page—Model League of Arab States**

http://192.203.180.62/mlas/saudi.html

MLAS is sponsored by the National Council on U.S.-Arab Relations, with support from the Arab League Information Center and the U.S.-Arab Chamber of Commerce. The Web site aims at providing links to information about all nations of the Arab League, the Arab world, and other countries of interest.

Information spans culture, language, politics, business, human rights, technology, travel, etc.

- ◆ **Saudi Arabia Page—University of Texas Middle East Network Information Service**

http://menic.utexas.edu/menic/countries/saudi.html

A virtual library and annotated guide to Web sites in and about Saudi Arabia. MENIC is one of 12 U.S. Department of Education National Resource Centers for Middle East Studies.

- ◆ **Saudi Arabia WWW Sites**

http://www.liii.com/~hajeri/saudi.html

A very good compendium of links relating to Saudi Arabia. Information is categorized under the headings General Information, Schools and Educational Institutes' Homepages, Commercial Companies, and Personal Homepages.

- ◆ **Saudi Arabia WWW Virtual Library**

http://www.arablink.com/saudi-arabia/saudi-arabia.html

This page is one of the best on Saudi Arabia. Lots of links, including Ask Bob the Librarian—an FAQs about the site that guides the user to the proper section. Includes a country profile, traveler's information, and much more.

Syria

- ◆ **Syria Page—Model League of Arab States**

http://192.203.180.62/mlas/syria.html

MLAS is sponsored by the National Council on U.S.-Arab Relations, with support from the Arab League Information Center and the U.S.-Arab Chamber of Commerce. The Web site aims at providing links to information about all nations of the Arab League, the Arab world, and other countries of interest. Information spans culture, language, politics, business, human rights, technology, travel, etc.

- ◆ **Syria Page—University of Texas Middle East Network Information Service**

http://menic.utexas.edu/menic/countries/syria.html

A virtual library and annotated guide to Web sites in and about Syria. MENIC is one of 12 U.S. Department of Education National Resource Centers for Middle East Studies.

◆ **Syria WWW Sites**

http://www.liii.com/~hajeri/syria.html

A good starting point for finding Syrian information on the Internet. Information is categorized under the headings General Information, Schools' and Educational Institutes' Homepages, Commercial Companies, and Personal Homepages.

Tunisia

◆ **Tunisia—Model League of Arab States**

http://192.203.180.62/mlas/tunisia.html

MLAS is sponsored by the National Council on U.S.-Arab Relations, with support from the Arab League Information Center and the U.S.-Arab Chamber of Commerce. The Web site aims at providing links to information about all nations of the Arab League, the Arab world, and other countries of interest. Information spans culture, language, politics, business, human rights, technology, travel, etc.

◆ **Tunisia—University of Texas Middle East Network Information Service**

http://menic.utexas.edu/menic/countries/tunisia.html

A virtual library and annotated guide to Web sites in and about Tunisia. MENIC is one of 12 U.S. Department of Education National Resource Centers for Middle East Studies.

◆ **Tunisia WWW Sites**

http://www.liii.com/~hajeri/tunisia.html

A good starting point for finding information about Tunisia. Information is categorized under the headings General Information, Schools and Educational Institutes' Homepages, Commercial Companies, and Personal Homepages.

United Arab Emirates

◆ **Emirates Internet's UAE Links**

http://www.emirates.net.ae/sites.html

Links from homepage of Emirates Internet, UAE's Internet service provider. Links: Government; Foreign Embassies; News/Media; General Information; Insurance Industry; Medical; Travel & Tourism; Hotels; Business; Directories; Art/Culture; Events; Universities; and Technology/Computers.

◆ **United Arab Emirates Page—Model League of Arab States**

http://192.203.180.62/mlas/uae.html

MLAS is sponsored by the National Council on U.S.-Arab Relations, with support from the Arab League Information Center and the U.S.-Arab Chamber of Commerce. The Web site aims at providing links to information about all nations of the Arab League, the Arab world, and other countries of interest. Information spans culture, language, politics, business, human rights, technology, travel, etc.

◆ **United Arab Emirates Page—University of Texas Middle East Network Information Service**

http://menic.utexas.edu/menic/countries/uae.html

A virtual library and annotated guide to Web sites in and about UAE. MENIC is one of 12 U.S. Department of Education National Resource Centers for Middle East Studies.

◆ **United Arab Emirates WWW Sites**

http://www.liii.com/~hajeri/uae.html

A good starting point for finding information about the United Arab Emirates. Information is categorized under the headings General Information, Schools and Educational Institutes' Homepages, Commercial Companies, and Personal Homepages.

Yemen

◆ **Yemen Page—Model League of Arab States**

http://192.203.180.62/mlas/yemen.html

MLAS is sponsored by the National Council on U.S.-Arab Relations, with support from the Arab League Information Center and the U.S.-Arab Chamber of Commerce. The Web site aims at providing links to information about all nations of the Arab League, the Arab world, and other countries of interest. Information spans culture, language, politics, business, human rights, technology, travel, etc.

◆ **Yemen Page—University of Texas Middle East Network Information Service**

http://menic.utexas.edu/menic/countries/yemen.html

A virtual library and annotated guide to Web sites in and about Yemen. MENIC is one of 12 U.S. Department of Education National Resource Centers for Middle East Studies.

Current Events

Regional

◆ **Arabic Newsstand**

http://www.liii.com/~hajeri/newsstand/arab-news.html

Provides, by country, links to daily, weekly and monthly newspapers and magazines. Language is specified for each title to which links are provided.

◆ **Global Newsstand**

http://www.mcs.com/~rchojnac/www/tgn.html#ME or / tgn.html#Africa

Contains links to publications from all over the world, by region. Middle East includes Bahrain; Iran; Israel; Jordan; Kuwait; Qatar; UAE; regional newspaper *Al-Ayyam*; UN News; Relief Web; and International Committee for the Red Cross. Africa includes: Egypt; Morocco; and Tunisia.

◆ **ReliefWeb**

http://www.reliefweb.int/

A project of the UN Department of Humanitarian Affairs, ReliefWeb provides information on disaster prevention, preparedness, and response. Includes news search—links to AP, Reuters, Excite, and InfoSeek News Center. Emphasizes refugee problems, especially the dislocation caused by the Arab-Israeli conflict.

Specific Countries

Iran

◆ **Iran Weekly Press Digest**

http://www.neda.net/iran-wpd/

An independent weekly bulletin devoted to social, political and economic affairs. The free online version is condensed, with the full magazine being available only to paid subscribers.

◆ **Neda Rayaneh Institute**

http://www.neda.net

Iran's largest Internet provider. Customer information and services. Includes links to English-language and Farsi publications, Pakistan business directory, and Export Show Room of Leading French Companies.

Jordan

◆ **Petra News**

http://accessme.com/Petra/

English version of the press releases of the Jordan News Agency.

Palestine

◆ **Palestinian National Authority**

http://www.pna.net

News, press releases, leaders' speeches and interviews, government information, foreign affairs, facts about Palestine and the PLO. Includes links to related sites.

Newsgroups and Listservs

Regional

clari.world.africa.northwestern

Usenet newsgroup for news and discussion of Morocco, Algeria, Libya, and Saharan countries.

clari.world.mideast

This is a Usenet newsgroup for discussion of news from the Middle East.

clari.world.mideast.arabia

Moderated, Usenet newsgroup for news of the Arabian Peninsula.

◆ **Cyberarab Mailing List**

Subscription address: majordomo@leb.net

Electronic mailing list on Arab life. To subscribe, send the message **subscribe CyberArab your name** to the above address.

◆ **MEIG-L**

Subscription address: listserv@uga.cc.uga.edu

Electronic mailing list dealing with Middle Eastern issues. To subscribe, send a message **sub MEIG-L your name** to the above address.

◆ **Middle East News**

http://menic.utexas.edu/menic/newsites.html

Provides links by country to Middle East media publications and newsgroups; provided by the University of Texas Middle East Network Information Service.

soc.culture.arabic

This is a Usenet newsgroup for discussion of technological and cultural issues, not politics.

soc.culture.berber

Usenet newsgroup concerned with the Berber language, history and culture.

soc.culture.maghreb

Usenet newsgroup for discussion of North African society and culture.

talk.politics.mideast

Usenet newsgroup for discussion and debate over Middle Eastern events.

Specific Countries

Algeria

♦ **ALGERIA-NET**

Subscription address: majordormo.msen.com

Electronic mailing list dealing with Algeria. To subscribe, send a message **sub ALGERIA-NET your name** to the above address.

♦ **Algnews**

Subscription address: listserv@gwuvm.gwu.edu

Electronic mailing list sponsored by the Algeria News Network. To subscribe, send a message **sub ALGNEWS your name** to the above address.

♦ **AMAZIGH-NET**

Subscription address: majordomo@mail.msen.com

Electronic mailing list dealing with the Berber language, history, and culture. To subscribe, send a message **sub AMAZIGH-NET your name** to the above address.

soc.culture.algeria

Usenet newsgroup concerned with topics "From A–Z about Algeria."

Egypt

clari.world.mideast.egypt

Usenet newsgroup for news of Egypt, moderated.

soc.culture.egyptian

Usenet newsgroup respecting Egypt, and its society, culture, heritage, etc.

Iran

clari.world.mideast.iran

Usenet newsgroup for news and discussion of Iran.

◆ **IWIDG**

Subscription address: listproc@u.washington.edu

Electronic mailing list that has discussions of Iranian women's issues. To subscribe, send a message **sub IWIDG your name** to the above address.

soc.culture.iranian

Usenet newsgroup for discussions about Iran and things Iranian/Persian.

Iraq

clari.world.mideast.iraq

Usenet newsgroup for news of Iraq, moderated.

soc.culture.iraq

Usenet newsgroup concerned with Iraq, its society, culture and heritage.

Jordan

◆ **JORDANNEWS-L**

Subscription address: listserv@netcom.com

Electronic mailing list with discussion of current events in Jordan. To subscribe, send a message **sub JORDANNEWS-L your name** to the above address.

soc.culture.jordan

Usenet newsgroup covering all topics concerning the Hashemite Kingdom of Jordan.

Kuwait

soc.culture.kuwait

Usenet newsgroup providing discussion of Kuwaiti culture, society and history.

Lebanon

soc.culture.lebanon

Usenet newsgroup for discussion about things Lebanese.

Palestine

clari.world.mideast.palestine

Moderated, Usenet newsgroup for news of the West Bank and Gaza.

soc.culture.palestine

Palestinian people, culture and politics.

Tunisia

◆ **TUNINFO**

Subscription address: listserv@psuvm.psu.edu

Electronic mailing list sponsored by the Tunisian Information Office, Washington, D.C. To subscribe, send a message **sub TUNINFO your name** to the above address.

◆ **TUNISNET—The Tunisia Network**

Subscription address: listserv@psuvm.psu.edu

Electronic mailing list of the Tunisia Network. To subscribe, send a message **sub TUNISNET your name** to the above address.

Newspapers, Magazines, and Newsletters

Specific Countries

Bahrain

◆ **Bahrain Tribune**

http://www.bahraintribune.com/

Daily newspaper in English. The initial page has summaries of the stories with links to the full report. Local and world news, feature columns, business news, and sports information are included.

Egypt

◆ **Cairo Press Review**

http://www.us.sis.gov.eg/pressrev/html/indexfrm.htm

English-language newspaper with headlines and editorials.

◆ **Egypt Magazine**

http://www.us.sis.gov.eg/public/magazine/

Monthly magazine with stories dealing with Egyptian politics, culture, economy, religion, literature, and more.

◆ **Egypt Today (monthly magazine)**

http://www.arabia.com/EgyptToday/

Monthly magazine covering art, books, film, food, pop music, and more. The current issue plus back issues are available online.

Iran

- ◆ **The Iranian**

http://www.iranian.com

Electronic magazine with many links to sites about Iran. Must register when accessing for first time.

Jordan

- ◆ **Jordan Times**

http://www.accessme.com/JordanTimes/

Daily newspaper in English published by the Jordan Press Foundation. Information provided includes local and world news, editorials and letters, the economy, sports, and more.

- ◆ **Jordan Today (monthly magazine, in English)**

http://www.arabia.com/JordanToday/

Monthly English-language magazine with an emphasis on social and cultural events in Jordan.

- ◆ **Melad**

http://www.arabia.com/melad/

Monthly Jordanian/English magazine on real estate and related topics.

- ◆ **The Star Online**

http://www.arabia.com/star/

Jordan's political, economic and cultural weekly magazine. This is a condensed version of the print publication; the cover story plus selected features are available on the Web. Both current and back issues of the online magazine are available from November 16, 1995, to the present.

Kuwait

- ◆ **Kuwait Times**

**http://www.paaet.edu.kw/Info/HomePage/shaheen/kt/
    current/kutoday.htm**

Daily English-language newspaper. The current issues plus back issues are available on the Web.

Lebanon

◆ **Future News**

http://www.dm.net.lb/future/news/index.html

General news magazine published on the Web dealing with Lebanon.

Libya

◆ **Libyan News Items**

http://www.peg.apc.org/~jamahir/news.htm

Monthly English-language magazine with major Libyan news stories.

Palestine

◆ **Jerusalem Times**

http://www.amin.org/biladi.htm

Weekly news magazine in English.

◆ **Palestine Times**

http://www.ptimes.com

Monthly political newspaper in English. Current and previous issues are available.

Qatar

◆ **Gulf Times**

http://www.gulftimes.com

English-language newspaper from Qatar.

United Arab Emirates

◆ **Al Shindagah**

http://www.dnic.com/shindagah/index.html

Monthly news magazine from United Arab Emirates in English. Business, environmental, and cultural stories are featured.

◆ **Gulf News Newspaper**

http://www.gulf-news.com/

Daily, English-language newspaper from United Arab Emirates.

◆ **Khaleej Times Newspaper**

http://www.khaleejtimes.com/

Daily, English-language newspaper from United Arab Emirates, with many graphics. Back issues for the current week are available along with the current issue.

◆ **Update**

http://www.sids.com/update/

Monthly English-language magazine from United Arab Emirates with a business and technology focus.

Yemen

◆ **Yemen Times**

http://195.94.0.34/yementimes/

Weekly newspaper and the only English-language newspaper published in Yemen. Current and recent back issues are available. There is a search engine available to help the user locate information at this Web site.

BUSINESS

Regional

◆ **Arab World Online**

http://www.awo.net/about/

This site is a joint venture of the National U.S.-Arab Chamber of Commerce, and Multitasking Online, an Internet marketing company. Many business and commercial resources are linked here, including: Region-wide Information; Commercial Directory; Business; Events; and Organizations. Country information includes export/import data; government contacts; exchange rates; articles about the country; and country-related sites.

◆ **Country Commercial Guides, U.S. Dept. of State**

http://www.state.gov/www/about_state/business/ com_guides/index.html

CCGs review commercial environments in foreign countries, using economic, political and market analyses. They can be searched by Geographic Region (Middle East and North Africa) for guides to Algeria, Bahrain, Egypt, Jordan, Kuwait, Lebanon, Saudi Arabia, Tunisia, United Arab Emirates, West Bank, and Yemen. At press time, most guides were located in the Gopher Research Collection, linked from the Web page. The State Department was also in the process of converting the guides to HTML format.

◆ **ISLMECON**

Subscription address: listserv%sairti00.bitnet@listserv.net

Electronic mailing list with discussions of Islamic economics. To subscribe, send the message **sub ISLMECON your name** to the above address.

◆ **Middle East/North Africa Business Homepage, U.S. Department of Commerce**

http://www.ita.doc.gov/mena/

Presented by the Commerce Department's Office of the Near East for use of American companies interested in business, trade and commerce in the region, this site includes news updates on U.S. government projects and programs that affect business and trade. Other links include Trade Promotion Programs, MENA Economic Summits, Country Commercial Guides, Ask the Experts, and Trade Resources.

Specific Countries

Egypt

◆ **Business Today—Egypt**

http://www.arabia.com/BusinessToday/

Online version of Egypt's premier business magazine. Published monthly in English, it contains information on economic issues, the stock market, listings of business partnership opportunities and more.

◆ **EG-VOICE**

Subscription address: listserv@lists.aiesec.org

Electronic mailing list of the AIESEC, the Association Internationale de Estudiants en Sciences Economiques et Comerciales, which is an international association of university students who work with the business sector to promote development of their countries. To subscribe, send the message **sub EG-VOICE your name** to the above address.

◆ **Egypt Business Center**

http://163.121.10.42/amman/main

Contains information on investing and doing business in Egypt.

◆ **Egypt WWW Index—Business & Economy Links**

◆ **Egypt WWW Index—Commercial Links**

http://pharos.bu.edu/Egypt/#business

http://pharos.bu.edu/Egypt/#commercial

This site contains a large index of links to Egyptian banks, companies, chambers of commerce, law firms, and investment assistance. From Boston University's megasite.

Jordan

- **Economic Perspectives**

http://www.arabia.com/ep/

Monthly magazine available in English dealing with the Jordanian economy.

Lebanon

- **Lebanon OnLine Resources**

http://www.lebanon.com/

Primarily business information and services. There is a search engine provided to assist you in locating information at this site.

Morocco

- **MA-VOICE**

Subscription address: listserv@lists.aiesec.org

Electronic mailing list of AIESEC, the Association Internationale de Estudiants en Sciences Economiques et Comerciales, which is an international association of university students who work with the business sector to promote development of their countries. To subscribe, send the message **sub MA-VOICE your name** to the above address.

Tunisia

- **TN-LC-MD (AISEC-Medina, Tunisia local list)**

Subscription address: listserv@lists.aiesec.org

Electronic mailing list of the AIESEC (Association Internationale de Estudiants en Sciences Economiques et Comerciales) which is an international association of university students who work with the business sector to promote development of their countries. To subscribe, send a message **sub TN-LC-MD your name** to the above address.

United Arab Emirates

- **Al-Bawardi Enterprises**

http://www.albawardi.co.ae/

Homepage of a 100 percent nationally owned company with interests in fuel, computers/telecommunications, food production, general contracting, and other fields.

◆ **Dubai Department of Tourism and Commerce Markets**

http://www.dctpb.gov.ae/

Includes Dubai travel and tourism information, visas, business, news updates, and other UAE Sites.

CULTURE AND HUMANITIES, GENERAL

Regional

◆ **Assyro-Babylonian, Canaanite/Ugaritic and Sumerian Mythology FAQs**

http://pubpages.unh.edu/~cbsiren/assyrbabyl-faq.html

http://pubpages.unh.edu/~cbsiren/canaanite-faq.html

http://pubpages.unh.edu/~cbsiren/sumer-faq.html

This is a fun, easy-to-follow guide to pantheons and mythologies, along with some regional history. Maintained by graduate physics student Christopher Siren.

◆ **Encyclopedia Mythica**

http://www.pantheon.org/mythica/areas/

Site contains short glosses on characters and elements from Persian, Mesopotamian, Hittite and other mythologies of interest; Egyptian mythology is expected to be added soon.

◆ **Fertile Crescent Homepage**

http://leb.net/fchp/

Dedicated to the culture, heritage and people in "the place where agriculture and civilization first arose, the birthplace of the alphabet, the place where great religions first uplifted the souls of mankind, the home of philosophers, saints, poets, explorers and conquerors."

soc.culture.assyrian

Usenet newsgroup for discussion of Assyrian culture.

soc.culture.kurdish

Usenet newsgroup for discussion of Kurdish culture.

Specific Countries

Egypt

- **RITSEC (Regional Information Technology and Software Engineering Center)**
http://www.ritsec.com.eg/
Association of information technology professionals in Egypt. A special program is CultureWare, products that integrates multimedia and text "to revive and help preserve the cultural heritage of the region."

Iran

- **Iranian Cultural Information Center**
http://persia.org
This index includes art, Persian songs, literature, Persian text editors, Iranian movie titles, recipes, calendars, software and yellow pages. There are also links to other Iran-related www/gopher/ftp sites.

- **Persian Flower—Persian Gardening and Horticulture Design**
http://www.anglia.ac.uk/~trochford/persgard/index2.htm
Background, history, climatic and cultural factors, techniques of Persian garden design.

Jordan

- **Jordan Antiquities**
http://www.arabia.com/joantiq/
Weekly news magazine that features articles about the antiquities of Jordan. The online magazine is an abbreviated version of the print one.

Kuwait
alt.culture.kuwait
Usenet newsgroup for discussion of Kuwaiti culture.

Saudi Arabia
alt.culture.saudi
Usenet newsgroup concerned with the life and times of the people of Saudi Arabia.

Syria
soc.culture.syria
Usenet newsgroup for the discussion of Syrian culture.

EDUCATION

◆ **Glyph for Windows**
http://www.ccer.ggl.ruu.nl/ccer/WINGLYPH.HTML
This site contains a description of a hieroglyphic text processing program that is run in Microsoft Windows. Price, ordering information, and an ftp downloading link are included. Students of Egyptology receive a 50 percent discount with documentation of their student status.

◆ **Muslim Students Association of the United States and Canada**
http://www.msa-natl.org/national/
Links include: Contact Information; Conferences; Chapter Affiliation; and Resources.

FINE ARTS

Architecture

◆ **Survey of Islamic Architecture**
http://rubens.anu.edu.au/islam2/index_1.html
The survey contains architectural images from Egypt, Egypt-Jordan, Jordan-Morocco, Morocco-Spain, and Spain-Syria. Although you can view the list of offerings, only one image per country is available for free viewing; you must pay a subscription fee to view the rest.

Art

◆ **NAHIA-L**
Subscription address: listserv@msu.edu
Electronic mailing list for North American historians of Islamic art history. To subscribe, send a message **sub NAHIA-L your name** to the above address.

◆ **Tel el Amarna Collection of M. A. Mansoor**
http://www.amarna.com/
Excellent collection of Egyptian art. There is a history of the collection, information about the exhibits and scientific reports dealing with the collection.

Music

alt.music.arabic

Usenet newsgroup dealing with Arabic music.

◆ **Master Musicians of Jajouka**

http://matisse.net/~jplanet/afmx/jajouka.htm

Information on Moroccan music.

rec.music.iranian

Usenet newsgroup for discussion of Iranian music.

GOVERNMENT, LAW, AND POLITICS

◆ **Embassies of Some Islamic and Arab Countries**

http://www.utexas.edu/students/msa/links/embassies.html

Maintained by the Muslim Students Association at the University of Texas, this directory listing of the U.S. embassies of many Arab and Muslim countries contains links to "those embassies which have homepages"—at press time, the only link was to the Saudi Arabian Embassy.

◆ **Issues**

http://www.arabia.com/issues/

Monthly English-language magazine with perspectives on the Middle East and world affairs.

◆ **Royal Embassy of Saudi Arabia (Washington, DC)**

http://www.saudi.net

Profiles of the country and its government; travel information; current press releases; and status report on relations with the U.S. Multimedia section includes video and audio clips and images.

Human Rights

◆ **Amnesty International**

http://www.amnesty.org

Amnesty International produces regular, in-depth reports on human rights violations in countries around the world. Click on Library for these links: A–Z Index of Publications by Country and Region; 1994–97 Country Reports Listed by Year and Continent; and Other Human Rights-related Sites.

◆ **Human Rights Watch**

http://www.hrw.org/home.html

Human Rights Watch conducts investigations of human rights abuses in some 70 countries around the world. Hot Spots contains current news updates. Gopher Menu contains country-specific, recent press releases under the Middle East division.

◆ **Salem Review**

http://leb.net/bcome/

Monthly magazine by the Boston Committee on the Middle East. Discusses issues of peace and justice in the Middle East. Back issues are available from the first issue in April 1997. There are extensive links to other relevant sources on the Middle East as well as information about U.S. foreign policy toward the area.

Organizations

◆ **Algerian Peace Association**

Subscription address: majordomo@mail.msen.com

Electronic mailing list of the association. To subscribe, send the message **sub APA your name** to the above address.

◆ **Arab-American Institute**

Email: aal@igc.apc.org

The Arab-American Institute is a Washington, D.C.-based group that lobbies on issues of concern to Arabs and Arab-Americans.

◆ **IRANPEACE**

Subscription address: listserv@yorku.ca

Electronic mailing list with a focus on how to bring freedom and peace to Iran. To subscribe, send the message **sub IRANPEACE your name** to the above address.

◆ **Kuwaiti POWs**

http://hsccwww.kuniv.edu.kw

Information from the Kuwait National Committee for Missing and POW Affairs (regarding Kuwaiti nationals held in Iraq), and a Kuwaiti perspective/chronology of the Gulf War. There is a search engine provided to help you locate information at this site.

HISTORY

◆ **ABZU: Guide to Resources for the Study of the Ancient Near East**

http://www-oi.uchicago.edu/OI/DEPT/RA/ABZU/ ABZU_REGINDX_MESO.HTML

From the University of Chicago's Oriental Institute, an index of Internet resources for the study of ancient Mesopotamia, including territory under the control of the modern state of Iran.

◆ **ANCIEN-L**

Subscription address: listserv@ulkyvm.louisville.edu

Electronic mailing list dealing with the history of the ancient Mediterranean area. To subscribe, send a message **sub ANCIEN-L your name** to the above address.

◆ **Mediterranean Civilizations**

http://yarra.vicnet.net.au/~focus/civimenu.htm

This site is concerned with major civilizations and ancient cities, religions, museums, ongoing archaeological excavations, mythology, art/music/science, and inventions and discoveries. Emphasis is on Turkey, Jordan, and Egypt, but relevant materials from the Louvre in Paris are also included.

◆ **MENA-H**

Subscription address: listserv@ulkyvm.louisville.edu

Electronic mailing list dealing with the history of the Mideast and Northern Africa. To subscribe, send a message **sub MENA-H your name** to the above address.

Archaeology

◆ **Akkadian Language**

http://saturn.sron.ruu.nl/%7Ejheise/akkadian/

Good source of information on Babylonian and Assyrian cuneiform texts as well as information about language and grammar and external links to virtual libraries and museums.

◆ **The Kelsey On_Line**

http://www.umich.edu/~kelseydb/

The Kelsey Museum of Archaeology, University of Michigan, provides illustrations and artifacts from ancient Mediterranean cultures and online brochures of recent exhibitions. Also includes link to maps of the ancient Mediterranean.

- **Louvre—Department of Egyptian Antiquities**

http://www.paris.org/Musees/Louvre/Treasures/Egyptian/

The great Paris museum houses an extraordinary collection of Egyptian artifacts. Images and textual information about some of the Egyptian antiquities owned by the Louvre. The thumbnail images can be enlarged by clicking on the image.

- **University of Memphis Institute of Egyptian Art and Archaeology**

http://www.memst.edu/egypt/main.html

This site provides a color tour of Egypt and a virtual exhibit of Egyptian artifacts.

- **University of Michigan Papyrus Collection**

http://www.lib.umich.edu/pap/HomePage.html

Includes link to APIS—Advanced Papyrological Information System—a joint effort by papyrologists at several American universities to integrate their collections in a virtual library. Don't miss Snapshots of Daily Life, which contains translations and pictures of personal letters from ancient Egypt.

LANGUAGE ARTS AND LITERATURE

Language Arts

- **ARABIC-L**

Subscription address: mailserv@byu.edu

Electronic mailing list dealing with the Arabic language. To subscribe, send the message **sub ARABIC-L your name** to the above address.

- **Arabic Language Tutorial**

http://philae.sas.upenn.edu/Arabic/arabic.html

From the Arabic Program at the University of Pennsylvania. Includes links to Arabic audio lessons and pictures from Arabic music films. Includes downloadable DOS software for assistance in learning Arabic.

- **ARACOM-L**

Subscription address: listserv@nic.surfnet.nl

Electronic mailing list for the International Association for Arabic Linguistics Compiling. To subscribe, send the message **sub ARACOM-L your name** to the above address.

- **Association for Persian Logic, Language and Computing**

http://www.cogsci.ed.ac.uk/~apl2c/home.html

Persian linguistics, logic, computing, natural language processing, philosophy of language, etc.

- **ITISALAT**

Subscription address: listserv@listserv.georgetown.edu

Electronic mailing list, title of which stands for "IT IS Arabic language and teaching." To subscribe, send the message **sub ITISALAT your name** to the above address.

Literature

- **Treasures of Persian Literature**

http://www.cit.ics.saitama-u.ac.jp/hobbies/iran/

Collection of classic Persian literature in original form and/or English translation.

POPULAR CULTURE

Music

- **Arab Music and Dance**

http://www-scf.usc.edu/~seelye/Musicpage.html

This site is concerned with music from groups throughout the region who combine traditional and contemporary sounds in Arabic.

Sports

- **Amr Haggag's "Latest Egyptian Soccer News and History of Egyptian Soccer"**

http://www.cen.uiuc.edu/~haggag/soccer.html

From the homepage of Egyptian student Amr Haggag. There is introductory material, a history of soccer in Egypt, and current feature stories.

Television and Film

- **Al-Manar TV**

http://www.almanar.com.lb/

Includes programming and news stories from Lebanon. The information is in Arabic and English.

- **Arab Film Homepage**

http://www.arabfilm.com

Contains indexes of movies, countries, new releases, ordering information, and home videos. Includes plot summaries and excerpts from reviews. Maintained by Arab Film Distribution.

◆ **Arab Radio & TV**

http://www.art-tv.net

Information is provided on programs and movies in Arabic and English.

◆ **Future TV**

http://www.dm.net.lb/future/

Includes information about programs, news, and sports from Lebanon.

◆ **LBC-TV**

http://www.dm.net.lb/lbcsat/

Information about programs, the weather, news, and sports from Lebanon. The news page can be heard by using RealAudio. Most of the information is available in both English and Arabic.

RELIGION

Baha'ism

◆ **Baha'i Resources via Internet**

http://www.bcca.org/srb/resources.html

This site is a compendium of Internet resources about Baha'ism. Links include introductory materials; scriptures; chat, mailing lists and newsgroups; and organizations.

Eastern Christianity

◆ **Assyrian Church of the East**

http://www.cired.org

Links include Theology, Relations with the Catholic Church, Relations with Eastern Churches, General Locations, Liturgy, and Syriac Documents.

◆ **The Coptic Network (Christian Coptic Orthodox Church of Egypt)**

http://cs-www.bu.edu/faculty/best/pub/cn/Home.html

Wealth of links to documents, creeds, history, art, language, music, etc. Also includes links to Orthodoxy and other Christian churches.

◆ **MARONET—The International Maronite Foundation**

http://www.primenet.com/~maronet/index.html

This site contains news, communiques from the Patriarch, church locations, and information about publications.

◆ **Melkite and Eastern Catholic Bibliography**

http://dshak12.wi.us/Melkite/biblio.htm

A bibliography of printed sources dealing with the Eastern Rite and the Melkite Church. The bibliography is divided into the following categories: Eastern Rite Sources, Sources Dealing Primarily with the Melkite Church, Parish Histories and Documents, Devotional and Liturgical Materials, and Materials Pertaining Specifically to St. George Melkite of Milwaukee.

◆ **ORTHODOX**

Subscription address: listserv@arizvm.ccit.arizona.edu

Electronic mailing list dealing with the Orthodox Church. To subscribe, send the message **sub ORTHODOX your name** to the above address.

◆ **Orthodox World Links (TheoLogic Systems)**

http://www.theologic.com/links.html

This is a large index of orthodox sites, including prayers and literature; organizations and foundations; art and architecture; news and mailing lists; patriarchates, archdioceses and dioceses; monasteries; parishes and missions; personal homepages; and educational resources.

◆ **Websites Related to the Study of the Eastern Churches**

http://www.music.princeton.edu/chant_html/east.html

Contains a helpful index of links, including Syriac, Coptic, Armenian, Georgian, and Ethiopic.

Islam

alt.islam.sufi

A Usenet newsgroup for discussions of the mystical dimensions of Islam.

alt.religion.islam

A Usenet newsgroup for discussion of the Islamic faith, unmoderated.

bit.listserv.muslims

A Usenet newsgroup for Islamic Information and News Network, moderated.

◆ **Cybermuslim: Guide to Islamic Resources on the Internet**

http://www.uoknor.edu/cybermuslim/

Cybermuslim is an extremely useful list of Internet resources containing a significant amount of information related to Islam and Muslims. Useful for educators, scholars and students. Whimsical and fun—includes welcome sound bites in various languages of the Muslim world; Qur'aan; activist resources; books and periodicals; Islamic software; schools and education; beliefs and houses of worship; cultural tours of Iran, Jordan, Kuwait, Saudi Arabia, and other countries.

◆ **Haqqani Foundation Homepage**

http://www.best.com/~informe/mateen/haqqani.html

This is the homepage of the Sufi Haqqani Foundation in America, an off-shoot of the Naqshbandi Sufi Order and contains links about tenets, teachings and practices of Islam and Sufism. Choice of languages from Arabic, English, French, Bulgarian, Greek and German. Includes link to As-Sunna Foundation of America, a pan-Muslim/pro-unity organization.

◆ **ISLAM-L**

Subscription address: listserv@ulkyvm.louisville.edu

Electronic mailing list on Islamic history. To subscribe, send the message **sub ISLAM-L your name** to the above address.

◆ **ISL-SCI**

Subscription address: listserv@vtvm1.cc.vt.edu

Electronic mailing list dealing with Islam and science. To subscribe, send a message **sub ISL-SCI your name** to the above address.

◆ **Quran Browser Basic Homepage**

http://goon.stg.brown.edu/quran_browser/pqeasy.shtml

This site allows you to conduct searches of the Quran by Sura number and verse and finds lists of passages containing a particular word or part of a word. It also allows for browses by list of sura names. Maintained by Richard L. Goerwitz, lead research programmer/analyst, Brown University Scholarly Technology Group.

soc.religion.islam

Discussion of the Islamic faith, moderated.

◆ **Sufi-Related Resources on the Internet**

http://world.std.com/~habib/sufi.html

Contains many links to resources about this mystical branch of Islam.

Zoroastrianism

◆ **AVESTA—Zoroastrian Archives**

http://www.avesta.org/avesta.html

Avesta are the most ancient scriptures of Zoroastrianism, founded by Zarathustra (Gr. Zoroaster) in Persia, and still practiced worldwide, especially in Iran. Complete texts are provided, as well as many Pahlavic scriptures (sacred literature preserved in Middle Persian language), Avestan language, and many other links.

SCIENCE AND TECHNOLOGY

Regional

◆ **MEH20-L**

Subscription address: listserv@vm.tau.ac.il

Electronic mailing list dealing with water issues in the Middle East. To subscribe, send a message **sub MEH20-L your name** to the above address.

◆ **Middle East Water Information Network**

http://www.ssc.upenn.edu/~mewin/

MEWIN is an international nonprofit organization, founded with assistance from the Ford Foundation in 1994, to improve management and conservation of water resources, and promote peaceful cooperation. Site includes links to other water and Middle East sources.

Specific Countries

Algeria

◆ **Algerian Scientists List**

Subscription address: majordomo@mail.msen.com

Electronic mailing list for Algerian scientists. To subscribe, send the message **sub AS your name** to the above address.

Egypt

eg.environment

Usenet newsgroup for the discussion of Egyptian environmental matters.

◆ **Egypt's Environment Information Highway**

http://www.ritsec.com.eg/ritsec/env/highway/

This is a Megasite that links many Egyptian environmental organizations.

Iran

◆ **Gozaresh**

http://gpg.com/gozaresh/

Scientific, economic and social monthly magazine.

◆ **Zirakzadeh Science Foundation**

http://gpg.com/MERC/org/zirakzadeh.html

Organization founded in 1993 to build a museum of science and technology in Iran.

Saudi Arabia

◆ **SAMATH**

Subscription address: listserv%saksu00.bitnet@listserv.net

Electronic mailing list which serves as a discussion forum for the Saudi Association for Mathematical Sciences. To subscribe, send the message **sub samath your name** to the above address.

◆ **SAPHYSIA**

Subscription address: listserv%saksu00.bitnet@listserv.net

Electronic mailing list for Saudi physicists. To subscribe, send the message **sub saphysia your name** to the above address.

Tunisia

◆ **TSSNEWS**

Subscription address: listserv@psuvm.psu.edu

Electronic mailing list for the Tunisian Scientific Society. To subscribe, send the message **sub TSSNEWS your name** to the above address.

◆ **Tunisia WWW Homepage**

**http://www-nt.e-technik.uni-erlangen.de/~younes/
   tunisian_home/tunisia**

Information about—and links to—education; science; research; Tunisian organizations, students and researchers worldwide; and other related resources. In English and French.

◆ **Tunisian Scientific Consortium**

http://www.rennes.enst-bretagne.fr/~hamdi/TSC.html

Listing of working groups and link to e-mail address to obtain more information about the groups. TSC is an independent, nonprofit organization of Tunisians involved in Science and Technology.

Health

◆ **American Lebanese Medical Association**

http://med-www.bu.edu/ALMA/Lebanon

Links to mission, bylaws and directors' contact information. Information about ALMA's first annual convention, held in Lebanon.

◆ **Egypt's Health Net**

http://www.idsc.gov.eg/health/

Egypt's Health Net is essentially a library of links to Egyptian healthcare providers, pharmaceutical and medical supply companies, medical societies and centers, and other health-related resources.

Information Technology and Telecommunications

Regional

◆ **Amr's Arabic Archive**

http://www.cen.uiuc.edu/~haggag/arabic.html

This is a downloadable Arabic software database and includes instructions for downloading.

◆ **BYTE—Middle East**

http://www.arabia.com/byte/

Monthly magazine available in both Arabic and English dealing with computer technology and its applications.

◆ **The Homepage of Nicholas Heer**

http://weber.u.washington.edu/~heer/

Concerned with Arabic and Persian computing, this site contains Arabic html files for testing various WWW browsers and links to sites about the Middle East and Islam.

Specific Countries

Bahrain

◆ **BATELCO**

http://www.batelco.com.bh/

BATELCO (Bahrain Telecommunications Company) is Bahrain's Internet service provider. The site, which is in English and Arabic, contains customer information and services, announcements and information for residents and visitors, software downloads, entertainment and news media information.

Egypt

◆ **Internet Access in Egypt**

http://pharos.bu.edu/Egypt/access.html

Status report on connectivity in Egypt. From Boston University's Egypt WWW Index.

◆ **RITSEC (Regional Information Technology and Software Engineering Center)**

http://www.ritsec.com.eg/

Association of information technology professionals in Egypt. Many professional and business-development resources. Also links to RITSEC's projects and special programs.

Iran

◆ **READER**

Subscription address: contact alex@dt.uh.edu

Electronic mailing list dealing with the use of Farsi and other scripts on the computer. To subscribe, send an e-mail request to the person and address above.

Kuwait

◆ **Kuwait.Net**

http://www.kuwait.net/

From Kuwait's sole authorized provider of Internet connectivity. Largely about telecommunications in Kuwait, it has links to local user and corporate client homepages, Web pages in and about Kuwait, and customer information and services.

Saudi Arabia

◆ **INTRNT-L**

Subscription address: listserv%sakacs00.bitnet@listserv.net

Electronic mailing list that serves as a discussion forum about Internet connectivity in Saudi Arabia. To subscribe, send the message **sub INTRNT-L your name** to the above address.

Syria

- **Internet Society of Syria**

http://leb.net/iss/

Nongovernmental organization. Links include Internet; Arabic organizations; Arabic personal homepages; Syrian Computer Society and Higher Institute of Applied Science & Technology (two government-sponsored organizations); ISS mailing list.

- **Internet Society of Syria Mailing List (ISS)**

Subscription address: majordomo@leb.net

Electronic mailing list dealing with Internet access in Syria. To subscribe, send the message **subscribe ISS your name** to the above address.

United Arab Emirates

- **Computer News—Middle East**

http://gpg.com/cnme/

Monthly magazine, in English. Previous issues are available back to April 1995.

- **Emirates Internet**

http://emirates.net.ae/

UAE Internet service provider, subsidiary of ETISALAT—Emirates Telecommunications Corporation. Customer information and services, links to sites about UAE. Arabic version available.

OTHER

Travel and Tourism

- **Egyptian Tourism Authority: Egypt Has It ALL**

http://163.121.10.41/tourism/default.htm

This site contains up-to-date tourism information, with lots of pictures.

- **Hotels and Resorts in Saudi Arabia**

http://www.webscope.com/travel/saudi.html

Information for the tourist or business traveler about hotel accommodations.

12

French Canadian Resources

VICKI L. GREGORY

INTRODUCTION

Although French Canadians reside in all the provinces of Canada, this chapter focuses on resources relating to French Canadian culture in the Province of Quebec and that portion of the current Maritime Provinces that constitute the former area of Acadia. From 1534 to 1763, New France, the French colonial holdings in North America, expanded to include the shores of the St. Lawrence River, Newfoundland, and Acadia (Nova Scotia), as well as much of the Great Lakes region and parts of the trans-Appalachian West. After 1763, the British took over the area from France, but the French settlers retained their language, religion, school system and laws. People of French origin now account for approximately 25 percent of the population of Canada and are firmly entrenched in the province of Quebec; in addition, sizable French Canadian communities exist in New Brunswick and Ontario and smaller communities are found in the western provinces.

Today, one of the most distinctive aspects of Quebec is, of course, its traditional insistence on maintaining its distinct French-influenced culture. By the time of the 1991 national census, the population of Quebec was just slightly shy of 7 million. Roughly 10 percent of these are people of British descent with another 10 percent being of continental European origin other than France. Beginning in the 1980s, Quebec witnessed an increased number of immigrants from Southeast Asia and from Haiti. However, roughly 80 percent of the population remain descendants of the French settlers who originally populated the region encompassed by the province. In a largely English-speaking country, the French Canadians maintain their language, their Roman Catholic religion, separate schools, and French civil law.

While many Québécois (as the inhabitants refer to themselves) historically had never fully reconciled themselves to either British rule or Anglo domination within Canada, the serious Quebec sovereignty movement began in earnest in the early 1960s; by 1965, a royal commission declared that a partnership between the French-speaking and English-speaking peoples was vital to the continued existence of Canada. Thus, in 1969, French and English were both declared the official languages of Canada. Also in that year, a provincial law was enacted in Quebec that guaranteed parents a choice between English and French schools for their children. Since 1980, a series of referenda have been held in Quebec on the question of Quebec sovereignty, i.e., the province's eventual withdrawal from Canada as an independent nation. These sovereignty proposals have all been defeated at the polls, but in the last referendum held in 1995 the proposition failed by a margin of less than 1 percent of those voting.

As you might imagine, since the French language is considered by Québécois as central to their culture, there are many Internet resources respecting Quebec and French Canadians that are available only in French. In the subject areas of science and technology, virtually all substantial Internet resources we found that applied to French Canada were available only in French. However, many Canadian Web sites on most subjects do make available both English and French versions. If a site initially loads in French, look for a button or hotlink labeled Anglais. Clicking on this button or link will load the English version of the Web page. The emphasis in this chapter, as in all the chapters in this work, is on sites available in English (even if the title of the site is in French); however, for those who can read French, be sure to look at Branchez-vous (**http://branchez-vous.com**), which is a Quebec-based site devoted to new resources on the Internet for French-speaking users. Recognizing that a significant part of what makes French Canada special is its language, be aware that many of the best Internet sites for information about French Canada are in French only; due to the emphasis of this book the French-only sites are not included in the lists of resources that follow.

For those seeking more information or updated information, there are many search engines available on the World Wide Web to assist you. Web sources listed in this chapter were found using InfoSeek, AltaVista, Excite, Lycos, Hotbot, and Yahoo. You can easily and obviously search for names of places, such as Montreal or Quebec, or names of specific organizations or types of organizations. However, when using a search engine to look for information about French Canada, it is often helpful to broaden your search to Canada in general. Many of the general Canadian sites are subarranged by province and the user can judge from the names and titles provided which sites are specific to the Province of Quebec. One especially good overall Canadian World Wide Web site well worth checking is Canadiana—The Canadian Resource Page (**http://www.cs.cmu.edu/Unofficial/Canadiana**). This Web page is arranged by broad subject areas, such as News and Information, Facts and Figures, Travel and Tourism, Politics and History, Science and Education, with linkages provided to every site listed. This site is regularly updated with new information and corrected links. A general site dealing with French-Canadian culture is the French-Canadian Culture Link Library available at (**http://frenchcaculture.miningco.com/mlibrary.htm**). This site is a constantly evolving index to useful and entertaining Internet resources, which is organized by categories such as Authors and Literature, Cuisine, Genealogy, History and Traditions, Music, and more.

Finally, the reader should note that this chapter is not intended to set forth a comprehensive bibliography, but rather a selective guide to what the author considers some of the best Internet resources on French Canada. Doubtless, opinions will differ as to what makes a given site "better" than some others, but keep in mind that Canadian organizations and government agencies are strong users of the World Wide Web, so the bibliography that follows should be viewed as an overview merely indicative of the wealth of resources that are available on a fascinating subculture of one of the largest and most important nations of the world.

GENERAL INFORMATION

Current Events

◆ **Canada NewsWire**
http://www.newswire.ca

Real-time news release database that contains a link to news releases from the Quebec Provincial Government and news releases from other firms and organizations in Quebec. Press releases are available in English, French, or both languages, and can be searched by keyword, organization, stock symbols, industry, category, and subject. Excerpts from *Canada's Business Report* are available in Streaming Audio. Hypertext links are provided to other related Canadian Internet resources as well as to archival copies dating back to 1995 of the quarterly newsletter *NewsWire*.

Newsgroups and Listservs

qc.general

Messages in this Usenet newsgroup are mostly about current events relating to Quebec and may be in either English or French.

Newspapers, Magazines, and Newsletters

◆ **Maclean's Magazine**
http://www.macleans.ca/

General Canadian news magazine site that is highly graphical. The cover story plus selected other features from the print version are included. There is a feature called Webpicks that is a selection of other Web sites related to the current week's cover story.

◆ **Montreal Gazette**

http://www.montrealGazette.com

The largest English-language daily in Quebec. Includes daily features and editorials. The site is updated each day by 2:00 A.M., Eastern Time. Two months of the Web pages are archived and accessible by date only; there is no subject search capacity for the archives.

◆ **Newsroom: Quebec Update**

http://www.mri.gouv.qc.ca/salle_des_nouvelles/ index.an.html

A biweekly electronic newsletter produced by the Quebec Ministére des Affaires Internationales, which provides information on many Quebec initiatives on the international scene as well as business and economic-related provincial information.

◆ **The Stanstead Journal**

http://www.tomifobia.com/journal/journal.html

The Internet edition of a weekly English-language newspaper with pictures. The site includes articles dealing with local news, feature columns, editorials, and special features.

BUSINESS

◆ **Designer's Web**

http://www.designers.qc.ca

Dedicated to Quebec's fashion industry, with photographs of the designers' collections as well as articles on fashion.

◆ **Quebec Business Directory**

http://www.quebecweb.com

Select the link to Business Directory. This site is devoted to Quebec businesses arranged in subject clusters and by region, and is also searchable in an alphabetical index. Although obviously not specific to French Canada, notable at this site is the Les Autruches de la Mauricie file, which gives information about ostrich products and general information about ostriches with color pictures.

◆ **Quebec Society: Socio-Economic Conditions**

http://www.gouv.qc.ca/societe/indexa.htm

From the Quebec Society page, clink on the hyperlink to Socio-Economic Conditions to find information on the labor market in Quebec, the employment situation, incomes, and taxes.

CULTURE AND HUMANITIES, GENERAL

◆ **Quebec Society**

http://www.gouv.qc.ca/societe/indexa.htm

Information is provided about the people of Quebec including the non-French-speaking minorities as well as the native peoples. There is a discussion of the family and the position of women in Quebec.

soc.culture.Canada

Messages in this Usenet newsgroup deal with all of Canada and its people, but it usually contains some messages dealing with the Quebec independence question. Messages in either French or English. Archived messages are available by FTP at **ftp://rtfm.mit.edu/soc.culture.canada**.

EDUCATION

◆ **Concordia University**

http://www.concordia.ca

Highly graphical page with information about the university, its departments and its libraries. There is a virtual tour of both the Webster and Vanier Libraries which allows the user to move around the library and click on various areas for additional information. For those using a text-based browser, there is a link provided for "graphically challenged browsers" so that all users can easily use the resources with or without the graphics.

◆ **Ecole Polytechnique de Montreal**

http://www.polymtl.ca/english.htm

Information is provided about the college's Graduate Studies and Research Division, the Technological Development Center, and its various research units and facilities. There is only a limited amount of information available in English (when compared to the version of the site provided in French).

◆ **McGill University**

http://www.mcgill.ca

McGill is an English-language university located in Montreal. The site provides information about McGill with links to the libraries and other parts of the university. Under the heading About McGill University, there is a virtual tour and A View of Montreal, which gives some historical and cultural information about the city.

◆ **Ministère de l'Éducation**

http://www.meq.gouv.qc.ca/gr-pub/com-ang.htm

Hyperlinks are provided to the full-text of recent laws, bills, and reports having to do with education in Quebec as well as to relevant English-language publications.

◆ **Quebec Studies Page**

http://www.well.com/user/mariita/quebec.html

This site is intended as a resource for American scholars of Quebec. Materials are arranged in three major sections: an introduction to Quebec; a general reference guide for researchers; and a listing by subject areas of resources for various areas within Quebec studies such as history, language, law, literature, native studies, etc. Most of the links are to French-only sites but there are bilingual English-French sites and a few English-only sites that contain valuable information about Quebec.

FINE ARTS

◆ **French-Canadian Culture: Traditional Québécois**

http://frenchcaculture.miningco.com/index.htm

The Web address brings you to an opening page. From there, choose For Francophone Music Lovers to go to the page for traditional music, which provides an introduction, plus it has links to other pages that offer an overview of traditional francophone music, including information about current groups performing this type of music.

◆ **Montreal Museum of Fine Arts**

http://www.mbam.qc.ca/a-sommaire.html

With a QuickTime viewer, the user can experience a virtual reality tour of the museum. Even without the special viewer, information as to current and upcoming exhibits, a history of the museum and its collections, a link to the virtual boutique shops of the museum and general information about the museum are available.

Art

◆ **Musée du Québec**

http://www.mdq.org/fr/anglais

Homepage of the Quebec art museum, which contains information about current exhibits, including a floor plan that allows the user to click on specific areas of the museum to obtain information about the works exhibited there, as well as general information concerning the museum's collection, arranged by period with color pictures of some of their most outstanding works. There is also an interactive memory game for children.

Music

◆ **Montreal Opera**

http://www.operademontreal.qc.ca/english/cadre-main.html

Provides an extensive history of the opera company in addition to a current schedule of performances, plus general news from the world of opera.

◆ **Montreal Symphony Orchestra**

http://www.osm.ca/html/home.html

Schedule of concerts, including the children's concerts, with information about the works being performed plus recent releases.

Photography

◆ **Shooting in Quebec: Picture Perfect Photo-Bank**

http://www.quebec-film.com

Select Shooting in Quebec for photographs of the Province of Quebec, including the cities of Montreal and Quebec; scenes from the countryside; including rivers, waterfalls, the Gaspe Peninsula and more. The site is intended for film producers, but the pictures may be of interest for many other uses.

GOVERNMENT, LAW, AND POLITICS

Government

◆ **Canadian Parliamentary Internet**

http://www.parl.gc.ca

Information about the role, history, and activities of the Canadian Senate, House of Commons, and the Library of Parliament is provided, along with parliamentary information and reference sources. There is also a link provided to related Gopher sites.

can.gov.announce

This Usenet newsgroup consists of press releases by the Canadian government, all of which are in both French and English.

can.gov.general

Discussions in this Usenet newsgroup about governmental issues dealing with Canada in general; however, French Canadian issues are discussed as well as other concerns.

◆ **Government of Quebec**

http://www.gouv.qc.ca/introa.htm

Official site of the Quebec Provincial Government, with hyperlinks to more specific content on other Quebec government sites and to private sites in Quebec. Information other than that offered on governmental sites is organized according to eleven themes including society, education, culture, business, tourism, institutions, etc. Official government links include the Prime Minister, the National Assembly, departments and institutions, the courts, etc.

◆ **National Assembly of Quebec**

http://www.AssNat.qc.ca/assnat/eng

Bills and statutes are available in French and English. The *Journal des débats* (Hansard) and the press conferences are not translated but recorded in full in French or English, as the case may be. Other documents provided at this site are in French only.

Politics

◆ **Bloc Québécois**

http://www.blocquebecois.org

Official Opposition in the Canadian Parliament and the party dedicated to Quebec sovereignty. Site contains press releases, the mission statement of the party, a section on milestones dealing with the question of sovereignty for Quebec as well as biographical profiles of the parliament members.

◆ **CAN-FUTS**

canfutures@chatsubo.com

This electronic mailing list provides a forum for the discussion of the future of Canada in light of the referendum for separation by Quebec, which was narrowly defeated (by less than 1 percent of Quebec's electorate participating in the referendum). The list is not moderated. Contact: Mike Gurstein at **mgurst@sparc.uccb.ns.ca**.

can.politics

This Usenet newsgroup deals with discussions of Canadian politics but with obvious Francophone (French speaking) or Quebec threads of discussion. Messages are either in French or English.

◆ **Perspective and History of Quebec Nationalism**

http://www.uni.ca/history.html

The site provides a French Canadian perspective on the question of Quebec sovereignty along with a timeline of nationalist history, with a more detailed timeline beginning with 1976.

- **qc.politique**

This Usenet newsgroups contains discussions of Quebec politics with messages predominantly in French but with English ones intermixed.

- **soc.culture.Quebec**

Messages in this Usenet newsgroup are in either French or English and deal extensively with the question of Quebec independence.

HISTORY

- **Acadian History**

http://frenchcaculture.miningco.com/msub12.htm

This site has links to information about the history of Acadia and the Acadians, including Acadians in Louisiana. There is genealogical information as well as a historical timeline.

- **The French Presence in Canada and in British Columbia**

http://www.culturalexpress.com/news/french/
   french1.shtml

Historical information is provided about the settlement of Acadia, Quebec, and British Columbia.

- **Museum of Civilization**

http://www.mcq.org

There are both French and English versions of this site. The focus is on Quebec history, with some color pictures of important items in the collection. A Quebec map with the location of the museum is provided.

- **Official Symbols of the City of Montreal**

http://ville.montreal.qc.ca/symboles/engl/symbola.htm

Explanations and historical information along with graphical representations of the coat of arms, flag, and logo of the city of Montreal.

- **Pointe-à-Callière: Montreal Museum of Archaeology and History**

http://www.musee-pointe-a-calliere.qc.ca/carrefour/
   calliere/indexan.html

The site opens with a drawing of the museum with the location of key areas noted. There is a schedule of activities as well as information about both the permanent and temporary exhibitions. Since it opened in 1992, the Pointe-à-Callière has managed the archaeological collections of the City of Montréal. The Museum's collections are an invaluable resource for research, outreach and educational activities. The remains, fragments and objects found at the Pointe-à-Callière and Place

Royale sites are the basis of the Museum's archaeological collection with artifacts from other archaeological excavations in Montréal being gradually added.

Genealogy

◆ **Acadian Genealogy**

http://frenchcaculture.miningco.com/msub10.htm

The genealogy homepage has links to various genealogical information, including a list of Acadian-Cajun surnames and researchers. There is also a link to a Cajun Chat Room from this site.

LANGUAGE ARTS AND LITERATURE

Language Arts

◆ **Balzac-L**

Subscription address: listserv@cc.umontreal.ca

An electronic discussion group dealing with teaching and research in the area of French, Québécois or Francophone literature. To subscribe send the message **subscribe balzac-l your name** to the above address.

can.francais

This Usenet newsgroup deals with the use of the French language in Canada. Messages are in either French or English. French culture plus Quebec separatism are often the subject of messages.

can.talk.bilingualism

This Usenet newsgroup deals with the subject of bilingualism in Canada. Messages are about either Canadian English or French and are available in either language. Since language is a political issue in Canada, this group might also be seen as a political one as well as one about language.

Literature

◆ **Canlit-l**

Subscription address: listserv@infoserv.nlc-bnc.ca

Bilingual electronic mailing list for those interested in Canadian adult and children's literature. To subscribe send the message **subscribe canlit-l your name** to the above address.

◆ **French-Canadian Authors and Literature**

http://frenchcaculture.miningco.com/msub7.htm

There is a link from this site to a list of books by and about famous French Canadians and of novels about French Canada at the Amazon Bookstore. Other features of this site include information about authors plus some online books and poetry. The language of the Web site is English but some materials are in French only.

◆ **French Canadian Literature**

http://www.library.ubc.ca/fren/welcome.html

Features of this site include a list of electronic sites and electronic mailing lists dealing with French Canadian literature plus a bibliography of books which includes series, handbooks and dictionaries, regional biographical dictionaries, and retrospective bibliographies and guides.

POPULAR CULTURE

◆ **Montreal Family Tour Guide: Festivals**

http://www.odyssee.net/~bigben/fest.html#fest

This site states that Montreal is truly a City of Festivals. Information is provided here on some of the many festivals in and around Montreal from Jazz to Hot Air Balloons, from Grand Prix Racing to the Montreal Marathon to the World Film Festivals.

◆ **Quebec Casinos**

http://www.casinos-quebec.com

Highly graphical site that is available in both English and French. Information is provided about all the casinos in Quebec-Montreal, Charlevoix, and Hull—with access maps and virtual tours (parts of which require a QuickTime viewer). From the Montreal Casino page, there are hyperlinks to all types of information about Montreal that tourists, whether or not they are interested in gambling, would find of interest.

Food and Drink

◆ **Favorite French-Canadian Recipes**

http://frenchcaculture.miningco.com/library/cookbook/blrec000.htm

This site has a selection of traditional French-Canadian recipes for both main courses and desserts. There is a recipe submission form if you have any recipes that you would like to share.

◆ **World Wine Encyclopedia: Quebec**

http://www.winevin.com/quebecxx.html

Information about the wines produced in Quebec, along with information concerning the vintners. The initial screen contains a map of Quebec with major wine producing areas identified. Information about price ranges and a sweetness index are also provided.

Music

◆ **AfterHour**

http://www.Hour.qc.ca

Contains information about the music scene in Montreal plus the online version of *Hour Magazine,* which is a Montreal weekly cultural magazine that contains a listing of shows and films. There is a hotlinked listing of shareware for both Macintosh and Windows plus other features geared toward leisure activities.

◆ **Montreal International Jazz Festival**

http://www.montrealjazzfestival.worldlinx.com

This site is available in both French and English and provides an overview of the festival with information about tickets, free concerts and other activities.

Sports

◆ **Mountain Biking in Quebec**

http://www.total.net:8080/~swsmith

Information is provided about major bicycle trails in the Montreal area as well as providing links to other Web resources of interest to bicyclists.

◆ **Quebec Winter Carnival**

http://www.carnaval.qc.ca

Annual event with snow sculpting, dogsled racing, automobile racing, canoe racing, cross-country skiing, snow soccer tournament, parades and more. Site is highly graphical with an opening photograph of the current advertising poster.

◆ **La Route Verte**

http://www.velo.qc.ca/route_verte/

This site is available in French or English and contains copies of La Route Verte bulletins where information is provided about the Route Verte, a 3,000-kilometer bicycle network in the province of Quebec. There is a discussion of the planning process for the bike paths including safety considerations and financing.

Professional Sports

alt.sports.baseball.montreal-expos

This Usenet newsgroup deals with the Montreal Expos baseball team. Messages are generally in English and contain information both in regard to the Montreal team and baseball in general.

alt.sports.hockey.nhl.mtl-canadiens

Discussions in this Usenet newsgroup concern the Montreal Canadiens NHL hockey team.

◆ **Montreal Canadiens**

http://www.habs.com

Contains news from the *Montreal Gazette* and *Slam! Sports* about the Montreal Canadiens NHL hockey team along with their schedule, individual statistics, team standings, team records against opponents, roster and record. There is a link to their farm team, the Fredericton Canadiens of the American Hockey League. Fans can also participate in live chat about the team.

◆ **Montreal Canadiens Sound Page**

http://www.geocities.com/Colosseum/8805/

Audiofiles dealing with the Canadiens' games. Files are either midi or wav files and require no additional software to be installed before listening.

◆ **Montreal Expos Official Web Site**

http://www.montrealexpos.com/en/index.htm

Schedule and ticket information, player information plus box scores and statistics for the current season are available.

◆ **Radically Canadian: The Official Site of the CFL: Montreal Alouettes**

http://www.cfl.ca/CFLMontreal

Information about the Montreal Alouettes of the Canadian Football League, which includes their schedule, results and standings in the league and other information relating to the team and the Canadian Football League.

Television and Film

◆ **Montreal World Film Festival**

http://www.ffm-montreal.org/

This site is available in French and English. There are a FAQ (Frequently Asked Questions), press reviews and press releases, registration information and other similar information for the present year's events as well as a short history of the festival and archival information concerning past winners from 1977 to the present.

SCIENCE AND TECHNOLOGY

◆ **Quebec Science and Technology**

http://www.gouv.qc.ca/techno/indexa.htm

Information is provided concerning research and development efforts in Quebec, including government investment in such activities. There is also a brief, general discussion of university and college level training and research.

◆ **Science and Technology Council of Quebec**

http://www.cst.gouv.qc.ca

The English version is an abridgement of the information provided by the site in French. There is a list of English-language publications of the Council along with annotations. Some of the documents can be downloaded, others must be ordered.

Information Technology and Telecommunications

◆ **Canadian Technology Network**

http://ctn.nrc.ca

The Canadian Technology Network (CTN) links federal and provincial government labs and agencies, universities, community colleges, industry associations, technology centers and economic development agencies with the mission of providing innovative Canadian companies with quick and personal access to expertise, advice and information. CTN provides a wide variety of information aimed at small and medium-sized businesses in order to assist them in linking up with other technology related organizations.

OTHER

◆ **Bibliothèque Nationale du Québec**

http://www.biblinat.gouv.qc.ca/

English-only readers should choose the English Summary. Information is provided there on the Library, its collections, services, publications, and cultural activities. IRIS, the bibliographic database, contains descriptions of more than 475,000 documents published in Quebec or about Quebec. The database, which is highly graphical, is also available at low resolution for challenged browsers.

Exhibits

◆ **Aquarium du Québec**

http://www.aquarium.qc.ca/english

Information is provided about the aquarium, with color pictures, a layout plan of the aquarium, plus a location map to help a visitor locate the aquarium. There is a list of links to other aquarium sites and to similar information around the world.

◆ **Guide to Canadian Museums & Galleries**

http://www.rcip.gc.ca/Museums/e_museums.html

Lists Canadian museums with information about their collections and about special exhibitions. To obtain a list of museums and galleries in Quebec, from the homepage select Canadian Museums & Galleries, and then do a search on Quebec. This guide provides links to the various museums' or galleries' home-pages. For Quebec organizations, these hotlinked homepages are only in French, but the guide itself is available in English.

◆ **Montreal Botanical Garden**

http://www.versicolores.ca/jardins-du-quebec/en/html/ montreal_botanical_garden.html

Information with pictures is provided about the gardens, greenhouses, and nature trails along with opening hours and admission prices.

Maps

◆ **Montreal Major Highways Map**

http://www.cum.qc.ca/cum-fr/visiteur/tranvisf.htm

Includes major roads and the locations of the two commercial airports.

◆ **Montreal Metro Map**

http://www.stcum.qc.ca/metro/mapmetro.htm

Map of the Montreal subway system with neighborhood maps that can be obtained by clicking on the nearest metro station location on the map.

◆ **Old Montreal and Old Port Area**

http://www.svpm.ca/map

Initial map allows the user to click on major landmarks to obtain an enlarged map of the surrounding area that includes street names, names of major buildings, and parking garages.

Organizations

- **American Council for Quebec Studies**

http://www.iccs-ciec.ca/info/assoc/e-aqs.html

This Council is an association of scholars and others with teaching, research and/or business interests in Quebec and French Canada. The Web site contains information about the activities of the society and its publications.

Travel and Tourism

- **Montreal E-Guide**

http://www.pagemontreal.qc.ca/meg/

This site is a guide to Montreal sights and activities, divided into three sections: general information, Montreal by category (arts and entertainment, museums, bars, hotels, and restaurants), and Montreal by district. Montreal by district includes a color map with the different areas labeled. Information about each district includes metro stations and links to the category section for information about museums, restaurants, walking tours, etc. for that particular area of the city.

- **Montreal Official Tourist Information**

http://www.cum.qc.ca/octgm/english/Welcome.html

Contains a tourist guide including attractions, information on exchange rates, restaurants, shopping, temperatures and transportation, plus a section on accommodations in Montreal as well as information about Montreal as a convention site. In addition, there is a live camera providing a continuously updated picture of the downtown skyline.

- **Province of Quebec Travel Guide**

http://www.iisys.com/www/travel/canada/quebec

Highly graphical site with information about entertainment, sightseeing, recreation and sports, Quebec artisans, and businesses. There is a section entitled Visit the City of Montreal with additional information about Montreal, including accommodations, restaurants, the weather, etc.

- **Quebec Government Official Tourist Site**

http://www.tourisme.gouv.qc.ca

Tourist type information about attractions, events, and activities in the Province of Quebec. In addition, there is some historical information as well as a virtual tour of Quebec. This site is highly graphical with pictures, maps, and colorful background images (which sometimes distracts from the text).

- ### Quebec Tourist Guide
http://www.quebecweb.com

Select the link to Tourist Guide. This portion of this site contains information about cities and areas in each region of the Province of Quebec. As an example, the portions dealing with Quebec City and its surrounding areas provide pictures of the area and some historical details, as well as descriptions of attractions, museums, festivals, etc. Similar information is also available for Gaspe, Montreal, Charlevoix, Iles-de-la-Madeleine, Bas Saint-Laurent, Chaudiere-Appalaches, Estrie, Montérégie, Laurentides, Nouveau Québec-Baie-James, and Saquenay-Lac Saint-Jean.

Weather

- ### The Source of Weather – Quebec Region
http://www.wul.qc.doe.ca/meteo/index_ang.html

The categories of information provided include meteorological services, weather forecasts, current weather, imagery, weather watches, weather elsewhere in Canada, and road conditions. Five-day forecasts are based on five geographical regions of Quebec province and are further divided by city or locale. Marine forecasts for the St. Lawrence Seaway are divided into three regions and include information about wind speeds. One section of the site deals with weather warnings and is divided into geographical areas and marine warnings. In season, agricultural forecasts are available for Western, Central, and Eastern Quebec. The site is highly graphical, including maps and pictures.

13

Cajun and Creole Resources

MARILYN H. KARRENBROCK STAUFFER

INTRODUCTION

I don't really remember how I first located the sites in this chapter. I had already begun to collect multicultural resources on the Web for a course I teach on Library Services to Special Populations. One night, while surfing the Web, I came across a Cajun site. As I remember, that first site was the Everyday Cajun Homepage (**http://www.pcis.net/papabear/**). I was charmed by its color and friendly style. The page has changed a lot since then, but these qualities are still there. I also liked the page because it had pictures of Terrebonne Parish, where I once lived. (Louisiana, with its French background, uses the term "parish," rather than "county," for the administrative districts immediately below the state level.)

Whether I found the page by accident, or entered the term Cajun in a search engine first, I did search for the term almost immediately. Primarily, I used Altavista as a search engine, although I used a few others also. I used Deja News to search for Usenet newgroups. One of the best ways to find information, however, is by following the many links found on the Cajun and Creole pages themselves. Cajuns are very gregarious; they seldom do anything alone. A house in the country isn't an isolated farmhouse or one on a large acreage; it is likely to be one of twelve or fourteen houses in a row along a bayou. Even the Cajun Web pages are linked to many others.

Early in my search, I came across The Cajun and Creole Pages, unfortunately gone now, the work of Cajun Shane K. Bernard and Creole Herman Fuselier. Any chronicle of the unusual culture of southern Louisiana must include Creoles as well as Cajuns. The two groups are so intertwined in the culture of the area that they cannot easily be separated. Therefore, I generally used the terms Cajun and Creole in my searches.

Just what is a Cajun? A Creole? There is general agreement about the first term—a Cajun is a descendent of the Acadians, those French people who settled in Nova Scotia, Canada, in the early seventeenth century. After the British took possession of Canada, the Acadians were expelled in 1755. Many of them found refuge in southern Louisiana, settling there in 1763. There the term *Acadian* gradually became *Cadien* and then *Cajun*. There are many definitions and explanations of the term on the Web. A simple, mildly humorous definition is found at Acadiana: Les Paroisses Acadiennes (**http://www.webcom.com/~gumbo/cajun-home.html**). Serious, often historical, discussions are found at What's a Cajun? at Boudreaux's Cajun Wharf (**http://home.cheney.net/~boudreau/ilo_lalinks.htm**), What Is a "Cajun"? at the Acadian Genealogy Homepage (**http://www.acadian.org/genealogy/cajun.html**), Cajuns—Who are They? at the Cajun Cooking Page (**http://www.lacajun.com/mslucy/cooking.htm**), Cajun Country at the Louisiana Department of Culture, Recreation, and Tourism (**http://www.crt.state.la.us/crt/profiles/cajuns.htm**), and The Cajun People at Cajun Cooking Cuisine (**http://shell.ihug.co.nz/~sofr/cajun_p.html**). A nostalgic version is found at I'm Proud to Be a Cajun at A Taste of Louisiana (**http://www.geocities.com/BourbonStreet/3076/cajun.htm**) and a light-hearted one at What's a Cajun at Cajun Country U.S.A. (**http://www.geocities.com/BourbonStreet/2374/whats.html**). The most popular explanation, based on the number of Cajun sites which link to it, is the humorous What Is a Cajun? at Cajun Brew (**http://rampages.onramp.net/~ndronet/cajunis.htm**). The same site also explains the other, controversial name for a Cajun (Cajuns and the Term "Coonass" at **http://rampages.onramp.net/~ndronet/conasse.htm**). As the writer says, "Basically, if you call me a coonass, you'd better be a close friend."

The meaning of the term Creole is not as clear-cut as that of Cajun. In the past it has referred to white people of mixed French and Spanish heritage; to French-speaking persons in Louisiana, whether white, of African descent, or mixed-race persons of color; and to light-skinned African Americans as opposed to darker-skinned ones. Today, it is occasionally used by white people of French-Spanish descent to describe themselves, but usually the term refers exclusively to African Americans living in Acadiana, the southern parishes of Louisiana. Extensive explanations of the term are given by Edward J. Branley in On Being Creole at The Gumbo Pages (**http://www.gumbopages.com/being-creole.html**), and by Shane K. Bernard in The Encyclopedia of Cajun Culture (**http://www.cajunculture.com/Other/creole.htm**).

The "big three" topics in Cajun and Creole pages on the Web are music, food, and history/genealogy. The first two have always been very important in the Acadiana culture. In the last thirty years, renewed interest in preserving the French language in Louisiana has led to interest in the Acadian background and the genealogy of its people. Tourism is another topic that is well represented on the Web; the unique culture and landscape of South Louisiana make it a popular vacation area. Of course, many other topics are also found. Many of the Cajun and Creole pages are among the most attractive I have seen on the Web, replete with clever graphics, lively animation, and toe-tapping music. There are many personal homepages which are worth viewing for these characteristics. A few of these are listed in this chapter; others can be found at The Cajun Ring Homepage (http://www.geocities.com/BourbonStreet/3785/cajunring.htm) and at many links on the pages listed below.

GENERAL INFORMATION

- **Acadiana: Les Paroisses Acadiennes**
http://www.gumbopages.com/cajun-home.html

Still under construction at press time, the site is primarily a collection of links to Cajun music, food, culture, tourism, festivals, and genealogical sites.

- **Boudreaux's Cajun Wharf**
http://home.cheney.net/~boudreau/index.htm

Cajun history, humor, and religion are found here. An interesting section called Cocodrie gives words to a song, set to the tune of "Kokomo," about one of the southernmost settlements in Terrebonne Parish. The Cajun Links are quite extensive and well-arranged by category.

- **Cajun Country, USA**
http://www.geocities.com/BourbonStreet/2374/cajland.html
http://www.geocities.com/~poboys/cajland.html

Both addresses will get you to the same page. Graphics intense (and with music!), these pages are devoted to such matters as What's a Cajun?, Cajun tourism, fun, food, sports, and Cajuns on the net.

- **A Cajun Homepage**
http://www.coonass.com/

This personal page has interesting information about growing up in St. Landry Parish, Louisiana, good photographs of the area, and a description and history of Opelousas, Louisiana. There are recipes and other information.

- **The Cajun Ring Homepage**
http://cust2.iamerica.net/madmark/

The Cajun Ring is a group of Web sites that are Cajun/Louisiana oriented. Sites share personal and cultural experiences and must be rated general. In a Ring, sites are connected so that Web surfers can click from one site to the next until they get back to where they started. Many personal sites not listed in this chapter can be found here. Such sites, while often colorful, usually do not contain material of interest to most other people. For a list of all Cajun Ring sites, see The Cajun Ring Friends at **http://amigonet.org/cajun/**.

◆ Cajun's Web Index

http://pcis.net/cajun/index.htm

Index to Cajun's Homepage of James L. Lambert, Jr., and other pages maintained by him and his family. Mostly personal and familial information, but there are some nice pictures of New Orleans and Cajun country under the link entitled Cajun's Louisiana Pics, Vol. 1.

◆ Encyclopedia of Cajun Culture

www.cajunculture.com

One of the most complete of the Web pages on Cajun culture, by Shane K. and Kara Tobin Bernard. The Encyclopedia discusses topics in an alphabetical list from Acadian to Zydeco. Some articles include pictures. Sources for all articles are given; a short citation is given at the end of each article, with full information found on the References page. (See Mission Statement.)

◆ Everyday Cajun Homepage

http://www.pcis.net/papabear/

Homepage of Cliff Hebert. Still under construction at the time of this writing, but under the Everyday Cajun Menu there are Cajun Recipes and Cajun Scenes from Terrebonne Parish, Louisiana.

◆ The Gumbo Pages

http://www.gumbopages.com/index.html

A former resident of New Orleans, Chuck Taggart, now host of Gumbo, a radio show in Los Angeles, provides extensive information on New Orleans and Acadiana, as well as other information on music and radio. This is one of the most extensive sites on Cajun and Creole information. It includes The Cajun and Creole Recipe Page and Acadiana: Les Paroisses Acadiennes, listed separately in this chapter.

◆ Lafayette Convention and Visitors Commission: FAQ's and Facts

http://www.cajunhot.com/html/facts.html

This page, part of the Lafayette Convention and Visitors Commission Web page listed in this chapter under Tourist Information, is chock full of information about the area and its cultures. You can see pictures of the Cajun and Creole flags, and don't miss the Live Oak Society page. There is much, much more. An outstanding resource!

◆ Louisiana: Acadiana ... Bayou Country ... Cajun Country

http://www.geocities.com/Heartland/Hills/2789/ html1.html

This is a personal page, but it is worth including here because of several things not found elsewhere. It has a history of the King Cake, a couple of lovely photographs of the waterways of the area, and a list of links, but the most useful part of the page is found under Louisiana Statistics. Despite its name, this page does not give statistics, but has excellent photographs of the state Capitol building, seal, flag, dog, bird, insect, flower, tree, and other things.

◆ **Louisiana State Library**

http://smt.state.lib.la.us/

The Louisiana State Library homepage has genealogical information, Louisiana state documents, and other information that may be of interest.

◆ **Louisiana, Where Y'at—Your Cajun Connection**

http://http.tamu.edu:8000/~n017ij/bcc.html

Excellent links to many matters about Cajuns and their culture and to tourist information for the state of Louisiana.

◆ **Welcome to Cajun Land!**

http://cust.iamerica.net/ccallais/

A personal homepage. Much of it is not of general interest, but Montegut, La., which is a history of Terrebonne Parish (taken from Le Terrebonne, by Sherwin Guidry), Superstitions on the Bayou, Cajun Christmas Songs!, and Marie Leveau give interesting information not found on other Web pages.

Newspapers, Magazines, and Newsletters

◆ **The Advocate Online**

http://www.theadvocate.com/

The Advocate is Baton Rouge's newspaper. Its online version is easy to read with lots of material. You can even see old Calvin and Hobbes cartoons there!

◆ **The New Orleans and Cajun Country Newsletter**

http://www.cajunews.com/

A monthly newsletter primarily about things Cajun, New Orleans and the rest of Louisiana are covered in less depth. The current issue is available on the Web or by e-mail, and recent issues are downloadable; look for Old Websites under the heading Downloadable Files.

◆ **The Opelousas Daily World Online**

http://www.dailyworld.com/

The Opelousas Daily World is another newspaper from Acadiana that has a useful online version.

- **South Louisiana's Internet Magazine**

http://www.houma.com/

Information about the city of Houma, Louisiana, its institutions and activities. Some pages are specific to the area; a few, such as the sports and the weather pages, link to general information sites. Not available from the home-page, but linked at the bottom of most of the other pages, is information about Terrebonne Parish (summary, history, and statistics), and the site of Houma, located on the Gulf of Mexico about an hour's drive west of New Orleans.

BUSINESS

- **Greater Lafayette Chamber of Commerce, Inc.**

http://www.lafchamber.org/

At this site, one can find out about the Chamber, locate businesses by category, and find a record of events for the next year.

- **The Louisiana Internet Mall**

http://www.icorp.net/lamall/home.htm

An Internet mall of five companies, four of which sell food products and one devoted to music.

- **The Rice Farm**

http://www.deltech.net/members/pat43/rice.html

This page describes rice farming in Southwestern Louisiana from planting through harvest. Photographs of the 1997 crop at various stages are included. This is part of a personal page called Grandma's Playhouse (**http://www.deltech.net/members/pat43/**) which has Cajun links.

- **Shop Southwest Louisiana**

http://www.shopswla.com/

A large virtual mall with a variety of products. Also has local information and links paged Cool Links and (from the Area Businesses page) one called Webbound Louisiana.

CULTURE AND HUMANITIES, GENERAL

- **Acadiana Culture**

http://www.net-connect.net/acadiana_info.html

Links to Cajun and southern Louisiana Web sites.

◆ **Action Cadienne—Cajun Action**

http://www.rbmulti.nb.ca/cadienne/cajun.htm

Action Cadienne is a nonprofit volunteer association dedicated to the promotion of the French language and the Cadien (Cajun) culture of Louisiana. The site is also available in French.

alt.culture.cajun

This Usenet newsgroup is devoted to Cajun culture and similar matters of interest. There are few messages posted at any one time.

◆ **Cajun Culture, Creole Culture—Louisiana's French Heritage**

http://www.lsu.edu/guests/poli/public_html/newla.html#Caj

Dozens of links to sites of interest. The Cajun/Creole section is part of a page called Selected Louisiana Resources on the Internet, maintained by Prof. James Bolner, Sr., of Louisiana State University; however, other sections of the page also have relevance.

◆ **Cajun Storyteller Revives an Old Tradition**

http://www.yall.com/thearts/quill/storytell.html

Biographical information about the Cajun storyteller, J. J. Reneaux, including two of her stories, one in text and one in RealAudio format. This site supplements Reneaux's own site, J. J. Reneaux, listed below.

◆ **J. J. Reneaux**

http://www.redhouse.com/jjreneaux/

Reneaux is a renowned Cajun storyteller, author, and musician. The Web page includes information about her books, audiotapes of stories, and her CD of Southern songs, Cajun, Country and Blue. The music from the CD is supposed to be available online, but when this book was written, it was unavailable due to a recent server change. However, short excerpts from the CD were available at Cajun Melodies, **http://www.yall.com/thearts/quill/ccb.html**. Reneaux's site is full of information and very attractive.

◆ **The Louisiana Folklife Center**

http://www.nsula.edu/departments/folklife/

The Louisiana Folklife Center is an agency of Northwestern State University of Louisiana at Natchitoches. Although this location is not in Acadiana, its interests include Cajun and Creole life. The Center sponsors the Natchitoches-NSU Folklife Festival each year; publishes a periodical, *Louisiana Folklife* (contents given); releases folklife-related recordings; and selects outstanding Louisiana folk artists for the Louisiana Hall of Master Folk Artists. Biographies of folk artists are listed by ethnicity, art form (including such unexpected ones as religious rituals, folk medicine, hunting and trapping, etc.), and geographical location. Louisiana's Traditional Cultures (**http://www.nsula.edu/departments/folklife/**

tradcult.html) is an article describing Louisiana cultures in detail. The whole site is not to be missed!

◆ **Louisiana Folklife Festival**

http://www.fon-insight.com/folklife/folklif.htm

The Louisiana Folklife Program is part of the Louisiana Division of the Arts, Department of Culture, Recreation, and Tourism. Its purpose is to preserve and promote Louisiana's folk culture, which is derived from many nations and cultures. The yearly Festival, now held in Monroe, Louisiana, celebrates the state's diverse heritages. The Welcome message tells of the history of the Festival, and handicrafts, food, music, narrations, participants, and the schedule at the Festival are described. In addition, the page called The Creole State gives a good description of the various ethnic groups found in the state.

◆ **"You See What I Say": The Mardi Gras Indians of New Orleans**

http://www.noline.com/indians.htm

A most intriguing look at an unusual culture—Creoles of Color (African Americans) who parade and dance in elaborate homemade costumes at Mardi Gras and other festivals. The custom is said to be based upon traditional ties between African slaves who were befriended by Native Americans and were sometimes adopted as members of the tribes. The tribes use a combination of West African and Native American motifs in the costumes. Click on all the links to see related interviews and pictures.

EDUCATION

◆ **Louisiana State University**

http://www.lsu.edu/

General information about the state's largest university, located in Baton Rouge.

◆ **Project Evangeline**

http://www.gumbopages.com/acadiana/evangeline.html

This educational project, funded from a variety of sources including Apple Computer, Council for the Development of French in Louisiana (CODOFIL), and various universities and individuals, has produced a multimedia computer CD-ROM program to teach students about Cajun heritage and culture. It has been distributed to schools across Louisiana and in other states. It is available in both English and French.

- **The University of Southwestern Louisiana**
  http://www.usl.edu/AboutUSL/introduction.html
  USL, at Lafayette, Louisiana, is the second largest university in the state. Its homepage gives information about enrollment, programs, athletics, and other general information.

FINE ARTS

- **Etc Arts Culture Communications Monthly**
  http://www.netwwworks.com/98etc/1jan/index.htm
  This arts magazine covers Baton Rouge, Lafayette, and New Orleans.

- **Festival International de Louisiane**
  http://fil.net-connect.net/
  The Festival International de Louisiane is an organization that since 1986 has produced an annual visual and performing arts festival that celebrates Southern Louisiana's cultural heritage and emphasizes its relationship with the rest of the French-speaking world, particularly the French, African-Caribbean and Hispanic influences. Programming includes music, theater, dance, visual arts, cinema and culinary arts.

Art

Visual Art

- **Chez Surette Art: Epic Historical Paintings by Surette**
  http://www3.ns.sympatico.ca/pat.emin/NSURETTE.HTM
  Nelson Surette is a Canadian painter of historical subjects. Among them are a series of six paintings showing the expulsion and return to Nova Scotia of the Acadians which can be seen at the University Gallery (**http://www3.ns.sympatico.ca/pat.emin/GALLERY.HTM**).

- **Dafford's Sight**
  http://www.mural.com/dafford_html/center.html
  Muralist Robert Dafford is a native of Louisiana. Among his works at the Gallery Acadien (**http://www.mural.com/murals_html/gallery.html**) are paintings that show the exile of the Acadians from Nova Scotia and their settlement of Louisiana. Other works by Dafford are also shown.

◆ **Guy's Homepage**

http://www.saia.com/guyhome/gfanguy.htm

Guy Fanguy is an artist from Houma, Louisiana, whose pictures are primarily drawings of typical Cajun scenes or humorous cartoon-like drawings.

HISTORY

◆ **The Acadian Memorial: St. Martinville, La.**

http://www.pwcweb.com/usapages/acadian/

The Acadian Memorial is located in the heart of Cajun country. It includes a mural of the founding of Louisiana by the French settlers exiled from Canada, a wall of names of the settlers, and an eternal flame symbolizing their ability to rekindle their culture in a new land. The site also has pictures and information about nearby sights such as the statue of Evangeline.

◆ **The Acadian Odyssey**

http://www.schoolnet.ca/collections/acadian/intro/

This site tells of the forced deportation by the British authorities of the French-speaking Acadians from Canada between 1755 and 1763. The people were sent to the English colonies along the east coast of North America, some going as far south as Georgia. Later, the ancestors of the present-day Cajuns emigrated to what is now Louisiana. This is a highly informative site with pictures and interesting graphics.

◆ **Acadian Odyssey**

http://www.teachnet.org/blueplate/dupuis/index.htm

Another version of Acadian history. It does not seem to be complete, since it ends before the deportation from Canada. There are topics listed in the sidebar-index that are not yet on the Web. Click on On Crawfish to read a tall tale about the origin of this mud bug. Notice that when you reach the page for this tale, you will enter in the middle of the page; look above the entry point as well as below.

◆ **The Center for Louisiana Studies, University of Southwestern Louisiana**

http://www.usl.edu/Departments/Center.La.Studies/
gopher://suze.ucs.usl.edu:70/11/
    Center%20for%20Louisiana%20Studies%20%28Louisiana
    %20History%29

The Center for Louisiana Studies was established in 1973 to promote a better understanding of Louisiana's history and culture. The Web site has an extensive description of the Center and its programs. The gopher site has bibliographies for Acadian, African American, Antebellum, Civil War, and Louisiana Indians which are useful for those wishing to learn about any of these topics in Louisiana history.

◆ **History of Terrebonne Parish**

http://www.rootsweb.com/~laterreb/histerr.htm

This page describes the history of Terrebonne Parish from prehistoric times until about 1855. Although the history is not complete, it is already very interesting. Related pages include Indians in Terrebonne Parish (**http://www.rootsweb.com/~laterreb/indian.htm**) and Terrebonne Parish Today (**http://www.rootsweb.com/~laterreb/today.htm**).

◆ **A Little Cajun History**

http://www.geocities.com/Heartland/2073/cajun.htm

Another history of the odyssey from Acadia to Louisiana, with an emphasis on the part played by religion. Be aware that the history begins on the second screen of the page.

◆ **Le Monument to Be Restored**

http://www.cajunews.com/monument.htm

The Ascension of Our Lord Catholic Cemetery in Donaldson, Louisiana, has been placed on the National Register of historic places. The tomb of the Bringier family, located near the entrance to the cemetery, is undergoing restoration. The Web site includes a history of the Bringier family and pictures of the massive tomb.

◆ **Ville Platte, Louisiana, Cajun Heartland USA**

http://www.geocities.com/Heartland/2073/vp.htm

This page leads to a short but interesting history of Ville Platte and one for its parish, Evangeline Parish.

Archaeology

◆ **Ancient Architects of the Mississippi**

http://www.cr.nps.gov/aad/feature/feature.htm

An extensive site, by the National Park Service (NPS), which describes the Moundbuilder civilization of the Lower Mississippi valley and the NPS efforts to save it through the Lower Mississippi Delta Region Initiative. There are many pages here and it is not always clear what is available. For full information, click on Next at the bottom of each page, as well as all links within the text. Nice maps and graphics.

◆ **Louisiana Division of Archaeology**

**http://www.crt.state.la.us/crt/ocd/arch/homepage/
    index.htm**

This extremely valuable site has three virtual books that combine text, maps, and pictures much as a printed book would do. Two of these books include projects in Acadiana. The first, Beyond the Great House: Archaeology at Ashland-Belle Helene Plantation, focuses on the growing and processing of sugar-cane and the day-to-day life of African Americans who served as slaves and later as laborers on the plantation, which was located in Acadiana. The second virtual book, Louisiana Prehistory, describes the Native Americans who lived in the area from 10,000 B.C.E. until about 1,500 C.E. Many of these cultures were located in Acadiana. Maps show the location of each site.

◆ **NPS Lower Mississippi Delta Project**

http://www.cr.nps.gov/seac/deltapro.htm

A poster showing the ancient Moundbuilder civilization called Ancient Civilizations—Forgotten Cultures heads this site. It is a public awareness project of the Southeast Archaeological Center (SEAC) of the National Park Service (the homepage, which contains much information about the Southeast outside Acadiana, is at **http://www.cr.nps.gov/seac/seac.htm**). One can view the text on the back of the poster and link to several other NPS or SEAC sites.

Genealogy

◆ **Acadian-Cajun Genealogy**

http://www.geocities.com/~timhebert/

Acadian and Cajun history and genealogy, genealogy links, and other information are found at this very useful site. Unfinished, but there is already an enormous amount of information and it is constantly being updated.

◆ **Acadian Genealogy Homepage**

http://www.acadian.org/

The main attraction of this site is a huge number of links to various Acadian resources. Most of them are part of this site, although there are links to other Web sites as well. Acadian is interpreted very broadly to include information about Canada, Maine, France, and other places as well as Louisiana. Much of the information consists of reprinted articles from various publications and is historical rather than strictly genealogical. The Web site author advertises a CD called In Search of Our Acadian Roots.

◆ **Acadian Roots**

**http://www.schoolnet.ca/collections/acadian/english/
eroots/eroots.htm**

This site from the Centre Acadien of Université Sainte-Anne, Church Point, Nova Scotia, includes information on first settlers and heraldry of Acadian family names. The background may make the site hard to read, but this can be solved by highlighting the text.

◆ **American-French Genealogical Society**

http://users.ids.net/~afgs/afgswhat.html

Founded in 1978, the AFGS is devoted to helping people of French-Canadian descent to trace their genealogy. The organization itself is located in Rhode Island, with headquarters in Pawtucket and a library in Woonsocket. From the library materials mentioned, it seems to be mainly concerned with those people of French-Canadian ancestry in the New England area.

◆ **Cajun Clickers Geneaology SIG**

http://www.intersurf.com/~cars/

The Cajun Clickers Genealogy SIG was founded in 1993 to promote the merger of technology and genealogy research. It is headquartered in Baton Rouge and has an impressive list of Web links.

◆ **Franco Gene**

http://www.cam.org/~beaur/gen/welcome.html

Formerly known as The Denis Beauregard Genealogy Pages and later as "Francétres," this site is dedicated to the genealogy of the French-speaking world, including Quebec, Acadia, Louisiana, France, Belgium, and Switzerland.

◆ **The Hebert Family**

http://www.geocities.com/Heartland/Hills/3061/hebert.htm

Hebert (pronounced A-bear) is the fifth most common Cajun surname in the United States and the most common in Louisiana (see Distribution and Population of Heberts, **http://www.geocities.com/Heartland/Hills/3061/hebdist.htm**). It is an Old French name, with French, German, and English variations which are detailed here. The site includes family history, heraldry, etc., as well.

◆ **Jeansonne/Johnson Family of Louisiana**

http://www.geocities.com/BourbonStreet/5075/index.html

A Web page devoted to the Jeansonne family (sometimes spelled Johnson) who are descended from William ("Billy") Johnson and Isabelle Corporon, who were married in Acadia in 1713. The site focuses primarily but not exclusively on the Louisiana branch of the family, but does not include persons surnamed Johnson who are not descended from the pair named above. The site describes the first four generations of the family and is a model for building an attractive genealogical Web page.

◆ **Louisiana USGenWeb Project**

http://www.flex.net/u/golden/la-state/la-state.html

This site is a database of genealogical and family history information from all the Louisiana parishes. Although the LA Parish Selection List gives access to Web pages for most of the state's parishes, not all have genealogical records entered yet. Some of the most interesting sites are listed on the main page.

◆ **Oldbears Index**

http://www.geocities.com/Heartland/9220/start.htm

This page has an index to over 12,000 Acadian and Quebec surnames, plus more information about Heberts.

◆ **Provincial Press: Reference Books by Winston De Ville**

http://www.provincialpress.com/

The site offers approximately thirty books by De Ville, a Fellow of the American Society of Genealogists. Many of the books would be of interest to Cajun families seeking their roots.

LANGUAGE ARTS AND LITERATURE

Language Arts

◆ **1915 Rue Bourbon—Introductory Cajun French**

http://www.geocities.com/BourbonStreet/1915/

This site attempts to teach the basics of Cajun French. It introduces pronunciation and the words for numbers, money, parts of the human body, and things seen in the backyard. Its approach to the language is more systematic than the other sites, but it does not deal with some common words and expressions of the area.

◆ **Cajun French Phrases**

http://www.allons.com/cajun.htm

Common Cajun French phrases used by everyone in Cajun country are explained here, with pronunciation.

◆ **How to Speak Local Tongue in New Orleans**

http://www.yall.com/yonder/cityscapes/no_lang.html

This article describes the differences between Cajun and Creole, defining Creole as the descendants of French or Spanish settlers. It also has a list of words common in New Orleans and Cajun country, ranging from andouille (sausage) to Zydeco (type of music).

◆ **See It & Say It in Louisiana**

http://www.crt.state.la.us/crt/sayit.htm

Another list of French phrases, with pronunciation, from the Louisiana Department of Tourism.

POPULAR CULTURE

◆ **Offbeat Magazine's Web Space**

http://www.neosoft.com/~offbeat/

Offbeat Magazine is the monthly music and entertainment magazine of New Orleans and Louisiana. Cajun and Zydeco music are well represented. The Web site features some of the articles, reviews, club listings, and columns from the current issue. Another version of the homepage can be found at **http://www.neosoft.com/~offbeat/home.html**; the text here takes up a larger area of the screen. These homepages do not link to earlier issues, but an index to articles that have appeared can be found at **http://www.neosoft.com/~offbeat/text/**.

Dance

◆ **Dancin' in South Louisiana**

http://www.tabasco.com/html/music_letsdance.html

This site, part of the TABASCO PepperFest page, not only gives instructions for the Cajun two-step, it even has an animation of the steps.

◆ **Learn to Zydeco Dance Tonite! Video Page**

http://www.erols.com/bpagac/video.html

This site briefly explains Zydeco music and dance and offers for sale an instructional video for Zydeco dancing.

Food and Drink

◆ **Cajun Brew: Home of the Ragin' Cajun Recipe Pages**

http://rampages.onramp.net/~ndronet/index.htm

All kinds of recipes donated by various people, plus basic techniques for making rice and rouxs.

◆ **Cajun Cooking: A Grocery Store of Products from Louisiana**

http://www.shopswla.com/webbound/sites/culture.html

This site sells almost anything you could want for Cajun cooking, including equipment and food products (although there are a limited number of brands available).

◆ **Cajun Crawfish at Frugé Aquafarms**

http://www.cajuncrawfish.com/

Boudreaux the Crawfish leads the viewer on a humorous tour of everything you ever wanted to know about the little Louisiana mud bug. The company sells crawfish by mail order in season.

◆ **Cajun Culture by Tony Chachere's Creole Foods: Nothing Is More Cajun**

http://www.cajunspice.com

The Web site of the first inductee to Louisiana's Chefs Hall of Fame. Much of the site is devoted to advertisements for products (cookbooks, seasonings, rice mixtures, gift baskets) but there are also recipes, Tony's Tales (personal stories), and one of the largest collections of Cajun links I have found (check under Fun Stuff).

◆ **A Cajun Family's Recipe Book: A Little Lagniappe from Delta Eagle Enterprise**

http://deltaeagle.com/index.htm

This site features more than 500 recipes from a Cajun family in Franklin, Louisiana. It also links to Bodin Foods, Inc. (**http://deltaeagle.com/bodin/bodin.htm**), which sells Cajun foods.

◆ **Cajun in the Kitchen**

http://users.accessus.net/~cajun/

Bob and Eve Broussard have provided a page for those cooks who say, "Cajun Yes ... Blackened No." Despite popular belief, burning and covering in pepper is not a characteristic of true Cajun food. The crawfish in the chef's hat leads to the recipes; the alligator with the accordion provides links to other sites that share the Broussard's philosophy about Cajun food. Great music and graphics! A fun page!

◆ **Cajun Land Seasonings**

http://www.icorp.net/cajun/main.htm

A full line of seasonings for Cajun dishes is offered for sale, along with cooking directions and recipes.

◆ **Chef Paul Prudhomme—"America's Favorite Chef"**

http://www.chefpaul.com

Chef Paul, who made Cajun food famous (albeit the blackened kind deplored by the Broussards), sells his seasonings and cookbooks at this site, but he also gives recipes and cooking tips and tricks.

◆ **Comeaux's Inc., Authentic Products of Cajun Louisiana**

http://www.lacajun.com/mslucy/cooking.htm

Another site selling many Cajun food products. It does describe many of the products less familiar outside Louisiana, something which many sites don't do. Don't bother to click on the product links—they simply lead to pictures, seldom ones of the product you are clicking on.

◆ **The Creole and Cajun Recipe Page**

http://www.gumbopages.com/recipe-page.html

Great recipes of all kinds from New Orleans and Cajun country, as well as other links to food and drinks on the Web. Links to information about Cajun and Creole cooking and the Cajun Food Craze give a history of Louisiana cuisine and how it has developed. Don't miss the special bonus, The Crawfish-Sea Urchin Tale.

◆ **The Gumbo Shop**

http://www.gumboshop.com/

The attractive homepage of this New Orleans restaurant includes menus, products to order, and a collection of secret recipes, including such New Orleans favorites as gumbo, jambalaya, and bread pudding with whiskey sauce.

◆ **Okra**

http://www.fatfree.com/foodweb/food/okra.html

Okra is a vegetable many people love to hate, but it is essential in the South, where it is used in gumbo and other recipes. This page gives basic information on selecting and preparing okra, including a few recipes.

◆ **Okra**

http://www.agric.gov.ab.ca/food/nutrit/veg08.html#top

This okra page gives, for example, nutritive values. No recipes are provided, however. Strangely enough, since okra is definitely a warm weather plant, this page comes from the Alberta (Canada) Agriculture Department; it seems they grow it in greenhouses there.

◆ **Okra**

http://www.produceoasis.com/Items_folder/Vegetables/Okra.html

Still another okra page, this site is by far the most attractive of the lot, but with very similar content. There is a place for recipes, but at the time this book was written, they were not yet there. A few interesting bits of trivia about okra are included.

◆ **Prejean's Restaurant**

http://www.prejeans.com/html/entrees.html

Prejean's Restaurant in Lafayette provides Cajun food, music, and dancing. The menu contains fish, shellfish, and crawfish, of course, but it also includes such delicacies as venison, alligator, and frog legs.

◆ **Pure Cajun Products**

http://www.purecajun.com/index.htm

One of the largest selections of products for authentic Cajun food on the Web. Also has cookbooks for sale. There are History of the Cajuns and Myths about Cajun Foods pages.

◆ **Southerners Love Odd Little Okla Pod**

http://www.yall.com/thesouth/vittles/okra.html?splasher

A humorous but informative article about the fuzzy, slimy vegetable that is essential for making gumbo.

◆ **Steen's Syrup**

http://www.steensyrup.com/

Steen's 100 percent Pure Cane Syrup has been produced in South Louisiana for over eighty-five years. At this site, you can read about its history, cook from a lengthy list of recipes, add your own comments and reminiscences, or order syrup for your table. There is also the largest set of Cajun/Creole links I have seen; it is very useful because it is listed by topic.

◆ **Tabasco PepperFest**

http://www.tabasco.com/

PepperFest is the Web page of the McIlhenny Company, makers of Tabasco sauce, the hot peppery sauce that is synonymous with Cajun food. Although this is, of course, primarily a food-related site, it is also much more. For instance, you can listen to Cajun music with RealAudio, learn to dance the Cajun two-step, or look at photographs of the Cajun Mardi Gras (for the two latter, see Dancin' in South Louisiana and Images from Cajun Mardi Gras in this chapter). You can even download a great screensaver!

◆ **Tailgating Across America**

http://206.1.91.150/tailgate/halftime.htm

Chef Joe Cahn, founder of the New Orleans School of Cooking, took a tailgate trip across America during the 1996 National Football League season. In the process, he taught fans how to tailgate and introduced them to New Orleans cooking. The site includes Cajun and Creole recipes. In the half-time section, Cahn gives a History of Louisiana Cooking and a Cajun Food Dictionary, along with other information.

◆ **A Taste of Louisiana**

http://www.geocities.com/BourbonStreet/3076/index.html

This site not only provides Char's extensive recipe collection, but also has links to the Louisiana Music page and the Louisiana, U.S.A. history page, which are each listed separately in this chapter.

◆ **The Web Is Cooking**

http://cust2.iamerica.net/madmark/0206food.htm

Nancy Regent's article from the *Baton Rouge Advocate* is subtitled Homepages Featuring Cajun Recipes Cropping Up on the World Wide Web. Regent discusses various recipe pages on the Web (links are given) and includes several recipes.

Humor

◆ **Boudreaux Jokes**

http://home.cheney.net/~boudreau/ilo_boudreaux.htm

An attractive page that pokes gentle fun at Boudreaux and his friend Thibodeaux. Do try the Dirty Joke at the beginning.

◆ **The Cajun Dictionary**

http://www2.cajun.net/~cajundict/

The Cajun Dictionary is a humorous compilation of Cajun dialect written by James Sothern and illustrated by Jerry Charpentier. The site includes a few examples, some pictures from the book, and an online order form.

◆ **Sleauxman's Cajun Humor Page**

http://web.wt.net/~slovacek/cajun_humor.htm

A few more Boudreaux jokes, plus You Know You're a Cajun If ... and A Cajun Mother's Letter to Her Son; the latter two are similar to those often attributed to other cultural groups.

Mardi Gras

◆ **History of the King Cake**

http://www.wlox.com/store/history.htm

King Cakes were originally served on Epiphany in honor of the Three Kings who visited the Christ Child on that day, according to Christian tradition. Today, the King Cake has become a vital part of Mardi Gras. Baked inside the cake is a tiny baby figure representing the Christ Child. The person who gets the baby must provide the King Cake at the next celebration.

◆ **Images from Cajun Mardi Gras**

http://www.tabasco.com/html/artsgames.html

Photographs by Sydney Byrd of the strange Cajun Mardi Gras, very different from the one in New Orleans, which, believe it or not, is more decorous and sophisticated than its Cajun cousin. Photographs here show the celebration in Eunice, Church Point, Basile, and Gheens. This site is part of the Tabasco PepperFest Page.

◆ **Krewe of Bacchus**

http://www.geocities.com/BourbonStreet/6737/bacchus.htm

Bacchus is one of the more popular parades at Mardi Gras. Started in 1969, it was the first krewe (Louisiana mystic social club) to open its celebration to tourists and to choose celebrities for its king. A list of kings for every year is available. Although the site is not complete, it is very attractive and interesting and has great music.

◆ **Mardi Gras Indians: Tradition and History**

http://www.MardiGrasNewOrleans.com/mardigrasindians/

The Mardi Gras Indians are African American clubs that parade at Mardi Gras, dressed in beaded costumes supposedly based on Native American regalia. The site gives the history of the Mardi Gras Indians and has interesting photographs.

◆ **Mardi Gras New Orleans**

http://www.MardiGrasNewOrleans.com/zulu/

Almost anything you could want to know about Mardi Gras can be found on these pages—history, do's and don'ts, pictures of recent past celebrations, memorabilia.

◆ **Traditional King Cake Recipe**

http://www.wlox.com/store/history.htm

A recipe for King Cake, plus a link to another page with a short History of King Cakes.

◆ **Zulu Social Aid and Pleasure Club, Inc.**

http://www.MardiGrasNewOrleans.com/zulu/

Zulu is the famous African American krewe that has been marching on Mardi Gras since 1909. The site includes a history of the krewe, the 1997 Proclamation of King Zulu LXXX, and a series of collector's posters that can be purchased.

Music

◆ **Acadiana Music**

http://www.net-connect.net/music/

At the time this was written, Acadiana Music was only begun, but it already had a couple of tunes (both an excerpt and the entire song) available for listening. The intent is to have a wide representation of Acadiana music available on the site in the future.

◆ **Allons à Lafayette! Historical Recordings of Cajun Music**

http://www.dirtynelson.com/linen/feature/60cajun.html

An article on the history, instruments, and recording of Cajun music.

◆ **Balladeer Music General Catalog: Cajun/Zydeco**

http://www.pond.net/~morgan/cat/cajun/cajun.html

Balladeer Music is a store selling CD and cassette music in Eugene, Oregon. It sells all kinds of diverse and hard-to-find music. This page lists Cajun and Zydeco recordings available from Balladeer.

◆ **Bayou Boogie (from Bayoubeat.com)**

http://www.bayoubeat.com/bayou_boogie/bayou_boogie.htm

This is one of two pages, both called Bayou Boogie, devoted to Herman Fuselier, sports editor of *The Opelousas Daily World,* who also writes a weekly column called "Bayou Boogie" about southwestern Louisiana music and hosts Bayou Boogie programs on radio and television. This page features some of Fuselier's radio programs. See also the Bayou Boogie page below. Bayoubeat.com (**http://www.bayoubeat.com**) had just begun construction at the time this chapter was written. It is apparently devoted to radio station KVPI in Ville Platte, Louisiana; at that time, Fuselier's page is the only one operational.

◆ **Bayou Boogie**

http://www.dailyworld.com/text/boogie.html

Another site featuring Herman Fusilier (see Bayou Boogie page above). This site features "Bayou Boogie" articles from *The Opelousas Daily World.* However, only a few of the available "Bayou Boogie" articles are listed on this page. Go to the index at **http://www.dailyworld.com/text/**; all the pages beginning with "boogie" are Fusilier's music columns, which feature Cajun, Zydeco, and Swamp Pop music.

- ◆ **Beausoleil avec Michael Doucet**

http://www.rosebudus.com/beausoleil/

Beausoleil has been called the "best Cajun band." In 1997, it received its eighth Grammy nomination for Best Traditional Music album. The site includes a biography of the band, a discography and tour dates.

- ◆ **The Birthplace of Jazz**

http://www.NewOrleansWeb.org/jazz.html

A little history of jazz, facts about the traditional jazz band, and links to an interview with Pete Fountain make up this page.

- ◆ **Bon Tee Cajun Accordians**

http://www.inetserv.com/~inetserv/cajun/

Cajun music would be lost without the accordion. Larry G. Miller handcrafts Cajun accordions in Iota, Louisiana. Several examples of Miller's work are shown at the top of the page, followed by a brief history of the Cajun accordion and a short biography of Miller.

- ◆ **Cajun and Zydeco Festival Index**

http://www.festivalfinder.com/cajun/cajun.indexed.html

No matter where you live in the United States, you are likely to find a Cajun or Zydeco festival nearby in this alphabetical list.

- ◆ **Cajun Zydeco Web Resources—Virtually Live from San Francisco**

http://www.slip.net/~arubinst/index.html

There is an active Cajun Zydeco music and dance scene in the San Francisco Bay area. This page provides information on clubs, bands, festivals, associations, and products (calendars, books, recordings) available in the Bay area and elsewhere.

- ◆ **The Chicago Cajun Connection**

http://home.earthlink.net/~cterra440/

Dates, times, and clubs where Cajun and Zydeco music, dances, and dance instruction are taking place in the Chicago area.

- ◆ **Gary Hayman's ZydE-Magic Cajun/Zydeco Web Page**

http://www.erols.com/ghayman/index.html

A huge collection of information about Cajun/Zydeco music and dance. Since Hayman lives in the Metro D.C./Baltimore/Northern Virginia area, he puts a slight emphasis on happenings in that area, but there is information about the Cajun/Zydeco scene worldwide. Dance instructions, bands, many articles, including a frequently updated ZydE-zine, and other items can be found.

◆ **The Grand Old Cajun Opry**

http://www.yall.com/yonder/gitaways/fred.html

Cajuns love to party, and Fred's Lounge in Mamou, Louisiana, is one of the places they do it best. Fred's is an institution in Louisiana; the governor came to celebrate its 50th anniversary, naming the day, Fred's Day. Open only on Saturday mornings, there is plenty of drinking, dancing, and Cajun music broadcast by station KVPI-AM all over Cajun country. Fred's is credited as "the birthplace of the French Renaissance in Louisiana." This is real old-time Cajun culture!

◆ **Louisiana Music**

http://www.geocities.com/BourbonStreet/3076/music.html

Favorite Cajun and Swamp Pop bands and their recordings are featured, as well as links to other Cajun/Louisiana bands. Listen to favorite tunes on the linked midi page.

◆ **Music Hot Off the Bayou**

**http://pathfinder.com/@@p@dfFAcAsAOw@bHL/time/
   magazine/domestic/ 1995/950508/950508.music.html**

The article from *Time* (May 8, 1995) is a good introduction to Cajun and Zydeco music.

◆ **Northwest Zydeco Music & Dance Association**

http://www.scn.org/rec/zydeco/index.html

A newsletter about Cajun and Zydeco music and dance in Seattle. Includes a calendar of events in the area, in other parts of the United States and in Europe. Interesting articles from the newsletter are also available.

◆ **The Original Southwest Louisiana Zydeco Music Festival**

http://www.zydeco.org/index.html

This festival, now fifteen years old, has brought Zydeco to the attention of people all over the world.

◆ **Pierre's Cajun Record Shop**

http://www.winningways.com/pierre/

This Baton Rouge shop specializes in recordings of Cajun, Zydeco, and Swamp Pop music, but it also sells Cajun books, cookbooks, art, and videos. You can listen to music excerpts in RealAudio and view works of art for sale.

rec.music.rock-pop-r+b.1950s

A Usenet newsgroup that features discussions of rock, pop, and rhythm and blues music from the 1950s. Discussions of Cajun, Zydeco, and Swamp Pop music may be discussed here.

◆ **Steve Riley and the Mamou Playboys**

**http://harp.rounder.com/rounder/artists/
riley_steve_the_mamou_playboys/mamouplayboys.html**

The Mamou Playboys is a popular Cajun band. The site features the group's newsletter and lists their schedule. A link to an online review at Hotwired includes short sound clips.

◆ **Swamp Pop Music Pages**

http://acs.tamu.edu/~skb8721/swamppop.htm

Swamp Pop is the third popular indigenous music form of South Louisiana (after Cajun and Zydeco), combining influences from rhythm and blues, country and western, and Cajun and black Creole Zydeco music. It reached its peak of popularity in the 1950s and early 1960s, but is seeing a resurgence in the 1990s. These Web pages include a discussion of Swamp Pop; a CD discography; a description and ordering information for Swamp Pop: Cajun and Creole Rhythm and Blues, a book by Shane K. Bernard, who also authored the Web pages; and a set of links to pages for articles, bands, radio stations, record companies, and more.

Sports

◆ **The LSU Fan Homepage**

http://www.lsufan.com/

Every true Cajun is a fan of the Louisiana State University Tigers. The emphasis is on football. There is even a very attractive LSU Tiger Stadium Wallpaper that can be downloaded, for a small price.

◆ **Mike Lane's Louisiana Fishing and Hunting**

http://www.rodnreel.com/

Basically a commercial site, this page lists charters and guides, marinas and launches, boat dealers, bait and tackle shops, etc. Despite the title, it seems to be almost entirely devoted to fishing.

Professional Sports

◆ **Louisiana IceGators**

http://www.icegators.com/

This is the official Web site for the professional hockey team in Lafayette, Louisiana. Everything you wanted to know is here—roster, statistics, schedule, ticket and radio information, merchandise, etc.

OTHER

+ **Common Birds of Louisiana**

http://www.intersurf.com/locale/birds/index.html#contents

Selections from a booklet by Mrs. S. Elizabeth Hewes, first published in 1941 for the Louisiana Department of Wildlife and Fisheries and republished in 1978. It consists of general information for children and adults, and includes the original illustrations.

Maps

+ **Lafourche.com**

http://lafourche.com

This page is an excellent example of a Web site for a local geographic area. It has a few nice photographs, a map, and links to many pages of local interest— historic places, local stocks, people, groups, businesses, schools, government, and local people abroad (which seems to mean other places in Louisiana and the United States).

+ **Maps and Geographical Information**

http://www.state.la.us/state/map.htm

This page has a good map of Louisiana parishes. The page has numerous links to other maps, geographical data, and even zip code information.

Travel and Tourism

+ **Cajun! Life: Information on the Heart of Louisiana**

http://www.cajunlife.com/

Events, festivals, attractions, accommodations and more of interest to tourists in southern Louisiana.

+ **Cam-Lyn Charters, Inc.**

http://www.cajunews.com/camlyn.htm

Fishing, duck-hunting, and relaxation along the Louisiana coast.

+ **Creole Nature Trail Natural Scenic Byway**

http://user.maas.net/~mosketer/creole.htm

This is a virtual tour of the 105-mile Creole Nature Trail in Cameron Parish in Southwest Louisiana. It has a good verbal description and interesting photographs of an ecologically varied area.

◆ **French Louisiana Bike Tours**

http://www.flbt.com/index.html

Four tours plus two self-guided ones are offered. They all include plenty of good Cajun food, but allow the traveler to choose an emphasis on Cajun music, wilderness areas, the Cajun Mardi Gras, or New Orleans and the River Road. The company is headquartered in Lafayette, Louisiana.

◆ **Gris-gris for the Wanderer**

http://www.yall.com/yonder/cityscapes/voodoo.html

Voodoo and swamps—tours of New Orleans and the swamps of Cajun country.

◆ **Le Guide Online!**

http://www.allons.com/

This is a complete visitor's guide to Acadiana. Not only does it list the usual restaurants, hotels, etc., but it gives some history of the region and even some insight into Cajun French words and phrases.

◆ **Inns and B&Bs in Louisiana**

http://www.inns.com/south/ai-la.htm

Information on inns and bed-and-breakfast facilities in Acadiana and other cities in Louisiana. Includes locations, rates, local sights, and visitors' comments. Some of the inns and B&Bs provide photos.

◆ **Jean Lafitte National Historical Park and Preserve**

http://www.nps.gov/jela/

Jean Lafitte National Historical Park and Preserve celebrates the heritage of Louisiana's Mississippi Delta. The park is made up of several physically separated sites: those at Lafayette, Thibodaux, and Eunice exhibit Cajun culture; the site at Charenton is on the reservation of the Chitimacha tribe of Native Americans and is devoted to their culture; the Barataria Preserve near New Orleans interprets the natural and cultural history of the swamp and marshlands of the region; the Chalmette Battlefield is the site of the 1815 Battle of New Orleans; and the New Orleans site in the French Quarter is the headquarters for the park. Complete information on the park is provided, including programs at each site. There is a link to a teaching unit on the park.

◆ **Lafayette Convention and Visitors Commission**

http://www.cajunhot.com/html/who.html

Formed in 1974, the Commission promotes tourism and coordinates marketing in Lafayette Parish. Much information about the city and parish, and many links to related pages.

◆ **Lagniappe Tours**

http://www.cajunews.com/tour.htm

Lagniappe Tours offers something "a little extra." Offered by the Foundation for Historic Louisiana, a preservation organization, the tours feature both famous landmarks and less-known ones. They are arranged to meet particular interests—nature, architecture, politics, cuisine, and many more.

◆ **Louisiana Department of Culture, Recreation and Tourism**

http://www.crt.state.la.us/

This is a rich source of information about Louisiana. Information about Cajun Country is found at **http://www.crt.state.la.us/crt/cajuncon.htm** and a scenic tour of the area at **http://www.crt.state.la.us/crt/photogallery/cajuns.htm**. There is much other information scattered about the site, and the whole is of great interest for all areas of the state.

◆ **Louisiana National Wildlife Refuges**

http://www.gorp.com/gorp/resource/us_nwr/la.HTM

Attraction in the Marshes has a general introduction plus profiles of three National Wildlife Refuges in Southeastern Louisiana—Cameron Prairie, Lacassine, and Sabine. The same sites are listed separately on the page also. Two other refuges, Atchafalaya and Barataria, are also in Acadiana. Complete directions on what to do and how to get there are given for each refuge. Some nice wildlife photographs are also included.

◆ **Louisiana Page Locale**

http://www.lapage.com/page/

The first thing you will see on this page is a map of Louisiana. Click on any parish (county) and you will get a larger map showing the surrounding area, followed by information, usually including Culture and Traveler's Guide, Geography and Statistics, and Community Links on the Web. Clicking on the small link that says Tourism Info will take you to a page featuring five areas of the state. One of these is Cajun Country. All kinds of information is given for each area and each parish within the area. Lots of information!

◆ **Louisiana Travel**

http://www.louisianatravel.com/

This page lists all kinds of tourist information by region, as well as giving a general calendar of events, outdoor information, festivals, and more.

◆ **"The Official" City of Eunice, Louisiana, Homepage**

http://www.orion-cs.com/eunice/

The Prairie Cajun Capital of Louisiana has a homepage that tells almost everything you could possibly want to know about the city. Addresses, people, place of interest, organizations, things to do; this site has it all! Don't miss the many festivals held in Eunice: City of Eunice and Surrounding Area Festivals at **http://www.orion-cs.com/eunice/festivals.html**.

◆ **Pack & Paddle**

http://www.packnpaddle.com/

Pack & Paddle, an outdoor specialty shop in Lafayette, Louisiana provides bicycle and canoe or kayak trips in French Louisiana. Complete descriptions of the trips are provided.

◆ **The Unofficial City of Eunice, Louisiana, Homepage**

http://stltcc.dyn.ml.org/users/eunice/index.html

Another page devoted to Eunice. Not as complete as the Official page listed previously, but has some useful information on tourist sights.

◆ **Where in the World Is Broussard**

http://www.beausoleil-broussard.com/

History, historic district, business opportunities, dining and accommodations, attractions, and fairs, festivals, and events of this city in south central Louisiana are listed.

Weather

◆ **Weather Underground: Louisiana**

http://www.wunderground.com/forecasts/LA.html

This page gives weather information for several Louisiana cities, including Baton Rouge, Houma, Lafayette, Lake Charles, and Morgan City in Acadiana.

14

Hawaiian American Resources

ARDIS HANSON

INTRODUCTION

Hawaii, the Pacific island U.S. state, is both the largest and the most populous jurisdiction in the Pacific region, with 6,425 square miles of land area and over 1 million inhabitants. The volcanic Hawaiian Islands, located approximately 2,400 miles from the U.S. West Coast, are the center of much trade, commerce, and industry for the Pacific as a whole. Honolulu is a major urban population center, but many Hawaiians also reside in rural and remote areas. Hawaii's population is highly diverse; indigenous Pacific Islanders constitute only a minority of its residents. Although Hawaii's cultural milieu is the result of overlay after overlay of varied cultural groups, the force of the original culture remains evident in the islands. Hawaiian cultural values and traditions embodied in such words as *aloha* (love), `ohana* (family), and *aloha `aina* (love of the land) are understood and respected widely throughout the society of the islands as a whole.

The Hawaiian language, `Olelo Hawai`i, is a Polynesian language spoken with only minor variations on all the inhabited islands of Hawaii. In the nineteenth century, Hawaiian became a written language and a language of government used in the courts, school system, legislature and government offices. It was also the most commonly used language of the general public and was the common language of communication among the different ethnic groups up until the establishment of American control. From 1897, the United States government forbade the use of Hawaiian and it was replaced with English in government activities, education, and in business. A Hawaii Creole language arose from the Hawaiian speaking public being forced to speak English, along with influence from the pidgin Hawaiian spoken by immigrants during the previous century. In 1978, Hawaiian was again made an official language by the State of Hawaii and government schools teaching in Hawaiian were reestablished in 1987. In 1990, the federal government of the United States established a policy recognizing the right of Hawaii to preserve, use, and support its indigenous language. An interesting note: Hawaiian is the first indigenous language to have its own computer Bulletin Board System (BBS), Leoki, available on the Internet.

Unfortunately, the Kanaka Maoli have benefited the least and suffered the most of all populations in Hawaii from the island's forced incorporation with the United States and the loss of sovereignty. The resurgence of native rights and the rise of the Nation of Hawaii is an attempt to have the Kanaka Maoli recognized as a tribal government, much the way Native American tribes are recognized on the mainland.

An assortment of cultural and scientific institutions in Hawaii provides a wide variety of opportunities for the appreciation and understanding of the fine arts, history, traditions, and sciences. The Bernice P. Bishop Museum, founded in 1889 in Honolulu, is a research center and museum dedicated to the study, preservation, and display of the history, sciences, and cultures of the Pacific and its people. The Honolulu Academy of Arts, often called the most beautiful museum in the world, houses a splendid collection of Western art, and its collection of Asian art is also one of the finest in the Western world. The active art, language, music, and drama departments in Hawaiian schools and colleges and at the University of Hawaii contribute to the expanding cultural life of Hawaii, while the state has several theater organizations, professional and amateur.

Hawaiian music is probably the first true world music, defined as a new form of music created from the integration of several cultures. When the Europeans arrived in Hawaii, they found a rich cultural history passed along by chants based on a two-note musical scale accompanied by percussive instruments. The ukelele was presented to Hawaiian King Kalakahua's royal court in 1879 by Manuel Nunes, a Portuguese craftsman; the Hawaiian guitar was invented by Joseph Kekuku in the 1890s. Slack key guitar, which is Hawaiian music played to an open chord on an acoustic wooden guitar, has enjoyed a revival in the 1990s.

In addition to the rich cultural life of the islands, Hawaii has one of the most diverse ecosystems in the United States. Its national, state, and county parks offer a range of activities and views, e.g., Hawaii Volcanoes, Haleakala, and the Waimea Canyon State Park. Surfing also originated in ancient Hawaii and is now practiced at some 1,600 recognized surf spots throughout the islands.

Two overview Web sites are Hawaiian~Index.com at **http://www.hawaiian-index.com/**. This site's tag line says "If it's about Hawaii—it's here" and that's a fairly accurate statement. From listings of local business, churches, culture, education, employment, environmental groups, food, dining, recipes, government, media, organizations, sports, and a telephone directory, almost anyplace with a Web site in Hawaii is listed here. Updated every few months, this is an excellent starting site to explore Hawaii. The second general listing of sites is Hawaii MAIN INDEX at **http://www.808.com/**, which contains a complete catalog of all the Web pages in Hawaii listed by Island, City and Category.

Although one can start with these pages, it is also important to remember the other areas to explore when surfing for Hawaiian resources. Polynesian history or voyaging sites, as well as federal space, astronomical, or oceanographic agencies, have sites dealing with their particular views of Hawaii. The sites that have been selected for this chapter are just that—selected. This is by no means a comprehensive list, rather it is a list of some of the best of Hawaii.

GENERAL INFORMATION

- ◆ **The Asian and Pacific Islander Population in the United States**
http://www.census.gov/population/www/socdemo/race/api.html

Basic census statistics of the Asian and Pacific Islander population within the United States.

- ◆ **The Bishop Museum**
http://www.bishop.hawaii.org/

No trip to Hawaii is complete without a visit to the Bernice Pauahi Bishop Museum founded in Honolulu in 1889, named for the Hawaiian princess who was the great granddaughter of Kamehameha I. Throughout its history, the museum's commitment has been the gathering and the dissemination of information on Hawaii and the Pacific. Its resources on the net include Quickcams and MPEG movies, photos, and audio of Hawaiian sayings, descriptions of past and current exhibits, and links to its Planetarium, ethnobotanical sites, and Electric Postcards.

- ◆ **Grant Opportunities for Minority Organizations**
http://web.fie.com/fedix/aid.html

This site lists federal grants available to minority organizations for a range of opportunities including small business, education, social services, and more.

- ◆ **Native Hawaiian Data Book 1996**
http://www.lava.net/~plnr/

Health, statistical, and other demographic information on the Kanaka Maoli.

Current Events

- ◆ **Ka `Upena Kukui (The Net of Light)**
http://www.aloha.net/~prophet/kaupena.html

Summarized from various island news sources, including independent interviews and research, radio and television broadcasts and local papers. Primarily covers news of the islands, concentrated in Honolulu. Archive available at site.

◆ **Pacific Islands Report**

http://pidp.ewc.hawaii.edu/PIReport/

Provided by Pacific Islands Development Program (PIDP), East-West Center, University of Hawaii and the Center for Pacific Islands Studies at the University of Hawaii at Manoa.

◆ **West Hawaii Today**

http://westhawaiitoday.com/

Originating in Kailua-Kona, Hawaii, this site contains another look at doings on the Big Island and is updated weekly.

Newsgroups and Listservs

◆ **The Hawai`i NewsList**

http://www.aloha.net/~prophet/NewsList/about.html

This is a free service, supported merely by the spirit of aloha, for people interested in the events and state of affairs in the islands. This list distributes nine Internet publications to your mailbox (some more consistently than others), all assembled by volunteers, covering different areas of Hawaii life. It features *Ka `Upena Kukui*—Hawaii's first online newspaper, *Hawai`i Sports News, The Lahaina News*, and Susan's Music Page. One stop shopping for the news of the day, of the moment, and of the people.

Newspapers, Magazines, and Newsletters

◆ **Hale Pai**

http://www.punawelewele.com/halepai/

The only Pacific American news journal serving the Pacific American Hawaiians, Samoans, Carolinians, Chamarros and Palauans with readership in the cities of western Washington, Oregon, California, Nevada, Alaska, the East Coast and Hawaii. Updated monthly, it fills the void left by the mainstream press to concentrate on indigenous issues.

◆ **Haleakala Times**

http://www.maui.net/~haltimes/home.html

Written by people in Haiku, Makawao, Kula, and many other Upcountry areas of Maui, it is a community-based newspaper with issues important to the community, small-town politics, ecology, and more.

◆ **Honolulu Star-Bulletin**

http://starbulletin.com/

Highlights of the current edition: news, business, features, community, and sports, archive of the past year's news, special reports, the *Star-Bulletin*'s stylebook. Users can choose either frames or no-frames format.

◆ **The Maui News**

http://www.maui.net/~mauinews/news.html

The Maui News made its debut as a weekly publication on February 17, 1900. Today, *The News* continues as an independent, Maui-owned newspaper and as "the truest possible servant of the community." Contains local news from around Maui, county news (comprising four islands: Maui, Moloka`i, Lanai, and Kahoolawe) in a brief form, and state news from the Islands. Three months of news are archived on the site.

BUSINESS

◆ **Business Hawai`i**

http://www.hcc.hawaii.edu/hspls/hbiz.html

A list of Hawaii's commercial sites and business related sites available on the World Wide Web. Has the various Chambers of Commerce, links to *High Technology Online Business Directory,* development corporations, small business organizations, tradeshows, exhibitions, and conferences. One major online resource is *Starting a Business in Hawaii* courtesy of the Hawaii State Department of Business, Economic Development and Tourism (DBEDT).

◆ **Focus on the Economy**

http://hotspots.hawaii.com/h4economy.html

Hawaii's H4 website also hosts an archive of this publication.

◆ **Hawaii Business Magazine**

http://www.hawaiibusinessmagazine.com/contents.html

Economic indicators, selected features, excerpts of current and archived articles, and links to the business sections of the *Honolulu Star-Times* and the *Maui News.*

◆ **Pacific Business News**

http://www.amcity.com/pacific/

Leading stories, this week in business, small business, industry, back issues, and a cyber business card exchange.

◆ **Small Business Hawaii**

http://www.hotspots.hawaii.com/sbh.html

This is your one-stop information source about Hawaii's most active, independent, small business advocacy organization, Small Business Hawaii (SBH). There is a lot of information here including the last 2½ years' worth of their monthly publication, *Small Business News*.

CULTURE AND HUMANITIES, GENERAL

◆ **A Brief Overview of Hawai`i**

http://www2.hawaii.edu/visitors/overview.html

Basic facts and a brief look at the eight islands, their individual insignias and emblems.

◆ **Hapa Issues Forum**

http://www.wenet.net/~hapa/

Hapa comes from the Hawaiian phrase *hapa haole,* which means "half white/foreigner." Once considered derogatory, it is now a simple way to describe a person of partial Asian or Pacific Islander ancestry. Hapa is a national non-profit organization that celebrates the mixed race Asian/Pacific Islander American experience.

FINE ARTS

◆ **The 24 "Canoe Plants" of Ancient Hawai`i**

http://hawaii-nation.org/nation/canoe/canoe.html

Imagine a culture without clay or iron, whose people trusted in 24 plants to be life sustaining. This site covers the plants and the place they had in ancient Hawaiian culture, with links to other sites of relevance to those plants.

◆ **Poakalani's Hawaiian Quilting Page**

http://www.poakalani.com/

Shares the tradition, heritage, and cultural significance of one of Hawaii's most treasured art forms.

◆ **State Foundation on Culture and the Arts**

http://kumu.icsd.hawaii.gov/sfca/

This Web site initially has been prepared to provide the basic information about Hawaii's state arts agency, its programs and their services. Good overview of what is happening to promote the arts in Hawaii. Uses frames to navigate the site.

Music

◆ **The Royal Hawaiian Band**

http://alaike.lcc.hawaii.edu/OpenStudio/frhb/

Created by royal decree, the Band has been a key player throughout the history and development of the Islands. Read about their history, the current bandmaster, and listen to selected recordings using RealAudio.

GOVERNMENT, LAW, AND POLITICS

◆ **Hawaii Legislative Reference Bureau Library**

http://www.hawaii.gov/lrb/lib.html

An incredible resource for legistative documents. Includes the Legislator's Handbook; Guide to Government in Hawaii; administrative rules, directories, and tables; legislative session and actions; a directory of Hawaiian state, county, and federal officials; and reports on the current legislative session. Once entered into the Web site, your browser must support frames to be able to read the documents and to navigate the site.

◆ **Hawaii State Government**

http://www.hawii.gov/

Links to sites in Hawaii's state government. New tool bar that links one immediately to media releases, the Governor's office, featured services, what's new, classes and calendars of the agencies, and a road map of the state.

◆ **Hawaiian Sovereignty Elections Council Homepage**

http://hoohana.aloha.net/hsec/

An in-depth look at the ongoing discussion of native Hawaiian governance. Includes the legislative history of the sovereignty bills, legal and historical documents, news articles, editorials, and comments.

◆ **Ka Lahui Hawaii: The Sovereign Nation of Hawaii**

http://www.kalahui.org/

Ka Lahui seeks inclusion of the Hawaiian people in the existing U.S. federal policy which affords all Native Americans the right to be self-governing and provides access to federal courts for judicial review. This site contains documents, a list of videos on Hawaiian culture, and more.

◆ **Nation of Hawai`i Homepage**

http://www.hawaii-nation.org/nation/

This site provides information about the restoration of the independence of Hawaii, along with cultural perspectives from her people. Includes history of

Hawaii, policy and legal documents substantiating sovereignty, photographs, and other areas of interest to the Kanaka Maoli (native Hawaiians). More on sovereignty is in the Politics & Government section.

♦ **The Office of Hawaiian Affairs**
http://hoohana.aloha.net/~oha/

The Office of Hawaiian Affairs is a trust entity for all individuals whose ancestors were natives of the Hawaiian Islands prior to 1778, and was established to manage and administer the resources held for the benefit of Hawaiians and to formulate policy for them. Although it has the status of a state agency, it is independent of direct governmental control. This site has information about sovereignty, education and business programs, grants, and *Ka Wai Ola o Oha,* an online newsletter specific to indigenous concerns.

♦ **Perspectives on Hawaiian Sovereignty**
http://www.opihi.com/sovereignty/

This site, sponsored by the Pacific Asia Council of Indigenous Peoples and Cyber Wave, Inc., covers historical/international analysis, historical documents, education, environment, society, health, citizenship, and economics of an independent Hawaii. An excellent site to understand the importance of the history and culture of a people.

HISTORY

♦ **Damien of Moloka`i**
http://shc.sscc.org/damien/damien_story.html

No story of the islands is complete without the story of Damien De Veuster, a priest in the order of the Fathers of the Sacred Hearts, more commonly known as Father Damien of the lepers of Moloka`i.

♦ **Different Voices, Different Choices**
http://naio.kcc.hawaii.edu/bosp/voices/index.html

This outgrowth of a journalism class at the University of Hawaii became a magazine about the voices of the many cultures that come together in Hawaii. Several essays are about race conflicts in Hawaii.

♦ **Life in Hawaii: An Autobiographic Sketch of Mission Life and Labors (1835–1881) by Titus Coan**
http://www.soest.hawaii.edu/GG/HCV/COAN/
    coan-intro.html

A view of Hawaii through the eyes of Titus Coan, an early Protestant missionary. Describes the Hawaiian Royalty from Kamehameha I to David Kalakaua and Queen Kapiolani, including his personal experiences with them, visits to the

Marquesas in the 1860s, with much sociological detail, brief descriptions of the other Hawaiian Islands in the mid-1800s and his experiences with, and impressions of, native Hawaiians of the time.

- ◆ **The Polynesian Voyaging Society (PVS)**

http://leahi.kcc.hawaii.edu/org/pvs/pvs.html

The cultural history of Hawaii and the migration and settlement of Polynesia are explored in this Web site, including current activities, newsletter, history of the seafaring Polynesians, wayfinding, canoes and canoe building, and the Isles of Hiva (Marquesas), from where it is believed the early Polynesians emigrated.

Archaeology

- ◆ **Petroglyphs**

http://www.aloha.net/~gberry/hawaii/pet.html

A petroglyph is an image carved in rock and is called a *kaha ki'i* in Hawaiian. How old are Hawaiian petroglyphs? Studies of the change in the sea level could place the oldest at about 640 B.C.E. This is an interesting look at what they are, what they mean, and the sites located throughout the islands. Includes an online dictionary. Requires a browser capable of supporting frames.

LANGUAGE ARTS AND LITERATURE

Language Arts

- ◆ **The Coconut Boyz Online Hawaiian Dictionary**

http://www.hisurf.com/cgi-bin/DM/dictionary.cgi

This online dictionary contains close to 5,000 Hawaiian-English and English-Hawaiian words. These are most of the frequently used words and definitions. In the Hawaiian language, most words have multiple meanings and sometimes hidden meanings. When the language is spoken, the understanding comes from the context of what is being said.

- ◆ **The Hawaiian Language**

http://www.volcanoalley.com/lang.html

Many Hawaiian words are mixed in with the everyday language. For example, it would not be uncommon for your waitress to ask you "Are you *pau?*," meaning "Are you finished?" This site contains both traditional Hawaiian and pidgin words and phrases used in sample sentences.

◆ **Ka `Ôlelo Hawai`i**

http://www.geocities.com/TheTropics/Shores/6794/

A comprehensive, informative, well-constructed resource on the Net for starting to learn Hawaiian, presented by a kama`aina, who has recently become passionately involved with learning and teaching Hawaiian.

◆ **Kualono**

http://128.171.15.130/OP/

The Kualono World Wide Web (WWW) at the University of Hawaii at Hilo–Hale Kuamo`o office exists primarily to service the Hawaiian-language-speaking communities worldwide. Although the majority of information is in the Hawaiian language, there are some resources in English for those interested in learning the Hawaiian language or in learning more about Hawaii's indigenous language. Resources include Hawaiian-language newspapers, a dictionary, True-Type Hawaiian fonts (which can be downloaded for the Mac or PC), resource organizations such as Hale Kuamo`o and Punana Leo, and a phonetic guide to the pronunciation of the Hawaiian language.

POPULAR CULTURE

◆ **H-4 HotSpots**

http://www.hotspots.hawaii.com/

A melange of Hawaii, this site offers a sampling of some of the "real" Hawaii, from community newspapers, over 154 pages of pictures of Hawaii; Internet Radio Hawai`i (Hawaii's First Online Hawaiian Music Site and Original RealAudio Partner Site); QuickTime VR on the H4; Wala'au (talk story), a chat room to help Hawaiian folks stay in touch.

Music

◆ **Hawaiian Jamz!**

http://www.mauigateway.com/~jamz/

This site is dedicated to promoting and preserving Hawaiian music and culture. Their RealAudio shows cover the widest range of Hawaiian music possible. Each show has a theme and lasts approximately one hour. Past shows are kept in their Hawaiian Jamz Archive. The latest version of the RealAudio Player is required to listen to the show.

◆ **Nahenahenet: The Sweet Sound of Hawaiian Music**

http://www.nahenahe.net/

The site for Hawaiian music resources on the Internet, with links to the Web sites of Hawaii's finest musicians, online CD stores, and many other Hawaiian music resources. It also sponsors the definitive Hawaiian music calendar, featuring special music events and regular gigs for musicians throughout the state. From here, one can link to the Na Hoku Hanohano site (the winners of the Hawaiian Music Awards) and to The Hawaii Academy of Record Arts (HARA).

◆ **Stevo's Hawaiian Music Guide**

http://members.aol.com/StevenA442/hawaimus.htm

The sole purpose of this page is to promote Hawaiian music, the most beautiful music on earth. Includes concert schedules and music sources for mainlanders, as well as musical instruments, artists' homepages, Hawaiian music radio shows and DJs, sheet music and audio clips.

◆ **Susan's Hawaiian Music Page**

http://www.nahenahe.net/susanmusic/

This Web site features actual music clips. Current and several back issues can be viewed here.

Sports

◆ **H3O Hawaiian Heavywater**

http://www.h3o.com/

Sending surfing to the world, and they deliver. QuickTime videos of major surfing celebrities, video clips of the month, photos, a beach break with skateboard news and world championship surf finals, music reviews, and wave watch. Also links to the ASP Tour and links to other surf sites.

◆ **Hawaii Winter Baseball**

http://www.fanlink.com/contents/leagues/hwb.html

Read all about the Honolulu Sharks, the West Oahu CaneFires, the Maui Stingrays, and the Hilo Stars and their season from this site. Has Pressroom, news caps, and player rosters.

◆ **HI Surf Advisory (HI=Hawai`i)**

http://www.i-one.com/hisurfad/

A local boy's view of the art of wave riding. Links to major surfing news and swell times; first-person accounts of pumping on the wall, cutbacks, rollos and spinners; video clips, stills, and surf art. One of the best designed Web sites I have seen.

◆ **The Kele (Navigator)**

http://www.holoholo.org/index3.html

This site, subtitled HoloHolo Hawaii Marine & Ocean Sports News, contains sailing news, surfing news, canoe club news, yacht club news, fishing news, diving news, windsurfing news, link to *The Marine Reporter,* and the islands' marine and business sports directory.

◆ **The Kona Ironman Triathlon**

http://www.sportsline.com/u/ironman/

No sporting event is quite as grueling as the Ironman Triathlon in Kona, Hawaii. This page's links give you the athletes, the history of the Ironman, and the race course. You need Shockwave to view the movie.

◆ **Maui WindCam**

http://www.maui.net/~bob/windcam.html

Prime windsurf area in Spreckelsville, updated hourly during the day. Also has current wind and temperature information. One of Maui's most popular pages.

SCIENCE AND TECHNOLOGY

◆ **Hawaii Catalogue of Web Pages: Science**

http://connect.hawaii.com/connect-bin/ index?Science_and_Nature

Links to everything from agriculture to space. Lists topics and corresponding number of sites. Includes academic, government, and private companies. Modeled after the popular Yahoo directory system.

◆ **The Hawaii Center for Volcanology**

http://www.soest.hawaii.edu/GG/hcv.html

The Hawaii Center for Volcanology (HCV) was conceived and created in 1992 as a cooperative effort involving over 80 scientists. This Web site is maintained solely by SOEST staff members. It contains online information about eruptive and seismic activity at Loihi seamount and Kilauea, a picture gallery provides photographs of the eruptions. An added feature is the online version of the book *Life in Hawaii,* by Titus Coan. First published in 1882, it describes the author's observations of active volcanism on the Big Island (Island of Hawaii) during the nineteenth century.

◆ **Hawaii in Space**

http://apollo-society.org/hawaii_space.html

This site has monthly SkyWatch, sunrise/sunset tables, meteor shower and other astronomical information, and satellite maps.

◆ **Hawaii Research & Technology**

http://www.hawaii.org/

Explore the diversity of science and technology in Hawaii and the ingenuity of its people. A wonderful site that walks you through some of the most interesting and cutting-edge projects going on in Hawaii, from optics to seagrass.

◆ **Hawaiian Astronomical Society**

http://www.hawastsoc.org/

The El Niño-Southern Oscillation (ENSO) climate cycle center in the U.S.-affiliated Pacific Islands (USAPI) conducts the necessary research and provides information products "translated" from highly technical scientific source materials into formats appropriate for the support of planning and management activities undertaken in the USAPI in such climate-sensitive sectors as water resources management, fisheries management, agriculture, civil defense, power utilities, coastal zone management, etc. Includes the Pacific Climate Information System (PCIS), climate, rainfall, and cyclone information and forecasts.

◆ **Hawaii's Endangered and Threatened Species Web Site**

http://www.bishop.hawaii.org/bishop/HBS/endangered/

This site includes the Biological Surveys of Hawaii (1994 to present), databases, publications list, and image files. See the latest up-to-date information on fungi, plants, and animals occurring in the Hawaiian Islands. It has the latest lists, images, and information on endangered, threatened, and extinct Hawaiian species.

◆ **HERN: Hawaii Education and Research Network**

http://www.hern.hawaii.edu/hern/HERN_home.html

Designed to explore the implementation and use of high speed networking to reform educational practice at multiple levels in Hawaii, this site has information on private and public telecommunications infrastructure, lists of resources that are searchable by keyword, and current projects being funded.

◆ **University of Hawaii Satellite Oceanography Laboratory**

http://www.satlab.hawaii.edu/satlab/

Real-time images and movies for meteorology and oceanography, satellite images of general interest, archived online oceanographic data including the TIWE—data from the Tropical Instability Wave Experiment; JGOFS—data from the Pacific Joint Global Ocean Flux Study Experiment; DUMAND—current data at the Deep Underwater Neutrino Detector Site; COARE—GMS–4 images from the Coupled Ocean Atmosphere Experiment; and LANAI—current meter data south of Lanai.

◆ **Virtually Hawaii**

http://satftp.soest.hawaii.edu/space/hawaii/index_orig.html

This site is maintained by the researchers at the University of Hawaii, Proxemy Research, Inc., Terra Systems, Inc., Hawaii and Private Company Sponsors. Incredible virtual views of Hawaii from a variety of sources, including instruments carried on aircraft, satellites and the Space Shuttle. The site also has tutorials on remote sensing (visible, radar and infrared), and an interactive spectral imager—see how a change in a color wavelength enhances features of interest on the ground. Finally, there is a remote image navigator to see remote sensing images of Hawaii with a range of special resolutions. The images are incredible.

◆ **Volcano Watch**

http:www.soest.hawaii.edu/hvo/

Volcano Watch is a newsletter from the Hawaiian Volcano Observatory (HVO) that has appeared weekly since 1991. As an experiment, the School of Ocean & Earth Science & Technology at the University of Hawaii at Manoa started making *VW* available online in the early days of the Web. As the archive grew, it made sense to continue it, leaving HVO free to develop a Web site which concentrates on current work. This site has maps, the latest earthquake epicenter maps, and recent images from Kilauea.

◆ **Waikiki Aquarium Virtual Tour**

http://www.mic.hawaii.edu/aquarium/vt.htm

The third oldest aquarium in the United States (1904), the Waikiki Aquarium offers a really remarkable tour. Click on gallery level, select the tank you wish to view, then select the creature in the tank you want to read more about and more information appears below.

Health

◆ **Asia and Pacific Islander American Health Forum**

http://www.igc.apc.org/apiahf/index.html

A national advocacy organization dedicated to promoting policy, program and research efforts for the improvement of the health status of all Asian and Pacific Islander Americans, covers issues in minority health including the impact of Medicaid and welfare reform on minorities, minority women's health, tobacco education, and HIV education and research.

OTHER

Travel and Tourism

◆ **The Aloha Insider**

http://www.theinsider.com/Aloha/

Island-by-island description of all the top things to do in Hawaii, over 100 original photographs taken expressly for *The Aloha Insider,* tips on surviving the rental car process, how to save money on hotel rooms, and book a discount hotel room in Hawaii (or anywhere). There is also a local bulletin board with tips on how to get the most out of Hawaii.

◆ **Driving & Discovering Hawaii**

http://www.discoveringhawaii.com/

One of the better e-zines with text and color photographs of places to see on each of the five main islands. Includes special and ongoing feature sections, a medical information section on native plants and animals that can cause injury, and a traveler's advisory. Very informative and nicely presented. Must have a frames-capable browser to view this site.

◆ **The Hawaii Show**

http://www.thisweek.com/

The Hawaii Show is produced by This Week Publications, publishers of Hawaii's premier visitor publications, with separate editions for each of Hawaii's four major tourist-visited islands, Kauai, Hawaii, Maui, and Oahu. Includes maps, packages, shopping, activities, accommodations, dining and entertainment, and a calendar of events.

◆ **Hawaii Volcanoes National Park**

http://www.nps.gov/havo/

Fact sheet on the park and links to other national park sites in the islands. Links to Volcano Watch (**http://www.soest.hawaii.edu/hvo/**) and Volcano World (**http://volcano.und.nodak.edu/**).

◆ **Molokai: The Most Hawaiian Island**

http://visitmolokai.com/index.html

Contains the history of Molokai, culture, activities and events, maps, a tour of the Molokai Ranch, Kalaupapa, and a spectacular photographic tour of the island.

Weather

◆ **Maui Weather Today**

http://hawaiiweather.com/mwt/

This site includes a live video cam from Maui's beaches; weather updates; links to surf, windsurf, and dive conditions; and weather forecasts by the month; satellite weather images of all the islands; and a tropical cyclones summary for the central north Pacific.

◆ **University of Hawaii Weather Service**

http://lumahai.soest.hawaii.edu/

Everything you need to know about the weather by region and type. Hawaiian and mainland weather, tropical and severe weather, an historical data page, and a forecast models page.

Site/Sponsor Index

I

L

Q

R

Contributors

D. Russell Bailey is the director of the Library and of Computer and Media Services at Green Mountain College in Poultney, Vermont. He has a Ph.D. in German Studies and in the past has taught in the East Asian Studies Program at Eckerd College in St. Petersburg, Florida. He conducted research pursuant to Fulbright Fellowships to Korea in 1990 and to Japan in 1994.

Emily K. Dunskar is a graduate assistant in the School of Library and Information Science at the University of South Florida and is a doctoral candidate in Educational Technology at the University of South Florida.

Alicia Barraqué Ellison is a reference librarian with the Tampa-Hillsborough County Public Library System in Tampa, Florida. She has worked with the Suncoast Free-net.

Paula Geist is a doctoral student in library and information science at the University of Texas at Austin. She has a background in fine arts and public librarianship, and her research interests include the information needs of special populations, information ethics, and information policy.

Vicki L. Gregory is associate professor in the School of Library and Information Science at the University of South Florida, where she teaches courses in collection development, library networks, and information science. Many of the contributors to this book were students in her Library Systems and Networks course, where the Internet resources bibliography project helped to generate the idea and form the foundation for this book.

Ardis Hanson is director of the Research Library at the Louis de la Parte Florida Mental Health Institute at the University of South Florida. As a first-generation

American and the mother of two children who are part Chamorro, Ms. Hanson has a keen interest in cultural legacies and continuity. She is active in the Multi-Cultural Mental Health Internship at the institute and recently participated in the Simposio Sobre Tecnologias Educativas: Enseñanza para el Siglio XXI in Meridia, Venezuela, where she introduced a low-cost library catalog searchable via the World Wide Web.

Sharon Peregrine Johnson is a librarian at Baylor University's Law School Library in Waco, Texas, where she works in acquisitions, Internet instruction, Web design, and development. She is also a graduate student in George Washington University's Technology Leadership program. Winner of the 1995 W. W. Newell Prize from the American Folklore Society, she frequently writes and presents workshops about folklore, Western Americana, and the Internet.

Thomas Keene is a public services librarian for the New Port Richey, Florida, Public Library. He has taught Web design and Internet courses at the University of South Florida.

Angelo F. Liranzo is a desktop business analyst at the Tampa Electric Company. He has worked as a foreign language teacher and as a business information specialist in the Tampa Bay area. Born in Santo Domingo, Dominican Republic, and raised in Brooklyn, New York, Mr. Liranzo has traveled widely throughout Spain, France, Germany, and Italy. He enjoys searching the Internet and sharpening his knowledge of Spanish, French, Portuguese, and related languages and cultures.

Cynthia A. Nuhn is an assistant professor and instructional services librarian at Eckerd College Library in St. Petersburg, Florida. She teaches the Senior Capstone class entitled "Quest for Meaning" at Eckerd College.

Claudia Rebaza is an information services librarian at the University of Southern Mississippi in Hattiesburg, Mississippi. Her professional interests include information literacy and academic publishing.

Suzanne M. Saunders is an adjunct instructor at the School of Library and Information Science, University of South Florida, Tampa, Florida, where she teaches Web design and Internet courses.

Marilyn H. Karrenbrock Stauffer teaches in the School of Library and Information Science at the University of South Florida. She was raised among Native Americans on the Ponca Reservation in Oklahoma, and has taught in communities that were at least 80 percent Hispanic/Latino in California, Cajun in Louisiana, and African American in South Carolina. She teaches a Services to Special Populations course that emphasizes services to racial and ethnic groups. In 1998, she led a federally funded Institute on Library Services to Migrant and Seasonal Farmworkers at USF.